# India Macroeconomics Annual
# 2006

# India Macroeconomics Annual
# 2006

Editor

Sugata Marjit

SAGE Publications
New Delhi ▪ Thousand Oaks ▪ London

*First published in 2007 by*

**Sage Publications India Pvt Ltd**
B1/I1 Mohan Cooperative Area
Mathura Road
New Delhi 110 044
www.indiasage.com

**Sage Publications Inc**
2455 Teller Road
Thousand Oaks, California 91320

**Sage Publications Ltd**
1 Oliver's Yard, 55 City Road
London EC1Y 1SP

Published by Vivek Mehra for Sage Publications India Pvt Ltd, typeset in 10/13 Aldine401 BT by Star Compugraphics Private Limited, Delhi and printed at Chaman Enterprises, New Delhi.

**Library of Congress Cataloging-in-Publication Data available**

**ISSN:** 0–973–290–X
**ISBN:** 10: 0–7619–3567–3 (PB)      10: 81–7829–727–2 (India–PB)
  13: 978–0–7619–3567–4 (PB)      13: 978–81–7829–727–9 (India–PB)

**Sage Production Team:** Gayatri E. Koshy, Rajib Chatterjee, Sanjeev Sharma and Santosh Rawat

# Contents

# Editorial Board

# Editor's Note

We are happy to bring out the current issue of *India Macroeconomics Annual 2006*, a joint venture of the Centre for Studies in Social Sciences, Calcutta and Sage Publications India Pvt. Ltd. This is the third issue of the annual partly funded by the Reserve Bank of India Endowment at the Centre for Studies in Social Sciences, Calcutta. We are also happy to inform the readers that *India Macroeconomics Annual* is now listed under the AEA Electronic Indexes, which are included in JEL on CD, *e-JEL* and EconLit.

The views expressed in the articles belong entirely to the authors and in no way implicate the Reserve Bank of India.

**Sugata Marjit**
Centre for Studies in Social Sciences, Calcutta

# Section I

# Politics and Contemporary Macroeconomy of India

SUGATA MARJIT
Centre for Studies in Social Sciences, Calcutta

DIBYENDU S. MAITI*
Centre for Studies in Social Sciences, Calcutta

This section addresses the *locus standi* of research on political economy issues in India. It argues that the tradition of research on political economy in India is over-burdened with discursive practices and that the quantitative analyses, albeit part of the mainstream discourse elsewhere, have not flourished in India. This article provides a survey of the contemporary, mainly quantitative, writings on political-economic issues in India. The second section offers a simple verification of the basic hypothesis that along with continued commitment towards liberalization, fiscal discipline in India is achieved mainly by keeping up a relatively 'populist' public expenditure. The last part uses an analytical model of re-distributive politics to show that the poor, although aware of what public investments can do for them in the long run and without having any preference for the present in terms of a sub-jective rate of discount, still favour pure income transfers and may not vote in favour of larger public investments.

**JEL Classification:** D72, E22, E62, H30
**Keywords:** Political economy, Governance, Corruption, Re-distribution, India

* We are deeply indebted to Pranab Bardhan, Partha Chatterjee, Maitreesh Ghatak, Abhirup Sarkar, Kausik Chaudhuri, Sugato Dasgupta, Pranab Kumar Das, Saibal Kar, Jyotsna Jalan, Vivekananda Mukherjee and Rongili Biswas for helpful discussions. We are also thankful to Siddhartha Chattopadhyay, Archita Banik and Nilendu Chowdhury for research assistance. The usual disclaimer applies.

# 1. Introduction

It is amazing that despite being a politically active democracy, Indian texts on economic policy often sidestep the issue of politics. While media and political analysts and historians often make political issues the focal point of their study, somehow Indian economics seems to be confined within the boundaries of clearly defined economic arguments, safely guarded by known parameters and variables. Quantitative analyses of the Indian political economy are relatively new and the volume of such work is really small compared to the better known discussions of India's political economy that are grounded in the discursive tradition. Obviously, this tradition is widely accessible since it does not go into the domain of explicit technicalities in terms of theoretical and applied model building, with the arguments mostly developed from contemporary and historical anecdotes with inputs from politics and sociology.

On the other hand, quantitative political economy does depend on explicit and often abstract modelling and are subject to appropriate statistical verifications. Consequently, issues discussed tend to be narrower and much more focussed. Such analytical rigour consequently becomes less accessible to readers at large and those who belong to various other disciplines. Somehow, this tradition of writing has not flourished in India, although such research in mainstream economics has made a considerable mark. Very recently, quantitative work on Indian political economy began to surface at a reasonable pace with quite a few interesting issues being discussed. The purpose of this article is to track down some of these works and the issues with which they are concerned also and to highlight potentially interesting future research ideas. We shall, however, deliberately refrain from repeating the analytical content of the contributions of Persson and Tabellini (1994), Drazen (2001) and many others simply because we are not interested in the 'political economy' as such or 'political economy of the developing world' in general. Our main task is to identify analytical themes in the context of the Indian economy.

This article is divided into three broad sections. The first is a survey of the contemporary, mainly quantitative, writings on political-economic issues in India. The second is a simple verification of the basic hypothesis that along with continued commitment towards liberalization, fiscal discipline in India is achieved mainly by keeping up a relatively 'populist' type of public expenditure. In other words, we argue that public capital expenditure and development expenditure have not been in tune with growing GDP, although such discrepancies have contributed towards maintaining fiscal discipline.

The last one provides an analytical model of redistributive politics where the poor, despite being aware of what public investments can do for them in the long-run and without having any preference for the present in terms of a subjective rate of discount, still favour pure income transfers and may not vote in favour of larger public investments.

# 2. Literature Review

This section discusses both discursive and quantitative approaches to research on the so-called 'Indian political economy'. While the discursive tradition generally deals with the issue of 'class and caste politics' and its economic outcomes, the quantitative tradition attempts to verify the economic impact of political variables. However, before we consider the recent developments in the quantitative approach, it would be appropriate to highlight some of the important contributions of the traditional approach (the discursive tradition) along with the contemporary issues in this area of research. Once again, we purposefully keep this coverage to a minimum, since this is not the major focus of our study.

## 2.1 The Discursive Tradition

This traditional approach deals, from time to time, with state intervention, mode of agricultural production and backwardness, inter-sectoral terms of trade and industrialization, poverty alleviation programmes, nationalization, reservation, economic reform and so on. During the 1970s and the 1980s the debate has been centred on the class and caste politics behind India's backwardness and sluggish growth. Most of the research highlights biased policy approaches catering to the dominant classes and unfavourable terms of trade as the reasons for underdevelopment. Further, it is argued that the semi-feudal mode of production relation has been responsible for the state of backwardness in agriculture, and consequently slows down the rate of capital formation. Scholars largely speak about the development of capitalism in the country, and the consequences of class segregation in society.[1] More-over, those who became privileged in the process (the industrial class, the rich peasants and the professionals in the public sectors), as noted by Bardhan (1984), have initiated political processes of distributive demands, rent-seeking and patronage disbursement leading to inefficient economic management and the consequent slow pace of development. Following the same trend

---

[1] Bhaduri (1973) and Patnaik (1987) are examples.

of analysis, recent studies by Bhattacharya (1999) and Chakrabarti and Cullenberg (2003) analyse the impact of reform in India and illustrate with evidence that the reforms have clearly accentuated the dependent nature of Indian capitalism.

Bardhan (2003) also highlights various kinds of disjuncture between the policy of economic reform and the ongoing political and administrative processes in India. His main observations may be summarized as follows:

(*i*) While any sustained economic reform and investment requires a framework for long-term policy, Indian political processes have been moving in the opposite direction, dealing with day-to-day politics and eroding most of the institutional insulations imperative for long-term economic management. In fact, the process of reform itself has become a popular agenda for all political parties. Interestingly, when not in power, a political party typically campaigns against the evils of reform, but makes visible turnarounds to follow the reform agenda once it holds power.

(*ii*) Corruption and malpractice, which are outcomes of the 'permit raj', are expected to come down with extensive deregulation. However, since some of the newer social groups, like cadres, have, through political oligarchy, snatched power (in place of other groups of upper classes and upper castes, bureaucrats and so on), corruption does not decline, with the abolition of system of permits and licenses, in recent years.

(*iii*) Reservation is deemed (more or less) by all political parties as an important issue for controlling a large section of people, which might ensure the possibility of their re-elections.

(*iv*) Very few substantive reforms have taken place in the agricultural sector. This is either due to the low volubility of organized farm lobbies (with a few exceptions) or due to the apprehension of the political risk associated with the moves for dismantling the existing structure of food, fertilizer, water and electricity subsidies in exchange for benefits from increased international trade.

(*v*) Political power is shifting more towards regional governments and regional parties, which makes national coordination on macro policy more difficult. Economic reform and increased competition possibly lead to increased regional inequality, which subsequently increases the tension between the better-off and the poorer states.

(*vi*) While the political power of regional governments is on the upsurge, their fiscal dependence on the Centre is also increasing. A significant part of the central transfers is discretionary. These central transfers and loans based on discretionary subsidies are often used more for political influence in selected areas than for the reason of fiscal or financial reform and/or of poverty removal.

(*vii*) Decentralization of governance, through the 73rd and the 74th constitutional amendments in the early 1990s, has raised hopes for better delivery of public services through local administration that is sensitive to local needs. But so far, the progress has been disappointing in most states both in terms of actual devolution of authority and funds, and the outcome of services thus delivered.

(*viii*) India's administrative structure is dominated by bureaucrats chosen on the basis of a generalized examination, with their career promotions based largely on seniority and not individual performances. However, there are no well-enforced rules and regulations for punitive actions against their ineptitude and/or malfeasance. Moreover, in large parts of the country, the judiciary (particularly at the lower end) is almost completely clogged by the enormous backlog of cases and the legal system is largely paralysed by delays and corruptions.

The above discussion demonstrates that Bardhan (1984, 2003) offers leading examples of research in the discursive tradition, which use economic arguments and anecdotal evidence to reflect on the politics of economic development. While Bardhan (1984) mainly looked at the major economic events in the post-independence period up to the 1970s, his recent work takes up economic reform as the focal point. We now turn to contemporary quantitative research on India's political economy, which is our main point of focus.

## 2.2. The Quantitative Tradition

### 2.2.1 *Federal System of Governance*

India is described as a quasi-federation, whose polity is of a nature which compels union to be a federation of states. The Constitution has bestowed a considerable amount of power to the Centre and it is commonly held that the constitutional provisions tilt the balance of power in favour of the union government. However, a balance is struck by means of a financial structure, which is more or less federal. To ensure control over the states in the political as well as the financial arena, the Union Government has in several occasions gone beyond the framework of the Constitution and tried to legitimize the centralization process through the device of certain policies and/or institutions (Biswas and Marjit 2005). The Constitution of India envisages the Finance Commission as the key institution responsible for dealing with fiscal imbalances both between the Centre and states, and among the states. However, the role of the Finance Commission has been circumscribed by the working of the Planning Commission, which has typically been put outside the Finance Commission's terms of reference. Furthermore, although the transfers made by the Planning Commission are based on some pre-defined formulae, there has been a tendency to use discretionary grants determined by the central ministries. Thus, the overall tendency on the part of the central government has been to exercise as much political control as possible over transfers to the states. Also, within each channel of transfers, there is anecdotal evidence on attempts to influence the outcome of the process. The pertinent issue, here, is the extent to which the effect(s) of such influences might be moderated through institutional reforms, in circumstances where these are believed to lead to inefficiencies or failure to meet equity objectives in the system of Centre-state transfers (Rao and Singh 2001).

From Rao and Singh (ibid.) and others, one gathers that some of the approaches on the political economy of federalism use bargaining analysis to focus on the formation and stability of the federation itself. An alternative branch of literature examines distribution and redistribution in the context of existing nations, without the threat of secession or break-up being considered. Again, bargaining perspectives are important in this genre of models. Inman and Rubinfeld (1997) provide a transactions cost analysis of the federal provision of public goods. They have focussed particularly on the role of legislative structures in determining this allocation. According to them, given a clear assignment of tasks, level of representation and legislative institutions, one can compare the economic efficiency of different combinations of these three institutional variables.

Building on the work of Breton and Scott (1978) and Baron and Ferejohn (1989), they make this comparison based on an assessment of different types of transactions costs, without explicitly treating the inter-governmental transfers in their analysis. Kletzer and Singh (1997, 2000) analyse a median voter model of a federation with taxation, representative government and inter-governmental transfers. In their model, the constituent units of the federation realise that transfers have to be financed by taxes, and are, therefore, interested in net transfers. Inman and Rubinfeld (1997) show with an example how coalitions may form to determine the winners and losers from transfers, based on factors such as income and agenda-setting power. These formal theoretical models, as well as the causal empiricism, have been the basis for several recent attempts to estimate political influences on Centre-state transfers.

Rao and Singh (2001, 2003) attempt to estimate the political influence on the Centre-state transfers for 14 major Indian states over the period between 1983–84 and 1992–93. They estimate linear, log-linear, and translog functions (with state specific fixed effects) taking (*a*) Statutory Transfers (sum of shared

Tax Transfers and Non-Plan Grants), (*b*) Grants for State Plan Schemes and (*c*) Discretionary Transfers (sum of Grants for Central Plan Schemes and Grants for Centrally Sponsored Schemes) as dependent variables,[2] and SDP (State Domestic Products), Per capita SDP and population as explanatory variables. There are two 'political' variables in the group of explanatory variable as well, namely (*a*) 'power', defined as the proportion of Members of Parliament (lower house only) from the ruling party, coming from a particular state and (*b*) 'alignment', a dummy variable that measures whether the same party is in power at the Centre and the state level. Major findings of Rao and Singh (2001, 2003) are the following:

(*i*) Lagged value of the 'alignment' variable (capturing the five years decision cycles for such transfers) has a positive and significant effect on grants to state plan schemes for all the three different specifications mentioned above.

(*ii*) The 'power' variable affects the 'statutory transfers' positively and significantly (only in the logarithmic specification).

(*iii*) Population and SDP have positive and significant impact on per capita transfers, which shows the impact of 'economic size' on political transfers. The result is, howerver, not robust across specifications.

Biswas and Marjit (2005) deal with the same issue and examine empirically the political influence, especially of political lobbying, on the disbursement of discretionary money[3] on the part of the central government over the period 1974–97 for 17 major states in India. They perform 'pooled regression analysis' and 'fixed effect panel regression analysis' using 'two stage least square' method for their estimations. In order to assess the impact of 'politics' on the disbursement made by the central government, they define some relevant political variables, such as—'Lobbying Power', 'Political Disturbance Dummy', 'Coalition Dummy', 'Reform Dummy', 'Voter Turnout Percentage', 'Index of Opposition Unity' and 'Income Index' for each state.[4] Moreover, keeping in mind the somewhat aberrant political history of the state of Punjab, they use a 'Punjab Dummy' as well in the pooled regression analysis, which is performed by regressing the residual (obtained from the regression of Money Disbursement Index on Income Index and time dummies for 18 years) on different combinations of the 'political variable'

[2] Transfers are taken in per capita terms.
[3] Same as the 'discretionary transfers' of Rao and Singh (2003).
[4] For definitions of these indices, see Biswas and Marjit (2002, 2005).

and the Punjab Dummy. Similarly, the panel regression also involves regressing the residual (obtained from the regression of Money Disbursement Index on Income Index and time dummies for 18 years and 17 states). Both methods retrieve similar patterns as far as the major results are concerned. In particular (*a*) for every level of lobbying done, discretionary money disbursement from the Centre to the state is higher in the politically disturbed years; (*b*) for every level of lobbying done, lesser amount of money is disbursed in coalition and reform years; (*c*) for every increase (decrease) in lobbying, disbursement for the state of Punjab increases (decreases) more than the other states. This speaks in favour of a different political background for Punjab compared to other states in India as the authors presume; (*d*) states with more powerful opposition and/or with higher voter turnouts, and/or greater lobbying power receive higher discretionary finance from the central government.

Earlier, Biswas and Marjit (2002) examined the political influence on the disbursement of Industrial Licenses (IL) and Letter of Intent (LI) for the Indian economy over the period between 1974 and 1994 for 14 major states in India.[5] While all the other studies devoted to this very topic examine the political influence on some 'pecuniary' disbursement, the novelty of this article lies in that it investigated the political influence on some 'nonpecuniary' disbursement made by the central government. The political variables were the same as those defined in Biswas and Marjit (2005). Using the procedure of 2SLS, they first performed two separate regressions taking IL and LI as the dependent variable and Income Index as the explanatory variable. Income variable turned out positive and significant for both regressions. Residuals obtained from these two regressions were then used to examine the political influence on the disbursement of IL and LI. They estimated different 'fixed effect' models taking different combinations of 'political indices'. Their main results may be summarized in the following manner: The 'Lobbying Power' (both in terms of the council of ministers and the members of parliament) have a significant positive effect on the disbursement of both IL and LI. However, as the lobbying power (in terms of the council of ministers) increases, disbursement of both IL and LI fall in the reform years as well as in the coalition years, but the politically disturbed years fetch more disbursement of IL for all the states. Higher value of Voter Turnout Ratio and Index of Opposition Unity in a state, at a certain point of time, fetches more IL and LI in favour of that state during that period. Disbursement

---

[5] In actuality, they have used data of 18 years. See Biswas and Marjit (2002) for detail.

of IL also improves in favour of a particular state if the ruling party of that state has an alignment/coalition with the ruling party at the Centre.

Dasgupta et al. (2004) examine the role of redistributive politics between central and the state governments by constructing a theoretical model. Here, the opportunistic party in power at the Centre with an aim to maximize the number of seats it can win in each state, uses its discretion to make grants to the state governments on the basis of some political considerations, viz., the degree of alignment between the incumbent party at the central and state level and whether a state is a swing or not. The model predicts that 'swing' states that are 'aligned' with the central government (state government and the central government are governed entirely by a single political party or they have at least one party in common) will receive more grants relative to non-swing states (states that are not aligned with the central government). The crucial assumption here is that the central grants are used for financing public projects in the states to generate goodwill for the central government. Since these grants from the Centre improve the level of welfare in the provinces, the incumbent in the state also reaps some of the benefits. As a result, if the incumbent in the state and the Centre happens to be the same party, then that party derives the entire electoral benefit of any additional expenditure given to the state and the state, therefore, receives more funding from the Centre. On the other hand, if the central and state governments are governed by two different political parties, then some of the electoral benefits generated from the central grants 'leaks' to the other party and this gives the central government less of an incentive to provide grants to such states. Indian data for the 15 states during the period between 1968–69 and 1996–97 shows that the 'aligned-swing' effect is large in magnitude and statistically significant in explaining the log value of 'per capita discretionary grants' distributed by the central government to the state governments. Dasgupta et al. (2004) also find that per capita net state domestic product (PCNSDP) does have a significant positive impact on the central transfers and one standard deviation increase in PCNSDP induces a 3.1 per cent increment in per capita central grants, though the impact of the 'Lobbying Power' turns out to be non-significant with expected sign.

In this context, studies by Rao and Singh (2001) and Chakraborty (2003) regarding 'redistributive politics' and 'central-state transfers' are also noteworthy. That political power in India is shifting more to regional governments and regional parties makes national coordination on macro policies rather difficult. For example, fiscal consolidation in general and a substantial reduction in the budget subsidies in particular, become difficult when the national government depends on the support of powerful regional parties that assiduously nurse their parochial interest lobbies with a liberal use of subsidies (implicit or explicit). It is also the case that a large number of entry taxes on goods, imposed by governments even in states that perform well economically (for example, Maharashtra and Tamil Nadu), make the reformer's aspiration to integrate the market at the all-India level rather distant. The states' fiscal dependence on the Centre is on the rise despite significant tilt of power in favour of regional self-governments, that is, the fraction of states' current expenditures financed by their own revenue sources have declined. A significant part of the central transfers is discretionary (for example, the numerous central sectors and centrally sponsored schemes). These and discretely subsidized loans are often used by the Centre more for political influence in selected areas than for the cause of fiscal or financial reform and poverty alleviation.

Using a similar framework and specification as the model in Rao and Singh (2001, 2003), Singh and Vasistha (2004) use some illustrative panel data on Centre-state transfers to examine how the economic and political importance of the states influence the level and composition of per capita transfers to the states, as well as the differences in temporal patterns of Planning Commission and Finance Commission transfers. Through the use of dummies they find evidence that states with indications of greater bargaining power seem to receive larger per capita transfers; and that there is greater temporal variation in Planning Commission transfers over different term periods. The study also includes political variables to correspond to the decision cycles of the Finance Commission and the Planning Commission. All regressions (both for linear and non-linear specifications) are performed alternatively using the four categories of transfers (in per capita terms and at 1981 prices).[6] Over-all, the results suggest that states with greater bargaining power, as proxied by political variables, tend to receive larger per capita transfers, and they support the observation on political influence on transfers, as studied by Biswas and Marjit (2002, 2005). The estimates reveal positive effects of the demographic size of the states and, in turn, suggest that population may well be an indicator of political influence solely due to the size of the state and independently of its political regime.

Recently, Chaudhuri and Dasgupta (2005) used annual data of India to examine whether the economic policies undertaken by the Government of India are influenced by the proximity of an election in the national legislative

---

[6] The four categories of transfers are: shared taxes, non-plan grants, grants for central plan schemes and grants for centrally sponsored schemes.

assembly as well as by the 'cohesion of central government' on economic policies. The authors collected data on (*a*) central government's tax revenue, (*b*) central government's spending on current account, (*c*) central budget deficit, (*d*) central government's investment on various kind of infrastructure and (*e*) central government's monetary policy. They did not find any evidence on the influence of the electoral cycle on corporate tax revenue, income tax revenue and custom tax revenue policies, although its influence on excise tax revenue and the income tax revenue policies were observable when some political variables were controlled systematically. The nature of government (single-party or coalition) did not have any significant impact on the tax revenue collection by the central government. They examined the presence of electoral cycles for the central government's total per capita developmental expenditure and obtained the following results:

(*i*) 'Election induced spending spurts' in broad components of current account expenditure is weak.

(*ii*) Electoral cycle is present for agricultural expenditure, quantity of publicly distributed foodgrains, fertilizer subsidy, central government budget deficit and the deposit rates of commercial banks.

(*iii*) Electoral cycle has no influence on real per capita money supply and deposit rates of the central bank.

(*iv*) The single-party central government spends more on current account expenditure than coalition central governments—however, the central government's budget deficit is not affected by the nature of government.

(*v*) Compared to its single-party counterpart, coalition central government invests more in infrastructure—however, the electoral considerations reduce their per capita expenditure on school and per capita expenditure on railway tracks.

In a similar exercise Chaudhuri and Dasgupta (2006) estimate a fixed-effect error-component model to examine the impact of political consider-ations (namely, the proximity of a state election and the extent of government cohesion) on the fiscal policy choices of state governments. For their esti-mation, they took fiscal policy variables (for example, the log of per capita own tax revenue) as the dependent variable and a matrix of explanatory variables comprising $\alpha_s$, $\delta_t$, $x_{st}$, Fragment$_{st}$, and Elec$_{st}$, where, $\alpha_s$ is a state fixed effect, $\delta_t$ is a year effect, $x_{st}$ is a ($k \times 1$) vector of explanatory variables (like log of per capita domestic product in state-year [$s, t$]), the proportion of the domestic product in state-year ($s, t$) that is derived from the primary sector, the literacy rate in state-year ($s, t$), and the per capita newspaper circulation in state-year $(s, t)$. These variables are chosen to control for state specific factors that affect both state governments' fiscal policy choices and government characteristics. Fragment$_{st}$ measures the proportion of financial year $t$ during which the state government has more than one pivotal party. Elec$_{st}$ (the election year dummy) is a zero-one variable that equals one if financial year $t$ is an election year in state $s$, and the error term $\varepsilon_{st}$ has been presumed to be orthogonal to all of the regressors. In Chaudhuri and Dasgupta (2006), a financial year $t$ is considered as election year in state $s$ if a state legislative assembly election is held in the second half of financial year $t$ or in the first half of the next financial year, as described in Alesina et al. (1993) and Reid (1998). They use data of 14 major states of India over the period between 1974–75 and 1994–95 for studying whether the fiscal policies of state governments are systematically affected by the proximity of scheduled state elections and the extent of government cohesion. Their major findings are the following:

(*i*) State governments raise less commodity tax revenues, spend less on the current account, and incur larger capital account developmental expenditures in scheduled election years than in all other years.

(*ii*) Authors detect no election-year spurts in current account expenditure (as predicted by Rogoff and Sibert [1988]) and no election-year contractions in capital account spending (as predicted by Rogoff [1990]) in their paper.

(*iii*) In relation to single-party governments, fragmented coalitions have lower levels of own non-tax revenue and current account expenditure.

### 2.2.2 *Political Business Cycles*

The relationship between the size of the government and the growth of the economy, and the impact of this relationship are on re-election are vibrant issues in public economics. Wagner (1976) is supposed to be one of the earliest studies on the impact of expanding government size and growth of a nation. According to this study, the development of a nation is accompanied by an increase in the size of the government (government expenditure). This is known as 'Wagner's Law'. Since there is no clear cut procedure for defining the 'growth of a nation' and the 'expanding government size', econometricians, in order to test the 'Wagner Hypothesis', have estimated different models by defining both the variables in different fashion, which begets different versions of the Wagner's Law (see Lalvani 2003b: 124). However, the study by Wagner and Weber (1977) fails to identify any such evidence in their study of 34 countries. Since then, several papers on the 'Wagner Hypothesis' have surfaced. These econometric studies on the 'Wagner Hypothesis' may be classified into two broad categories: the 'non-parametric method' of estimation using the 'Multiple Rank F-test' and the 'parametric method of estimation' using time series and cross-section analysis. Holmes and Hutton (1990) find no evidence in favour of the 'Wagner Hypothesis' for India over the period between 1950 and 1981. The study by Bhat and Nirmala (1991) uses both the parametric as well as the non-parametric method of estimation and finds evidence of a reverse causality of the Keynesian type (i.e., government expenditure causes output growth) for India over the period between 1969–70 and 1988–89. Mohsin and Bhat (1992) find evidence of a bi-directional causality between per capita national income and government expenditure over the period between 1950–51 and 1989–90 for India. Therefore, there is no universal consensus either in favour or against the 'Wagner Hypothesis' for India. This is by and large true for other countries as well (see, for example, Lalvani 2003a).

Another issue that attracts econometricians is the theory of 'political budget/business cycle'. According to this theory an opportunistic incumbent political party attempts to manipulate policy instruments prior to elections in order to increase the probability of being re-elected. There are two different stands in this literature. One is the pre-rational expectation theories (Nordhaus 1975; Lindbeck 1976), which suggest large cycles in output and employment during the time of election (along with cycles in macroeconomic policy variables and inflation). The other is propounded by the post-rationalists (Rogoff and Sibert 1988; Rogoff 1990; Persson and Tabellini 1990) who claim that there would be an increase in budget deficit, money supply (via the monetization of deficit) and inflation during the election time but deny the presence of a significant political business cycle. Sen and Vaidya (1996) test the empirical implications of these theories for the Indian economy. They find evidence of a distinct increase in both budget deficit and its monetization in the years leading to an election. An evidence of a pre-election increase in the price of the manufactured products has also been identified. No evidence has been, however, found in favour of an electoral cycle in output and price level. Lalvani (2003b) examines the significance of the 'political cycle' for India over the entire period between 1950–51 and 1990–91 and also during the 1980s separately using the technique of 'mean growth rate', 'partial adjustment' and 'time varying parameter' technique. She finds evidence of 'political manipulation' for those macroeconomic variables on which governments have some discretionary power, when she uses the 'mean growth rate technique'. However, she does not find any evidence in favour of the political budget cycle for revenue deficit when she uses the technique of 'partial adjustment' and 'time varying parameter'. This directly contradicts the result previously obtained by Sen and Vaidya (1996). Lalvani (2003b) provides two explanations for this contradiction. According to this paper, the contradiction happens due to the choice of dummy variables that capture the effects of politics. Sen and Vaidya (1996) use single dummy variables. A string of dummy variables are, however, required, as noted by Lalvani (2003b) for explaining the issue more succinctly. Second, Lalvani (ibid.) perceives that 'learning on the part of the citizens' is responsible for not throwing in results which would indicate election time manipulations of key fiscal variables by politicians.

### 2.2.3   *Political Stability and Stagnation*

One of the interesting issues in the recent literature has been the impact of political instability on economic growth. As it is well known, India is a large democracy and experiences a periodical shifts in the political parties that form the government at the centre and at the provincial levels. There are also shifts from one-party dominance to multi-party coalitions. In this context, Lalvani (2003b) investigates the impact of political instability on economic growth on the basis of certain theoretical premises. Siermann (1998) discusses the adverse effects of political instability on growth, which are the 'adverse policies view' and the 'social unrest argument'. Any arbitrary change under uncertainty has an adverse effect on the saving rate, as noted by Venieris and Gupta (1986) whose central argument is that the politicians are likely to promote their own interests. This view is nothing but the argument of rent seeking, which had been as demonstrated by Tullock (1967). Krueger (1974) estimates the value of rents for India in 1964, which is around 7.3 per cent of national income. Within the 'adverse policies view', Alesina and Tabellini (1988) show that uncertainty about fiscal policies results in risk-averse individuals, who are hesitant about making new investments. Capital flight is seen to reduce domestic investment, and hence restricts economic growth. Tornell and Velasco (1992) argue that poor protection of property rights causes low investment.

Disagreements between various decisions makers (Alesina and Drazen 1991) and ideological differences between them (Frey and Schneider 1978) have an adverse effect on fiscal policy. Under political instability, coalitions of different groups of policy makers and minority government are seen to be more vulnerable. For example, left-wing governments favour expansionary policies accepting higher budget deficits, while others may not agree with this. As a result, policy makers in a more unstable political system are expected to behave more myopically and discount future. If the probability of the incumbent government to be re-elected is small, the government hesitates to undertake painful policies that threaten inflation, and cannot mobilize internal recourses effectively by redesigning tax system (Cukierman et al. 1992). While almost all empirical studies observe an inverse relationship between political instability and growth, Pindyck and Solimano (1993) do not find any relationship between them in their study.

Lalvani (2003a) examines the relationship between 'political instability' and growth for 14 major states in India using a 'pooled regression analysis' for the period between 1981–82 and 1998–99.[7] Regressing real state domestic product on political instability with a set of other control variables, for example, internal debt, tax revenue, grants from Centre, growth rate of capital outlay, urbanization and literacy rate, she finds that frequent changes in governing parties in the various states adversely affect growth rates and fiscal health of the Indian states.

The general presumption is that the political stability of a government depends on the success of economic development as an outcome of the policy implemented by the incumbent party. However, Sarkar (2006) explains the unusual political stability in West Bengal under the Left Front rule since 1977, despite relative economic stagnation. The Left Front government (that is, the alliance of CPI[M], RSP, Forward Block and CPI) came in power in West Bengal in 1977 by securing almost 47 per cent of the total vote in the Assembly elections. This share increased to almost 50 per cent in the Assembly elections of 1987. Although the Left Front's share of votes fell in the 1990s, it never went below the level they obtained in 1977. The Left Front's political success in the 1980s, as noted by Sarkar (2006), can be largely attributed to the phenomenal rise in agricultural production in West Bengal due to the introduction of 'high yielding boro rice cultivation'. This, coupled with the huge success of land reforms, and the decentralization of rural power via the 'panchayati raj' account for the political success of the Left Front in the 1980s. However, the 1990s became the decade of economic stagnation for West Bengal. The 1990s experienced not only a reduction in agricultural and industrial production, but the number of beneficiaries of land reform also fell rapidly, when compared to that of the 1980s. Despite these unfavourable aspects, the Left Front has not only been able to secure their position in state-level politics, but has also been able to maintain huge margins over their oppositions in different elections. According to Sarkar (2006), rapid informalization of the economy is the major reason behind the political stability of West Bengal.

---

[7] In Lalvani (2003a), 'political instability' is defined as a binary variable taking value unity in the year when a chief minister in a state is appointed between elections and zero otherwise.

Though the performance of the 'formal' industrial sector of the state deteriorated, the 'informal' sector grew rapidly over the last 20 years, thus making the people of West Bengal more vulnerable and dependent on the political parties for their survival in a regime where political support is available only in exchange for political allegiance. However, informalization alone would not have been able to do the trick as the experience of the rest of India demonstrates.[8] One must also consider the penetrating organization of the Left Front along with its role of a surrogate legal system that has kept the system stable in West Bengal for so long. Therefore, as he points out, a strong political organization is indeed necessary to reap the fruits of informalization. Both informalization and a strong organization are necessary to bring about political stability. One question comes up at this stage: Since informalization helps the ruling coalition to remain in power, does the CPI(M)-led Left Front consciously hinder growth of the formal sector in the state? While there is no conclusive evidence as to whether the government has consciously pursued a policy of hindering the growth of the formal sector, it is also true that it certainly has the incentive to do so. It may, however, be noted that the political society of the Left Front in West Bengal has not been confined to people surviving on the margins alone. The party organization has extended to cover a whole variety of people including school, college and university teachers and government employees. Hence, the question is really about the desirability of a strong party organization. An efficient party organization may certainly improve the welfare of the people if there are no distortions in the system, particularly the formal sector, and if the legal systems are well developed. But in the absence of that, an efficient political organization might backfire. It is also to be noted that according to Marjit and Kar (2005), the informal economy has flourished in every state all across India, but nowhere can one observe such sustained political stability as in West Bengal.

### 2.2.4  Interest Groups, Government Size and Growth

The theory regarding the impact of 'satisfied' voters or interest groups on economic growth was proposed by Olson (1982) and extended by Bardhan (1984) for India. Karnik and Lalvani (1997) examine the validity of the Olson-Bardhan hypothesis for 19 Indian states separately between 1982–83 and 1985–86 (for cross section regression analysis) and over the entire period (from 1982–83 to 1985–86 for pooled cross section time series analysis). They use per capita state expenditure (PCEXP) and per capita state revenue (PCREV)

---

[8] The informal sector grew not only in West Bengal, but throughout India.

as measures of government size, and the variable AGE as a proxy for 'interest group' for both the analyses.[9] They did not obtain conclusive results. While the pooled regression analyses have given evidence in favour of the Olson-Bardhan hypothesis, the cross section regression analysis contradicts the claim of the stated hypothesis.

The farm lobby is probably the most clearly identified 'interest group' in India that manipulates government policies. Karnik and Lalvani (1996) examine the nexus between this interest group and the performance of state governments with respect to Indian agriculture on the following two contexts: impact of interest group on the distribution of agricultural land, and its impact on the supply of public goods for agriculture. In their study (based on 16 Indian states over the period between 1982–83 and 1985–86), the supply of public goods for agriculture is measured by total expenditure by state governments on water, power and irrigation as a proportion of its total expenditure. The number of 'large land holdings' and 'area under large land holdings' are taken as proxy for 'agricultural interest group'. They undertake a simple 'Spearman's Rank Correlation' exercise (for 1985–86) to uncover the impact of the 'agricultural interest group' on agricultural subsidies provided by the state governments and also estimate an 'error component' model based on panel data for examining the impact of the agricultural lobby on the distribution of public goods for agriculture. Both the regression and the correlation analyses provide strong evidence of the existence of 'pressure' exerted by 'agricultural interest groups' on the framing of agricultural policy in India.

It is generally considered that a populist government, for the purpose of securing re-elections, dares to undertake policies that can hurt its own 'interest groups', but still manages to improve the level of welfare for a large number of people. Karnik (2002) derives a condition subject to which the government can undertake new reform policies without being afraid of losing elections. He also examines this condition empirically in the Indian context and shows that if the government reduces its amount of total subsidies and redistributes the money in education, and health, it generates an enormous number of beneficiaries. Consequently, the probability that an incumbent government gets re-elected could even increase by productive redistribution of public resources rather than the case where the government merely succumbs to the pressures from 'interest groups'.

[9] There are some other control variables too. See Karnik and Lalvani (1997) for details.

In a later study, Karnik (1996) explains the reason(s) why structural adjustment programmes in most developing countries do not resemble the Indian experience. In particular, the author tries to examine the impact of the structural adjustment programmes on economic growth by estimating the effect of reduction in government expenditure on private corporate investment and private household investment over the years between 1961–62 and 1988–89. As Karnik (ibid.) describes, while in the short-run, the government has to reduce its expenditure to contain its fiscal deficit, a populist government finds it difficult to curtail its non-developmental expenditure and subsequently reduces its developmental expenditures. The increment in non-developmental expenditure coupled with a reduction in developmental expenditure has a deleterious impact on economic growth. While an increment in non-developmental expenditure increases the amount of public debt in the following year's national budget (precisely the case for India in the 1980s), reduction in developmental expenditures hampers private corporate investment. In Karnik (ibid.), the relationship between government's expenditure and private investment has been examined using the technique of OLS and 'optimal control' for the Indian economy over the period between 1961–62 and 1988–89.

Results obtained from OLS show significant positive impact of both developmental and non-developmental expenditure on changes in public debt, which in turn has a negative impact on household investment. Private corporate investment is affected negatively by non-developmental expenditure and positively by developmental expenditure incurred by the government. Results obtained from the 'optimal control' analysis are also similar in character. Therefore, reduction in developmental expenditure due to political compulsions have an adverse impact on private investment and hence on economic growth. Again, while deficit in the fiscal front is financed either by borrowing or by monetization, the Government of India, however, pursues the first alternative to avoid inflationary pressure so as to maintain its political support. This results in a precipitous increase in public debt that ultimately hampers economic growth by affecting private investment adversely.

A different line of theoretical research on India's political economy looks at the role of redistributive politics, corruption and quality of public investment. Marjit et al. (2004) argue that the poorer the region, the greater the incentive for the incumbent government to go for a lower quality of labour-intensive public investment projects, such as low quality roads. On the other hand, in richer regions, the distribution of 'employment benefits' become costly, thus leading to more corruption and yet, better investment. They show, that in India, the ratio of capital to non-capital expenditure on roads is positively related to the state level income. Marjit and Mukherjee (2006) demonstrate that in democracies where the legal tax-transfer mechanism cannot be implemented efficiently, informal economic activities or redistributive 'transfer' mechanism to contain poverty and local investment will take place within the state. Thus, less egalitarian nations may impose lower tax but will also endure a weak-governance structure, somewhat contrary to the tradition of the median voter theorem. In a related paper, Marjit et al. (2006) have recently argued that trade-related reforms can expand or contract the size of the informal sector depending on the type of reforms. Hence, reforms may not necessarily contract unrecorded activities.

# 3. Fiscal Discipline in India

Redistributive policies usually hurt economic growth. This seems to be the consensus of those who have contributed to the contemporary literature on politics and economic growth. Papers by Alesina and Rodrik (1994) and others, well summarized in Persson and Tabellini (1994), articulate this view quite convincingly. While the argument rests fundamentally on the 'median voter' model, the theoretical papers by Banerjee and Newman (1993) and Galor and Zeira (1993) indicate different results. According to their studies, proper redistributive policies in this class of models can enhance human capital accumulation and hence eliminate poverty traps. The argument they put forward is that the voter, in an economy characterized by significantly skewed distribution of income, will favour a capital income tax, which will in turn hurt growth. The voter ignores the fact that such taxes can finance human capital accumulation by the poor. If that is the case, greater inequality should also call for pro-poor growth initiatives. Hence, the causal impact of inequality on growth should not be negative. The empirical exercises in Alesina and Rodrik (1994) demonstrate that it may not be the case after all and somehow inequality does not help the accumulation process. Therefore, more unequal societies should try to mend their social conditions before they launch a growth promoting strategy.

One issue that seems to be neglected in the literature has to do with the rationality of the 'poor' or the median voter. If the median voter believes that public investment in social and physical infrastructure, financed by taxing the rich, will improve their long-term income, then again, inequality will lead to more fruitful public investments and hence growth. It is quite true that the developing world in general has very poor infrastructure. Even one of the fastest growing developing countries such as India has remarkably inadequate infrastructural facilities and requires huge public investment. For example, paved roads as a percentage of total roads in the country accounts for only 57.3 per cent, while other growing countries (except Bangladesh and Pakistan) register at least 75 per cent as of 2002 (Table 1). An almost similar situation can be observed in case of the power facility in India. People having access to electricity, as a percentage of the total population, is only 43 per cent and per capita electricity consumption is 380 kwh in 2002. This is much lower than the per capita electricity consumption in other countries and India is comparable only with Pakistan. Moreover, almost one-fourth of the total electricity generated in India and Pakistan is lost due to transmission and distribution failure, which is quite high compared to others.

TABLE 1

**Infrastructure and power facilities in some east and southeast Asian countries, 2002**

| Country | Road paved (% total road) | Access to electricity (% population) | Power consumption per capita (kwh) | Transmission and distribution losses (% of output) |
|---------|---------------------------|--------------------------------------|-------------------------------------|-----------------------------------------------------|
| Bangladesh | 9.5 | 32.5 | 100 | 21 |
| China | – | 98.6 | 987 | 7 |
| India | 57.3 | 43 | 380 | 26 |
| Korea | 76.7 | – | 6,171 | 6 |
| Malaysia | 77.9 | 96.9 | 2,832 | 6 |
| Pakistan | 59 | 52.9 | 363 | 26 |
| Singapore | 100 | 100 | 7,039 | 9 |
| Sri Lanka | 81 | 62 | 297 | 18 |
| Thailand | 98.5 | 82.1 | 1,626 | 7 |

**Source:** *World Development Indicators, 2005*, World Bank.
**Note:** – Not available.

The infrastructure in India is poor because of inadequate investment. The capital expenditure, as a percentage of total expenditure in India, largely designated for infrastructure development, is not only low compared to the recently growing major East and Southeast Asian countries, but has also declined from 11.21 per cent in 1990 to 8.93 per cent in 2001 (Table 2). Although per capita expenditure on information and communication technology in

India increased from US$ 4.8 in 1992 to US$ 19 in 2001, still it is substantially below that incurred by other growing countries (Table 3).

TABLE 2

**Share of capital expenditure to total expenditure (%) in some East and Southeast Asian countries, 1990–2001**

| Year | India | Korea | Pakistan | Singapore | Sri Lanka | Thailand | Malaysia |
|------|-------|-------|----------|-----------|-----------|----------|----------|
| 1990 | 11.21 | 15.02 | 11.55 | 23.60 | 21.39 | 18.25 | 24.18 |
| 1991 | 11.35 | 15.87 | 17.04 | 22.55 | 23.20 | 21.68 | 16.47 |
| 1992 | 10.90 | 13.10 | 19.66 | 23.01 | 21.77 | 25.64 | 20.27 |
| 1993 | 11.38 | 13.21 | 14.89 | 23.82 | 25.07 | 30.00 | 20.08 |
| 1994 | 11.67 | 15.16 | 15.03 | 18.39 | 19.30 | 32.29 | 20.05 |
| 1995 | 11.25 | 19.99 | 16.08 | 22.82 | 21.30 | 34.53 | 22.69 |
| 1996 | 10.42 | 22.63 | 14.66 | 29.25 | 17.69 | 35.98 | 18.90 |
| 1997 | 9.70 | 21.66 | 12.43 | 30.01 | 19.23 | 44.59 | 22.98 |
| 1998 | 9.34 | – | 11.93 | 37.21 | 21.34 | 49.35 | – |
| 1999 | 9.11 | – | 11.01 | 32.34 | 22.55 | 48.59 | – |
| 2000 | 7.90 | – | 9.38 | 26.96 | 21.04 | 25.76 | – |
| 2001 | 8.93 | – | 7.49 | 26.20 | 18.36 | 22.19 | – |

**Source:** Ghosh and De 2005.
**Note:** – Not available.

TABLE 3

**Per capita expenditure on information and communication technology (US$), 1992–2001**

| Year | China | India | Korea | Singapore | Thailand | Malaysia |
|------|-------|-------|-------|-----------|----------|----------|
| 1992 | 6.7 | 4.8 | 339.1 | 1,200.3 | 56.4 | 143.3 |
| 1993 | 8.2 | 5.3 | 362.6 | 1,364.3 | 58.8 | 161.8 |
| 1994 | 9.8 | 6.6 | 411.1 | 1,594.5 | 65.7 | 179.6 |
| 1995 | 16.6 | 7.8 | 513.7 | 1,920.4 | 75.2 | 220.7 |
| 1996 | 20.2 | 7.2 | 669.2 | 2,176.7 | 86.9 | 256.7 |
| 1997 | 22.3 | 8.2 | 605.1 | 2,385.7 | 72.7 | 248.3 |
| 1998 | 31.4 | 13.2 | – | 2,348.2 | 52.1 | 214.7 |
| 1999 | 38.2 | 15.6 | – | 2,030.5 | 62.5 | 231.8 |
| 2000 | 46 | 17.7 | – | 2,103.6 | 70.8 | 259.1 |
| 2001 | 52.7 | 19 | – | 2,110 | 75.6 | 262.1 |

**Source:** Ghosh and De 2005.
**Note:** – Not available.

If the poor are interested in proper investment of resources raised by taxing the rich, the government should be more eager in doing that instead of funding short-run redistributive programmes. Technically speaking, lump-sum redistribution of tax proceeds as subsidies, which provide direct transfers to the poor, may not actually help them in the long run. Instead, proper investment of resources in infrastructure is likely to improve their income in the long run. Yet, there is a feeling, at least in India, that successive governments always prefer pure redistributive schemes to the promotion of public investment in infrastructure. This is true both for the central and the state governments. In the following sub-section, we try to examine the fiscal situation of India and observe how this has changed, (especially) after the adoption of liberal policies since early 1990s. In particular, we show that in the post-reform period, the capital and development expenditures have taken on the burden of adjustment for the maintenance of the so-called fiscal discipline.

## 3.1 Fiscal Scenario of Governments

Since the early 1990s, the Government of India emphasized the reduction of fiscal deficit, which loomed as large as 6 per cent of GDP in 1991–92—the period of severe economic crisis in India. This section presents a comparative study of the fiscal situation in the country between the pre-reform and post-reform periods.

Gross Fiscal Deficit (GFD) is defined as the difference between the sum of revenue expenditure, capital outlay and loans and advances net of recovery and the sum of revenue receipts and receipts through disinvestments, that is,

$$\text{GFD} = [R_E + C_O + L_R] - [R_R + D_L] \tag{1}$$

where, $R_E$ = revenue expenditure;
$C_O$ = capital outlay;
$L_R$ = loans and advances net of recovery;
$R_R$ = revenue receipt;
$D_L$ = receipts through disinvestments.

Dividing each term in equation (1) by the nominal GDP, we get

$$[\text{gfd}] = [r_E + c_O + l_R] - [r_R + d_L] \tag{2}$$
$$= [e] - [r],$$

where, the lower case letters indicate each term as a proportion to GDP.

We have reported the figures of government expenditures as a share of GDP in Tables 4–8. Now, GFD to GDP ratio (gfd) can be reduced either by reduction in the share of expenditure to GDP [*e*] and/or an increase in the share of receipt to GDP [*r*]. As per the empirical information provided in the tables and figures, the share of receipts to GDP [*r*] has not declined. It has, in fact, increased from 9.51 per cent in 1980–81 to 11.94 per cent in 1989–90 and then marginally declined to 10.48 per cent in 2002–03 (as depicted in Figure 1 and Table 4). On an average, it declines (though marginally) from an average of 10.91 per cent in the pre-reform period (1980–81 to 1991–92) to an average of 10.22 per cent in the post-reform period (1992–93 to 2002–03). Moreover, the share of expenditure to GDP [*e*] has gradually increased from 15.88 per cent in 1980–81 to 20.07 per cent in 1989–90 and then sharply declined to 16.94 per cent in 2002–03. Figure 1 portrays the declining trend of total receipts along with the total expenditure and GFD. Decreasing total expenditure becomes imperative if the government intends to reduce the GFD when government receipts are not increasing. Figure 2 also shows that the share of expenditure to GDP falls drastically from an average of 18.47 per cent in the pre-reform period to an average of 16.58 per cent in the post-reform period. As a result, 'gfd' has initially increased from 6.38 per cent in 1980–81 to 8.74 per cent in 1990–91 and then declined to 6.47 per cent by 2002–03. In other words, 'gfd' falls marginally from an average of 7.56 per cent in the pre-reform period to an average of 6.36 per cent in the post-reform period for the central government.

On the other hand, the fiscal situation of the state governments also replicates that of the central government barring marginal exceptions. Unlike the situation at the Centre, the share of expenditure to GDP for state governments has increased from 15.71 per cent in 1980–81 to 17.10 per cent in 2002–03 and on an average it has increased marginally from 16.56 per cent in the pre-reform period to 16.65 per cent in the post-reform period. However, the share of receipt to GDP for state governments has dropped and, as a result, the share of GFD to GDP increased from 3.23 per cent to 3.79 per cent on an average between these two periods. One can get the trend at the all-India level by adding up both the share of receipts and expenditure to GDP for the central and the state governments. It should be easy to observe that the resultant trend is similar to that of the central government.

Now, the important question is which sector in the economy has faced effective curtailing of expenditure, in view of controlling the overall expenditure? Broadly speaking, the total expenditure of the central government

TABLE 4

**Expenditure, receipt, and gross fiscal deficit of governments (% of GDP)**

| Year | Central government | | | State government | | | All India | | |
|---|---|---|---|---|---|---|---|---|---|
| | *e* | *r* | *gfd* | *e* | *r* | *gfd* | *e* | *r* | *gfd* |
| Pre-reform period | | | | | | | | | |
| 1980–81 | 15.88 | 9.51 | 6.38 | 15.71 | 12.52 | 2.85 | 31.59 | 22.02 | 9.23 |
| 1981–82 | 15.58 | 9.88 | 5.70 | 15.24 | 12.14 | 2.67 | 30.81 | 22.01 | 8.37 |
| 1982–83 | 16.55 | 10.28 | 6.27 | 15.80 | 12.46 | 2.94 | 32.35 | 22.75 | 9.21 |
| 1983–84 | 16.48 | 9.92 | 6.56 | 15.69 | 12.09 | 3.20 | 32.17 | 22.01 | 9.76 |
| 1984–85 | 18.36 | 10.54 | 7.82 | 16.46 | 12.31 | 3.68 | 34.82 | 22.85 | 11.50 |
| 1985–86 | 19.99 | 11.23 | 8.76 | 16.73 | 13.39 | 3.01 | 36.73 | 24.63 | 11.77 |
| 1986–87 | 21.36 | 11.89 | 9.47 | 17.43 | 13.74 | 3.33 | 38.78 | 25.63 | 12.80 |
| 1987–88 | 20.28 | 11.73 | 8.55 | 17.81 | 13.92 | 3.55 | 38.08 | 25.66 | 12.10 |
| 1988–89 | 19.69 | 11.52 | 8.17 | 16.76 | 13.32 | 3.08 | 36.44 | 24.84 | 11.25 |
| 1989–90 | 20.07 | 11.94 | 8.14 | 16.67 | 12.91 | 3.52 | 36.74 | 24.85 | 11.66 |
| 1990–91 | 19.49 | 10.76 | 8.74 | 16.98 | 13.01 | 3.68 | 36.47 | 23.76 | 12.41 |
| 1991–92 | 17.89 | 11.73 | 6.17 | 17.44 | 13.67 | 3.21 | 35.33 | 25.40 | 9.37 |
| Average* | 18.47 | 10.91 | 7.56 | 16.56 | 12.96 | 3.23 | 35.03 | 23.87 | 10.79 |
| Post-reform period | | | | | | | | | |
| 1992–93 | 17.27 | 11.30 | 5.97 | 16.92 | 13.53 | 3.10 | 34.19 | 24.83 | 9.07 |
| 1993–94 | 17.36 | 9.65 | 7.71 | 16.46 | 13.51 | 2.64 | 33.82 | 23.16 | 10.35 |
| 1994–95 | 16.78 | 10.49 | 6.29 | 16.92 | 13.33 | 3.02 | 33.70 | 23.82 | 9.31 |
| 1995–96 | 15.91 | 10.30 | 5.61 | 16.00 | 12.75 | 2.93 | 31.91 | 23.04 | 8.54 |
| 1996–97 | 15.55 | 10.19 | 5.37 | 15.76 | 12.29 | 3.00 | 31.32 | 22.48 | 8.36 |
| 1997–98 | 16.09 | 9.70 | 6.40 | 15.83 | 12.25 | 3.18 | 31.92 | 21.95 | 9.58 |
| 1998–99 | 16.81 | 9.72 | 7.09 | 15.93 | 11.04 | 4.65 | 32.74 | 20.76 | 11.74 |
| 1999–2000 | 16.40 | 10.44 | 5.97 | 17.20 | 11.80 | 5.21 | 33.60 | 22.24 | 11.18 |
| 2000–2001 | 16.54 | 10.27 | 6.27 | 17.64 | 12.55 | 4.72 | 34.18 | 22.82 | 10.99 |
| 2001–02 | 16.73 | 9.91 | 6.81 | 17.37 | 12.36 | 4.64 | 34.10 | 22.27 | 11.45 |
| 2002–03 | 16.94 | 10.48 | 6.47 | 17.10 | 12.37 | 4.55 | 34.04 | 22.85 | 11.02 |
| Average** | 16.58 | 10.22 | 6.36 | 16.65 | 12.53 | 3.79 | 33.23 | 22.75 | 10.14 |

**Source:** *Handbook of Statistics on the Indian Economy 2003–04*, RBI and own calculations.
**Notes:** * Pre-reform average (1980–91)
　　　** Post-reform average (1992–2002)
　　　*e* Expenditure to GDP (%)
　　　*r* Receipt to GDP (%)
　　　gfd Gross Fiscal Deficit to GDP (%)

can be broken down into two categories—the revenue expenditure and the capital expenditure. The data on the share of revenue expenditure to GDP and the share of capital expenditure to GDP are given in Table 5. Both the total revenue expenditure and the total capital expenditure can be further broken down into developmental expenditure and non-developmental expenditure. This means that the sum of revenue expenditure and capital expenditure is (almost) equal to the sum of developmental expenditure and

# FIGURE 1

**Expenditure, receipts and gross fiscal deficits of central and state governments and all-India, 1980–81 to 2002–03**

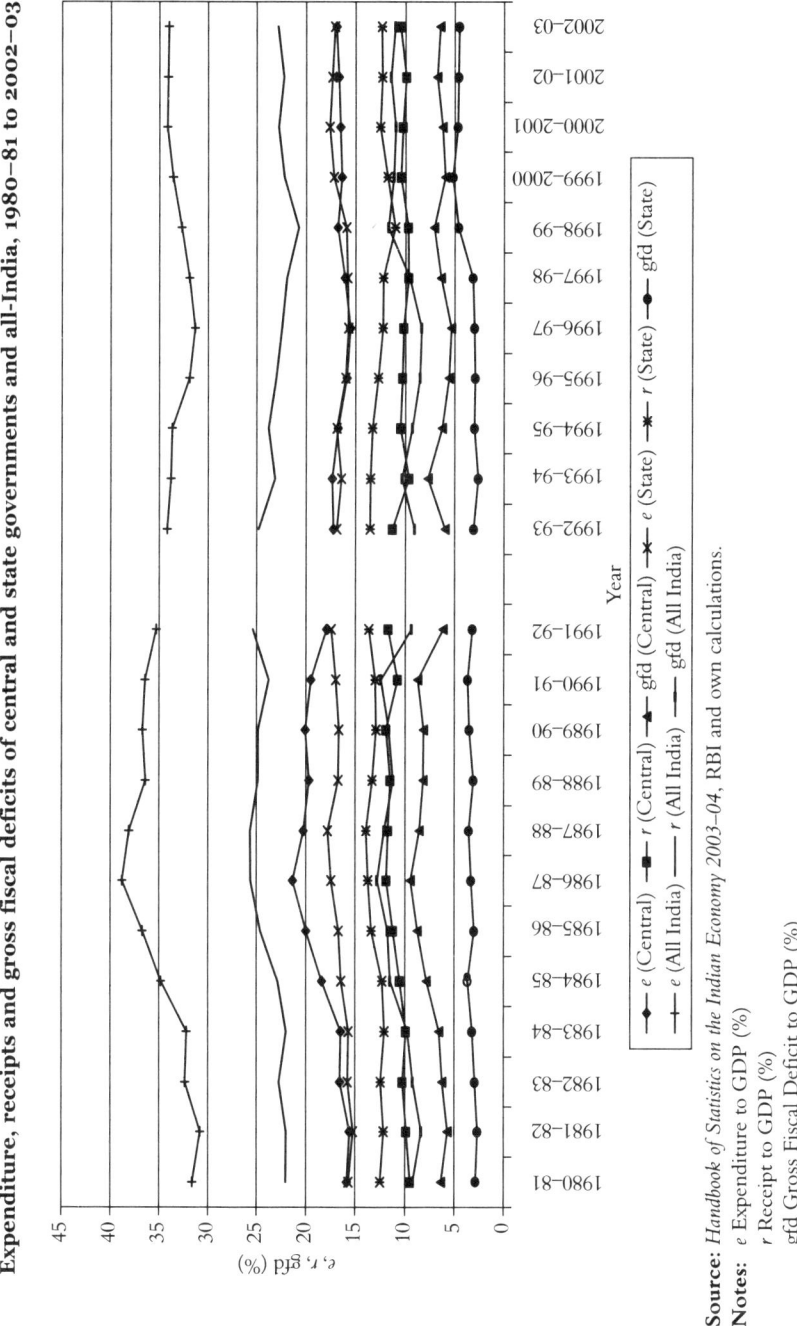

**Source:** *Handbook of Statistics on the Indian Economy 2003–04*, RBI and own calculations.

**Notes:** *e* Expenditure to GDP (%)

*r* Receipt to GDP (%)

gfd Gross Fiscal Deficit to GDP (%)

## FIGURE 2

**Pre- and post-reform average of expenditure, receipts and gross fiscal deficits at central, state and all-India levels**

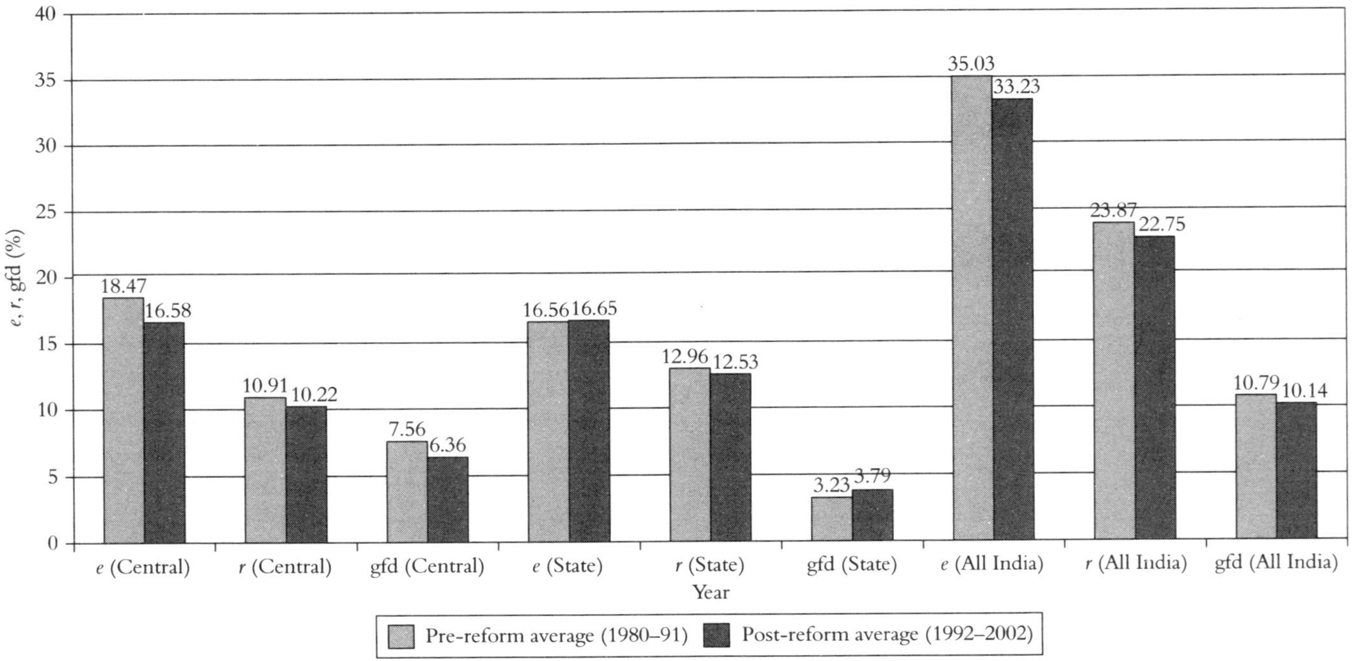

**Source:** *Handbook of Statistics on the Indian Economy 2003–04*, RBI.

**Notes:** *e* Expenditure to GDP (%)

*r* Receipt to GDP (%)

gfd Gross Fiscal Deficit to GDP (%)

non-developmental expenditure. It can be observed from Table 5 that the share of revenue expenditure to GDP for the central, state and all-India levels has increased from 11.07 per cent, 11.38 per cent and 22.45 per cent respectively in 1980–81 to 15.15 per cent, 14.83 per cent and 29.98 per cent in 2002–03, respectively for central, state and all-India levels (see also Figure 3). In other words, it registers a rise of almost 2 per cent on an average, from 26.08 per cent in the pre-reform period to 28.06 per cent in the post-reform period for the all-India level (Figure 4). Particularly, the share of capital expenditure to GDP for the central, state and all-India levels experiences a rapid fall from an average of 5.46 per cent, 3.51 per cent and 8.97 per cent, respectively, in the pre-reform period to an average of 2.78 per cent, 2.39 per cent and 5.17 per cent respectively in the post-reform period for central, state and the all-India level. The reduction in both the share of capital outlay to GDP and the share of Loans and Advances (net of recovery) to GDP has also been observed continuously (Figures 3 and 4). Therefore, Figures 3 and 4 together show that while attempting to curtail expenditure, the government essentially reduces the share of capital expenditure, while the share of revenue expenditure, which mainly represents the salaries and wages of the public sector employees, increases each year. Table 6 depicts the data on the shares of developmental expenditure and nondevelopmental expenditure with respect to GDP for the Indian economy over the period between 1980–81 and 2002–03. The table shows an increase in the share of non-developmental expenditure at the central, state and all-India levels from an average of 8.99 per cent, 3.92 per cent and 12.91 per cent, respectively, in the pre-reform period to an average of 9.64 per cent, 5.62 per cent and 15.26 per cent, respectively, in the post-reform period. During the same period, the share of developmental expenditure came down from 11.12 per cent, 12.49 per cent and 23.61 per cent to 8.24 per cent, 10.83 per cent and 19.07 per cent respectively for the central, state and the all-India levels. A time series plot showing the declining (increasing) trend for the share of developmental expenditure (non-developmental expenditure) can be observed from Figure 5. In a nutshell, therefore, the rising trend in the share of non-developmental expenditure co-exists with a decline in the share of development expenditure spanning the entire post-reform period (see also Figure 6).

The share of government expenditure on some of the important developmental and non-developmental heads is presented in Table 7, which shows that the rate of expenditure in all the important sectors including infrastructure (except housing) has declined in the post-reform period. This is also evident in Figure 7. The share of expenditure in agriculture and allied,

TABLE 5

**Expenditures of governments at central, state
and all-India levels (% of GDP)**

| Year | Central government | | | | State government | | | | All India | | | |
|---|---|---|---|---|---|---|---|---|---|---|---|---|
| | RE | CO | LR | CE | RE | CO | LR | CE | RE | CO | LR | CE |
| Pre-reform period | | | | | | | | | | | | |
| 1980–81 | 11.07 | 2.36 | 2.45 | 4.81 | 11.38 | 2.46 | 1.88 | 4.34 | 22.45 | 4.82 | 4.33 | 9.15 |
| 1981–82 | 10.13 | 2.76 | 2.68 | 5.44 | 11.23 | 2.36 | 1.65 | 4.01 | 21.36 | 5.12 | 4.33 | 9.45 |
| 1982–83 | 11.06 | 2.75 | 2.75 | 5.50 | 11.94 | 2.19 | 1.67 | 3.86 | 22.99 | 4.95 | 4.41 | 9.36 |
| 1983–84 | 11.20 | 2.63 | 2.65 | 5.28 | 11.98 | 2.15 | 1.55 | 3.70 | 23.19 | 4.79 | 4.20 | 8.98 |
| 1984–85 | 12.43 | 3.03 | 2.89 | 5.92 | 12.73 | 2.21 | 1.52 | 3.73 | 25.16 | 5.24 | 4.42 | 9.65 |
| 1985–86 | 13.59 | 3.07 | 3.33 | 6.40 | 13.13 | 2.19 | 1.42 | 3.60 | 26.73 | 5.25 | 4.75 | 10.00 |
| 1986–87 | 14.68 | 3.33 | 3.34 | 6.67 | 13.68 | 2.26 | 1.50 | 3.75 | 28.36 | 5.58 | 4.84 | 10.42 |
| 1987–88 | 14.61 | 2.94 | 2.73 | 5.67 | 14.27 | 2.11 | 1.43 | 3.54 | 28.88 | 5.05 | 4.16 | 9.20 |
| 1988–89 | 14.30 | 2.71 | 2.68 | 5.39 | 13.80 | 1.87 | 1.09 | 2.96 | 28.09 | 4.58 | 3.77 | 8.35 |
| 1989–90 | 14.66 | 2.70 | 2.72 | 5.42 | 13.75 | 1.82 | 1.10 | 2.92 | 28.41 | 4.51 | 3.82 | 8.34 |
| 1990–91 | 14.39 | 2.37 | 2.73 | 5.10 | 14.05 | 1.81 | 1.13 | 2.93 | 28.44 | 4.18 | 3.86 | 8.03 |
| 1991–92 | 13.97 | 1.94 | 1.99 | 3.92 | 14.63 | 1.71 | 1.10 | 2.81 | 28.60 | 3.65 | 3.08 | 6.73 |
| Average* | 13.01 | 2.72 | 2.75 | 5.46 | 13.05 | 2.09 | 1.42 | 3.51 | 26.05 | 4.81 | 4.16 | 8.97 |
| Post-reform period | | | | | | | | | | | | |
| 1992–93 | 13.77 | 2.02 | 1.48 | 3.50 | 14.29 | 1.58 | 1.05 | 2.63 | 28.06 | 3.61 | 2.52 | 6.13 |
| 1993–94 | 13.84 | 1.69 | 1.83 | 3.52 | 14.00 | 1.59 | 0.86 | 2.46 | 27.84 | 3.29 | 2.69 | 5.98 |
| 1994–95 | 13.32 | 1.62 | 1.84 | 3.46 | 14.01 | 1.89 | 1.03 | 2.92 | 27.32 | 3.52 | 2.87 | 6.38 |
| 1995–96 | 13.03 | 1.31 | 1.56 | 2.88 | 13.51 | 1.72 | 0.77 | 2.49 | 26.54 | 3.04 | 2.33 | 5.37 |
| 1996–97 | 12.78 | 1.14 | 1.63 | 2.77 | 13.59 | 1.41 | 0.77 | 2.18 | 26.37 | 2.55 | 2.40 | 4.95 |
| 1997–98 | 12.97 | 1.26 | 1.86 | 3.12 | 13.43 | 1.64 | 0.76 | 2.40 | 26.40 | 2.90 | 2.62 | 5.52 |
| 1998–99 | 13.55 | 1.18 | 2.09 | 3.27 | 13.77 | 1.44 | 0.71 | 2.15 | 27.32 | 2.62 | 2.80 | 5.42 |
| 1999–2000 | 14.19 | 1.37 | 0.84 | 2.21 | 14.87 | 1.45 | 0.89 | 2.34 | 29.05 | 2.82 | 1.73 | 4.55 |
| 2000–2001 | 14.66 | 1.31 | 0.58 | 1.88 | 15.38 | 1.64 | 0.62 | 2.26 | 30.03 | 2.95 | 1.20 | 4.15 |
| 2001–02 | 14.58 | 1.28 | 0.86 | 2.15 | 15.22 | 1.56 | 0.60 | 2.15 | 29.80 | 2.84 | 1.46 | 4.30 |
| 2002–03 | 15.15 | 1.30 | 0.50 | 1.80 | 14.83 | 1.62 | 0.65 | 2.27 | 29.98 | 2.91 | 1.15 | 4.06 |
| Average** | 13.80 | 1.41 | 1.37 | 2.78 | 14.26 | 1.60 | 0.79 | 2.39 | 28.06 | 3.00 | 2.16 | 5.17 |

**Source:** *Handbook of Statistics on the Indian Economy 2003–04*, RBI.

**Notes:** * Pre-reform average (1980–91)
** Post-reform average (1992–2002)
RE Revenue Expenditure to GDP (%)
CO Capital Outlay to GDP (%)
LR Loans and Advances of recovery to GDP (%)
CE Capital Expenditure to GDP (%)

mining, manufacturing and construction, transport and communications
and, finally, health has sharply declined during post-reform period. Moreover, almost all states in India registers sharp decline of capital expenditure
as a percentage of both total expenditure and net state domestic products
(Table 8).

# FIGURE 3

## Trends of expenditures at the central, state and all-India levels, 1980–81 to 2002–03

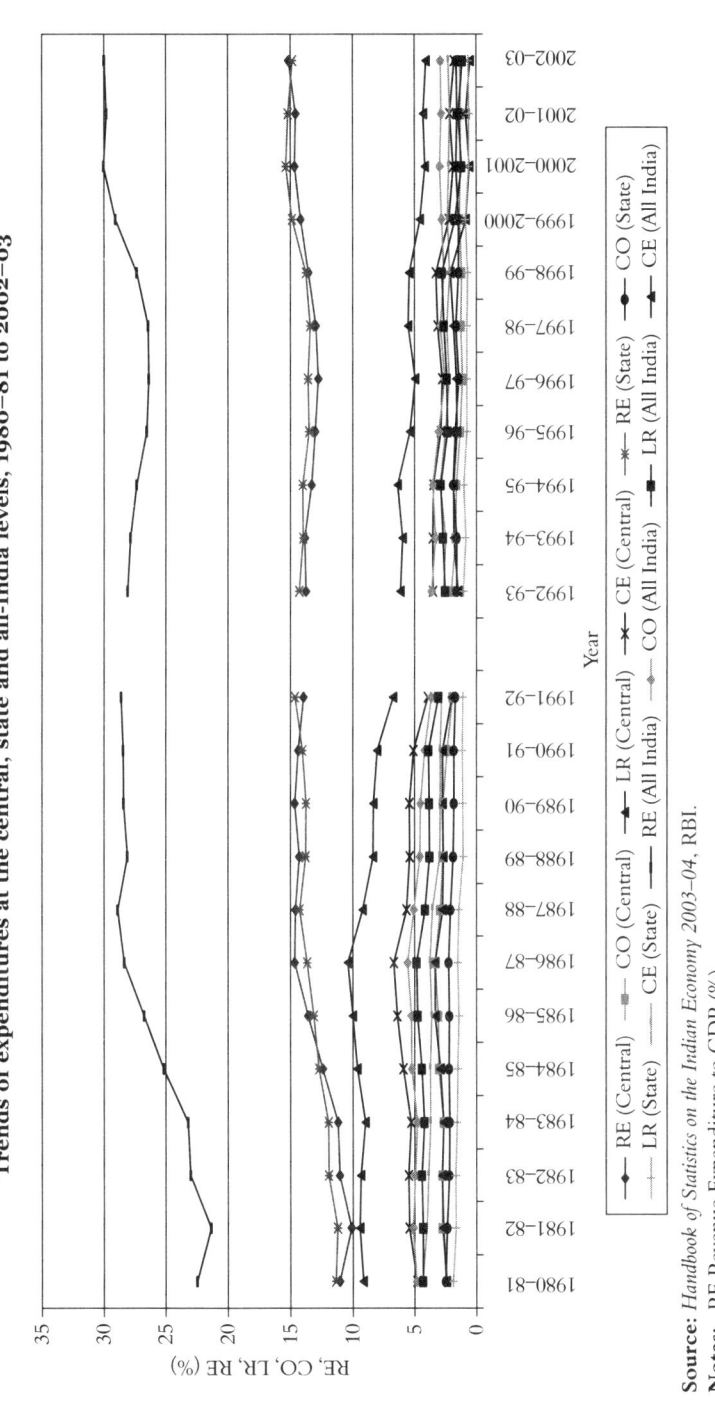

**Source:** *Handbook of Statistics on the Indian Economy 2003–04*, RBI.

**Notes:**
RE Revenue Expenditure to GDP (%)
CO Capital Outlay to GDP (%)
LR Loans and Advances of recovery to GDP (%)
CE Capital Expenditure to GDP (%)

# FIGURE 4

## Expenditures at the central, state and all-India levels in the pre- and post-reform periods

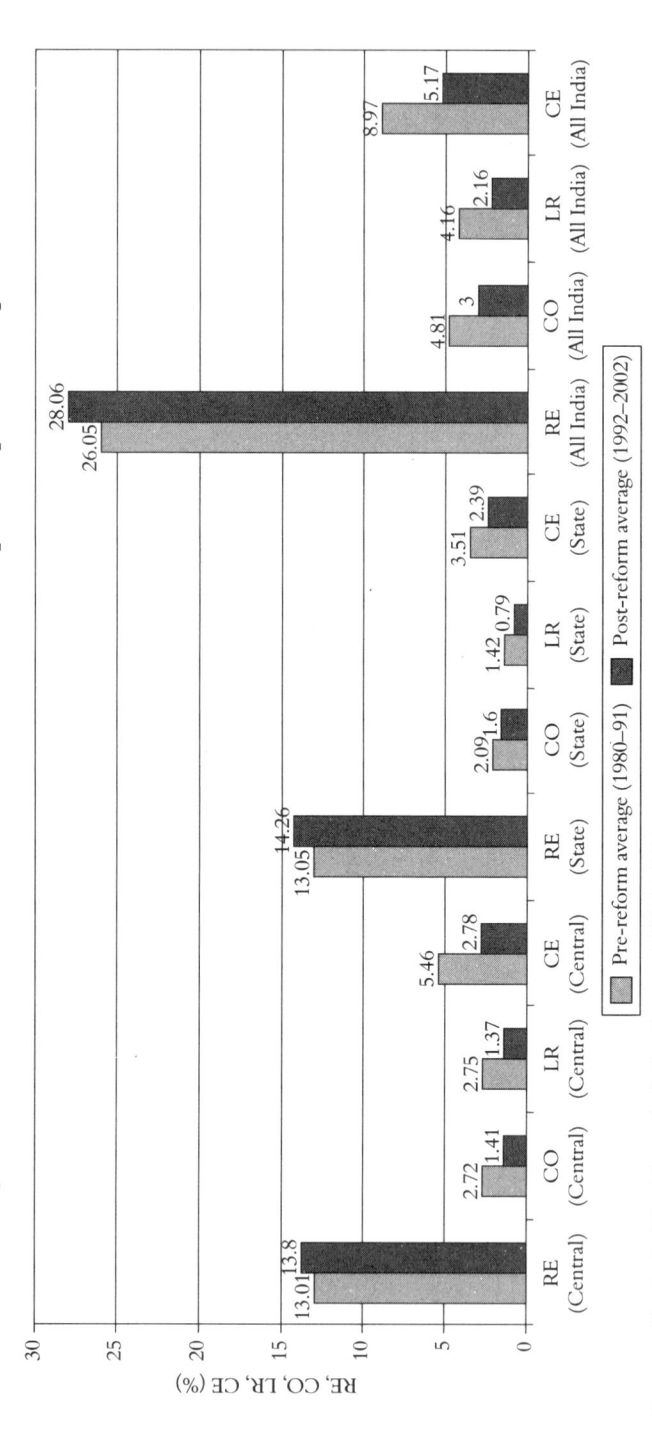

**Source:** *Handbook of Statistics on the Indian Economy 2003–04*, RBI.

**Notes:** RE Revenue Expenditure to GDP (%)
CO Capital Outlay to GDP (%)
LR Loans and Advances of recovery to GDP (%)
CE Capital Expenditure to GDP (%)

**TABLE 6**

**Developmental and non-developmental expenditure
of governments (% of GDP)**

| Year | Central government | | State government | | All India | |
|---|---|---|---|---|---|---|
| | DE | NDE | DE | NDE | DE | NDE |
| Pre-reform reform | | | | | | |
| 1980–81 | 10.24 | 7.58 | 12.26 | 3.30 | 22.50 | 10.88 |
| 1981–82 | 9.07 | 8.32 | 11.81 | 3.29 | 20.88 | 11.60 |
| 1982–83 | 9.64 | 9.38 | 12.18 | 3.47 | 21.82 | 12.85 |
| 1983–84 | 9.77 | 9.25 | 12.07 | 3.47 | 21.84 | 12.71 |
| 1984–85 | 12.29 | 8.32 | 12.55 | 3.75 | 24.85 | 12.06 |
| 1985–86 | 13.19 | 8.38 | 12.72 | 3.85 | 25.90 | 12.23 |
| 1986–87 | 12.76 | 9.37 | 13.24 | 4.03 | 25.99 | 13.40 |
| 1987–88 | 11.57 | 9.58 | 13.43 | 4.22 | 25.01 | 13.79 |
| 1988–89 | 10.97 | 9.38 | 12.41 | 4.20 | 23.39 | 13.58 |
| 1989–90 | 12.38 | 9.37 | 12.13 | 4.40 | 24.51 | 13.76 |
| 1990–91 | 11.48 | 9.66 | 12.40 | 4.42 | 23.88 | 14.08 |
| 1991–92 | 10.07 | 9.37 | 12.66 | 4.61 | 22.73 | 13.97 |
| Average* | 11.12 | 8.99 | 12.49 | 3.92 | 23.61 | 12.91 |
| Post-reform period | | | | | | |
| 1992–93 | 9.73 | 9.00 | 11.97 | 4.77 | 21.69 | 13.77 |
| 1993–94 | 9.27 | 9.42 | 11.44 | 4.87 | 20.71 | 14.28 |
| 1994–95 | 9.03 | 8.99 | 11.38 | 5.40 | 20.41 | 14.39 |
| 1995–96 | 7.87 | 9.19 | 10.70 | 5.16 | 18.56 | 14.35 |
| 1996–97 | 7.58 | 9.02 | 10.52 | 5.09 | 18.10 | 14.11 |
| 1997–98 | 7.98 | 9.20 | 10.45 | 5.16 | 18.43 | 14.36 |
| 1998–99 | 8.59 | 9.41 | 10.29 | 5.41 | 18.88 | 14.82 |
| 1999–2000 | 7.36 | 10.14 | 10.67 | 6.28 | 18.02 | 16.41 |
| 2000–2001 | 7.35 | 10.42 | 11.11 | 6.27 | 18.46 | 16.69 |
| 2001–02 | 7.70 | 10.41 | 10.47 | 6.67 | 18.18 | 17.09 |
| 2002–03 | 8.21 | 10.83 | 10.12 | 6.70 | 18.34 | 17.53 |
| Average** | 8.24 | 9.64 | 10.83 | 5.62 | 19.07 | 15.26 |

**Source:** *Handbook of Statistics on the Indian Economy 2003–04*, RBI.
**Notes:** * Pre-reform average (1980–91)
       ** Post-reform average (1992–2002)
       DE Developmental Expenditure to GDP (%)
       NDE Non-Developmental Expenditure to GDP (%)

Therefore, the discussion reveals that both the share of expenditure and that of receipt with respect to GDP have demonstrated an increasing trend till the mid-1980s, which resulted in an increasing trend in GFD to GDP ratio as well. A downward trend in each series can be observed since the late 1980s and early 1990s as the government attempts to contain gfd. In order to reduce expenditure, as the discussion shows, the government has merely reduced its expenditure meant for the developmental purposes, but has shied away from reducing its revenue expenditure.

**FIGURE 5**

**Trend of development and non-development expenditure (%) and the central, state and all-India levels, 1980–81 to 2002–03**

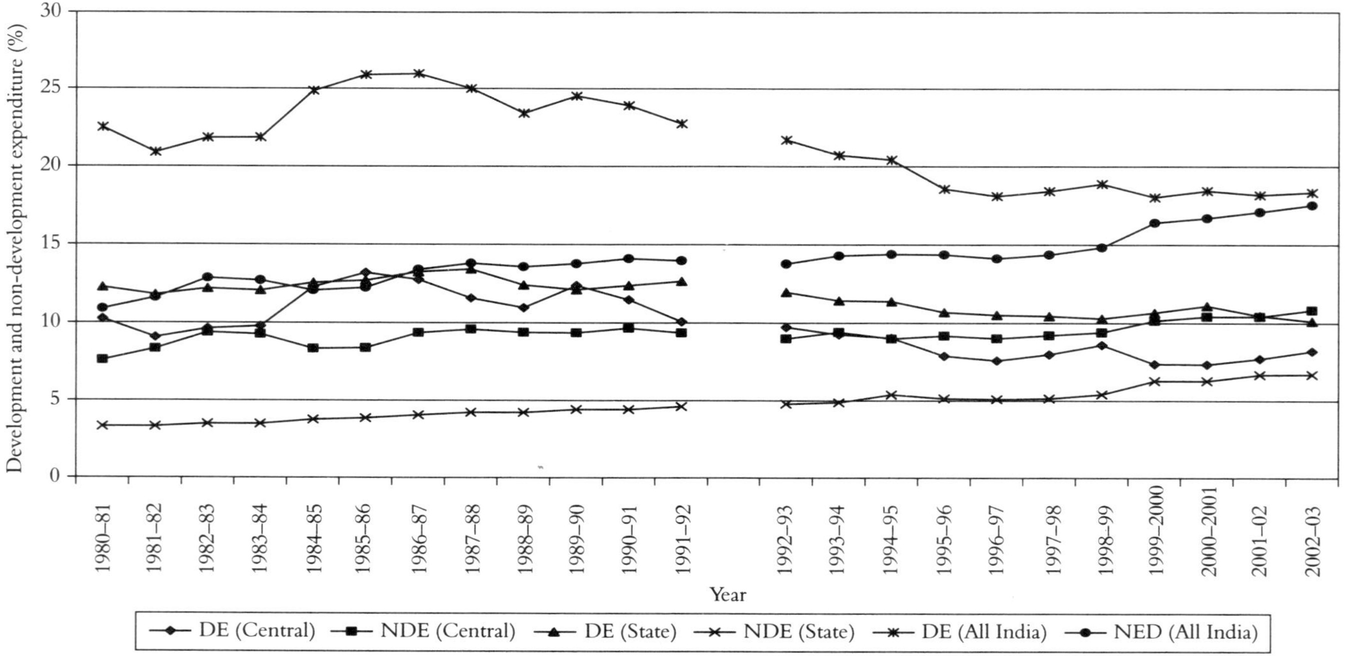

Legend: DE (Central) · NDE (Central) · DE (State) · NDE (State) · DE (All India) · NED (All India)

Y-axis: Development and non-development expenditure (%)

X-axis: Year (1980–81 to 2002–03)

**Source:** *Handbook of Statistics on the Indian Economy 2003–04*, RBI.
**Notes:** DE Developmental Expenditure to GDP (%)
NDE Non-Developmental Expenditure to GDP (%)

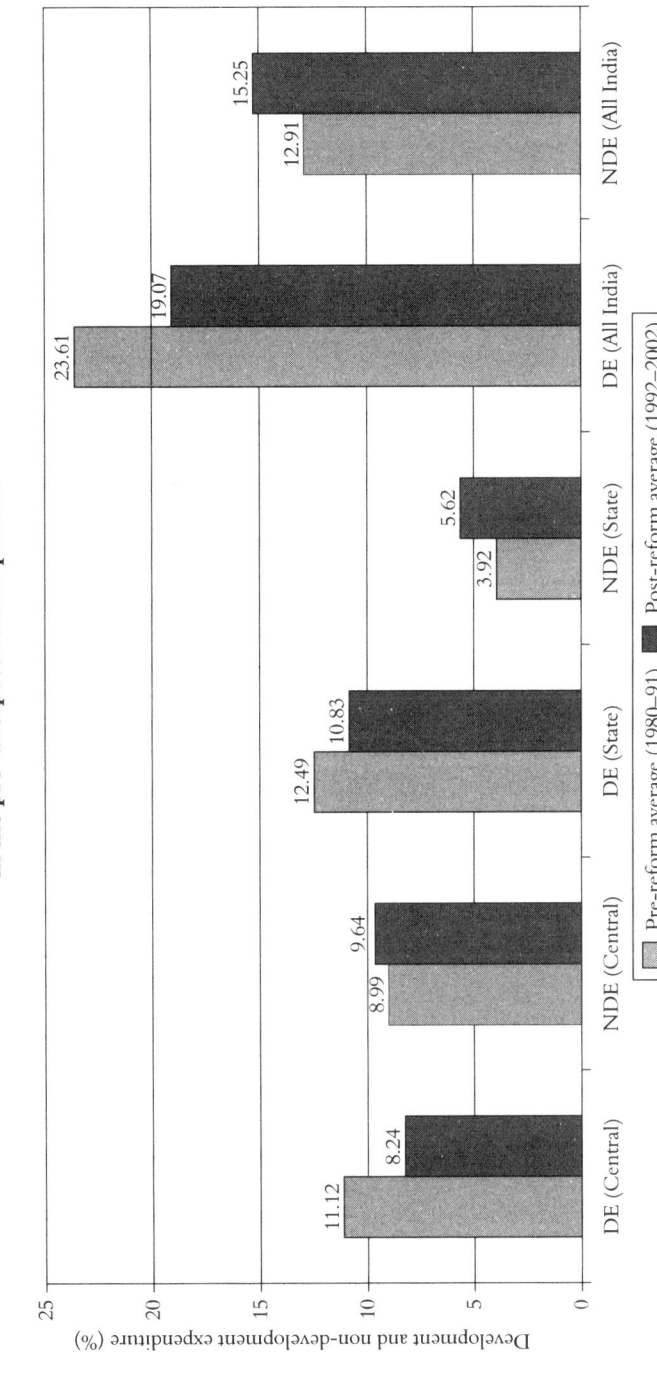

**FIGURE 6**

**Development and non-development expenditure (%) at the central, state and all-India levels in the pre- and post-reform periods**

Legend: Pre-reform average (1980–91) | Post-reform average (1992–2002)

DE (Central): 11.12, 8.24
NDE (Central): 8.99, 9.64
DE (State): 12.49, 10.83
NDE (State): 3.92, 5.62
DE (All India): 23.61, 19.07
NDE (All India): 12.91, 15.25

Development and non-development expenditure (%)

**Source:** *Handbook of Statistics on the Indian Economy 2003–04*, RBI.
**Notes:** DE Developmental Expenditure to GDP (%)
NDE Non-Developmental Expenditure to GDP (%)

TABLE 7

**Major components of government expenditures (% of GDP)**

| Year | Defence | Education | Health | Housing | Agriculture and allied | Mining, manufacturing and construction | Transport and communication |
|---|---|---|---|---|---|---|---|
| Pre-reform period | | | | | | | |
| 1981–82 | 0.285 | 0.026 | 0.027 | 0.050 | 0.078 | 0.095 | 0.041 |
| 1982–83 | 0.296 | 0.028 | 0.033 | 0.064 | 0.093 | 0.096 | 0.037 |
| 1983–84 | 0.293 | 0.027 | 0.035 | 0.065 | 0.110 | 0.089 | 0.036 |
| 1984–85 | 0.299 | 0.031 | 0.036 | 0.075 | 0.152 | 0.118 | 0.036 |
| 1985–86 | 0.319 | 0.032 | 0.036 | 0.087 | 0.137 | 0.109 | 0.041 |
| 1986–87 | 0.375 | 0.034 | 0.036 | 0.112 | 0.147 | 0.111 | 0.041 |
| 1987–88 | 0.376 | 0.049 | 0.035 | 0.117 | 0.141 | 0.100 | 0.037 |
| 1988–89 | 0.350 | 0.054 | 0.033 | 0.104 | 0.150 | 0.100 | 0.036 |
| 1989–90 | 0.326 | 0.045 | 0.027 | 0.137 | 0.139 | 0.105 | 0.049 |
| 1990–91 | 0.300 | 0.043 | 0.030 | 0.111 | 0.151 | 0.103 | 0.035 |
| 1991–92 | 0.276 | 0.039 | 0.028 | 0.103 | 0.142 | 0.073 | 0.032 |
| Average* | 0.318 | 0.037 | 0.032 | 0.093 | 0.131 | 0.100 | 0.038 |
| Post-reform period | | | | | | | |
| 1992–93 | 0.258 | 0.038 | 0.030 | 0.104 | 0.145 | 0.050 | 0.031 |
| 1993–94 | 0.276 | 0.032 | 0.030 | 0.115 | 0.098 | 0.036 | 0.031 |
| 1994–95 | 0.250 | 0.033 | 0.028 | 0.115 | 0.092 | 0.033 | 0.026 |
| 1995–96 | 0.247 | 0.035 | 0.026 | 0.116 | 0.086 | 0.032 | 0.023 |
| 1996–97 | 0.237 | 0.034 | 0.022 | 0.099 | 0.083 | 0.036 | 0.020 |
| 1997–98 | 0.252 | 0.037 | 0.025 | 0.097 | 0.091 | 0.027 | 0.028 |
| 1998–99 | 0.248 | 0.045 | 0.024 | 0.094 | 0.094 | 0.030 | 0.028 |
| 1999–2000 | 0.267 | 0.044 | 0.030 | 0.089 | 0.099 | 0.038 | 0.034 |
| Average** | 0.254 | 0.037 | 0.027 | 0.104 | 0.098 | 0.035 | 0.028 |

**Source:** IMF, *Government Finance Statistics Yearbook*, different issues.
**Notes:** * Pre-reform average (1980–91)
      ** Post-reform average (1992–2000)

## 3.2 The Relation between Public and Corporate Investment

One related and striking issue in this context is the impact of declining share of capital expenditure and development expenditure on private corporate investment. This becomes rather important especially when the government lowers the rate of public investment on infrastructure development. In this sub-section, we perform two separate cointegration analyses for the Indian economy between 1970–71 and 2002–03. We use two sets of data comprising variables to examine the long-run relationship between private and public investment. The two sets of data and their vairables are:

(*i*) Gross fixed capital formation to GDP for the private corporate sector ($I_{PC}$), capital expenditure of the central government as a percentage of GDP

## FIGURE 7

## Central government expenditures by sectors as percentage of GDP in the pre- and post-reform periods

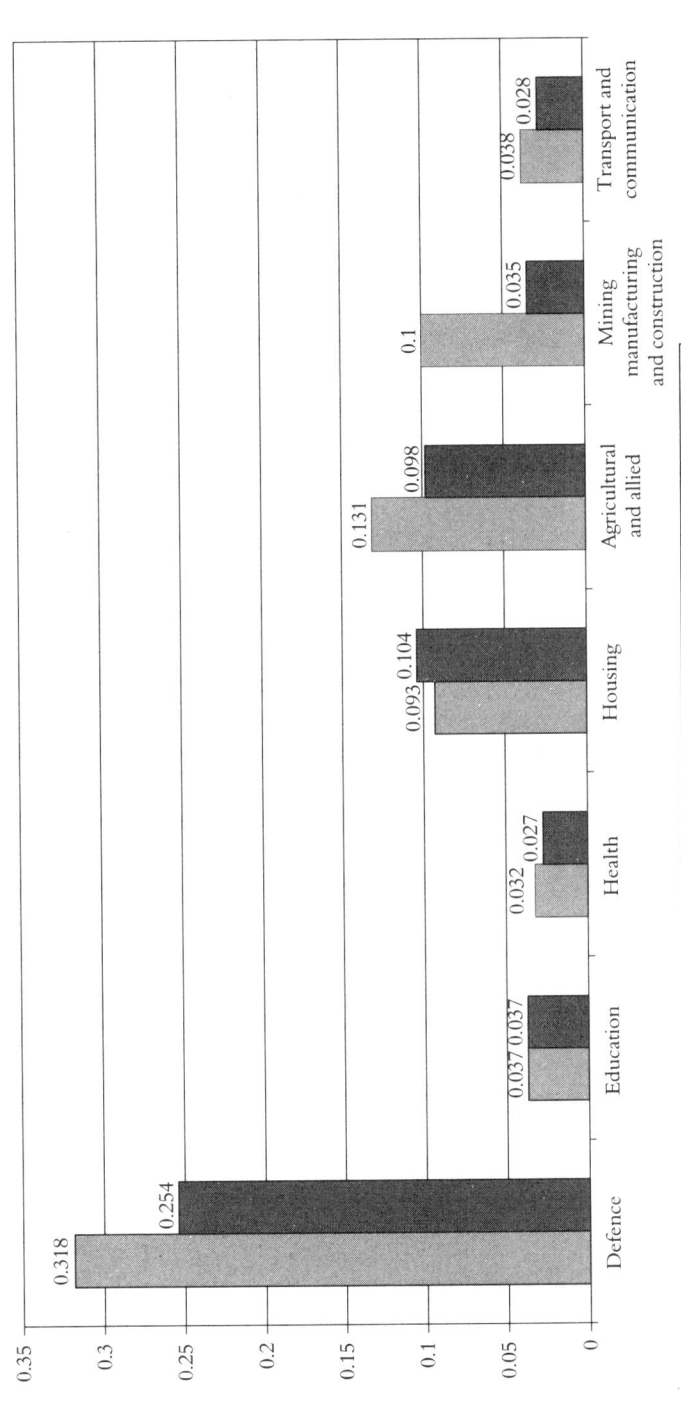

Pre-reform average (1980–91)   Post-reform average (1992–2000)

**Source:** IMF, *Government Finance Statistics Yearbook*, different issues.

## TABLE 8

### Capital expenditure as percentage of total expenditure and net state domestic products by major states in India

| Major states | Capital expenditure (% of total expenditure) | | | | | Capital expenditure (% of net state domestic product) | | | | |
|---|---|---|---|---|---|---|---|---|---|---|
| | 1980–81 | 1985–86 | 1990–91 | 1995–96 | 2000–2001 | 1980–81 | 1985–86 | 1990–91 | 1995–96 | 2000–2001 |
| Andhra Pradesh | 27.86 | 18.65 | 16.35 | 25.78 | 17.96 | 5.567 | 4.309 | 3.276 | 5.135 | 3.997 |
| Assam | 52.86 | 21.86 | 28.58 | 18.54 | 15.91 | 15.856 | 4.636 | 7.356 | 4.741 | 4.295 |
| Bihar | 48.15 | 29.27 | 21.38 | 10.20 | 15.35 | 12.344 | 6.383 | 5.301 | 4.399 | 5.956 |
| Gujarat | 37.37 | 24.87 | 25.37 | 18.91 | 18.89 | 7.484 | 4.904 | 5.218 | 3.312 | 5.712 |
| Haryana | 34.03 | 35.03 | 19.35 | 12.56 | 21.59 | 6.198 | 7.233 | 3.445 | 2.942 | 4.087 |
| Himachal | 44.44 | 30.06 | 19.38 | 18.97 | 17.66 | 18.886 | 12.993 | 7.814 | 7.516 | 7.808 |
| Jammu and Kashmir | 36.07 | 33.06 | 38.19 | 29.58 | 14.61 | 13.351 | 13.856 | 24.122 | 15.157 | 8.932 |
| Karnataka | 31.27 | 27.51 | 20.24 | 18.50 | 15.15 | 6.624 | 7.085 | 4.458 | 3.848 | 3.191 |
| Kerala | 21.95 | 26.58 | 16.33 | 16.80 | 9.66 | 4.466 | 7.316 | 4.119 | 3.101 | 1.994 |
| Madhya Pradesh | 36.07 | 27.89 | 19.54 | 13.71 | 11.45 | 7.434 | 6.114 | 3.952 | 2.566 | 2.636 |
| Maharashtra | 26.63 | 21.65 | 18.74 | 19.69 | 11.39 | 4.171 | 4.262 | 3.156 | 2.990 | 2.287 |
| Manipur | 55.63 | 36.98 | 32.19 | 23.67 | 18.12 | 40.182 | 22.239 | 18.333 | 13.610 | 9.948 |
| Meghalaya | 42.45 | 28.00 | 42.03 | 25.45 | 24.19 | 21.162 | 13.955 | 11.248 | 11.451 | 10.302 |
| Nagaland | 44.34 | 25.19 | 23.58 | 18.73 | 17.46 | 63.117 | 25.985 | 20.443 | 11.763 | 8.769 |
| Orissa | 38.34 | 29.03 | 28.21 | 15.55 | 20.08 | 8.874 | 5.979 | 8.097 | 3.631 | 6.543 |
| Punjab | 32.73 | 40.77 | 25.87 | 19.54 | 16.99 | 5.464 | 8.716 | 4.777 | 4.000 | 4.079 |
| Rajasthan | 25.25 | 28.05 | 77.87 | 23.62 | 14.05 | 5.116 | 7.213 | 6.205 | 6.179 | 3.502 |
| Sikkim | 30.70 | 25.38 | 30.08 | 11.21 | 19.42 | 24.490 | 21.239 | 23.517 | 26.127 | 20.756 |
| Tamil Nadu | 31.67 | 25.89 | 14.80 | 12.93 | 10.99 | 6.726 | 5.710 | 3.219 | 2.325 | 2.130 |
| Tripura | 38.98 | 26.73 | 18.88 | 20.51 | 18.78 | 19.180 | 13.291 | 11.470 | 9.788 | 8.236 |
| Uttar Pradesh | 35.68 | 30.55 | 22.07 | 15.54 | 15.40 | 6.177 | 6.002 | 4.962 | 3.249 | 3.617 |
| West Bengal | 28.16 | 24.01 | 14.93 | 17.92 | 17.34 | 4.142 | 3.728 | 2.597 | 2.804 | 3.596 |

**Source:** *Handbook of Statistics on the Indian Economy 2003–04*, RBI.

(*CE*) and Prime Lending Rate (*PLR*) of term lending institutions and (*ii*) gross fixed capital formation to GDP for private corporate sector ($I_{PC}$), developmental expenditure of the central government as a percentage of GDP (*DE*) and Prime Lending Rate of term lending institutions (*PLR*).[10]

Required stationarity tests (by Augmented Dickey Fuller and Philips Perron tests) for each variable have been run before performing the cointegration exercises. Each variable (other than PLR)[11] comes out integrated of order one (that is, I[1]). Each system comes out cointegrated with unique cointegrating vector. Results of the cointegration exercise, as reported in equations (3) and (4), imply that there exists a relationship of equilibrium among private corporate investment, government expenditure (both for capital expenditure and developmental expenditure) and PLR in the long run. The rate of private corporate investment is negatively related to PLR and positively related to both capital expenditure and developmental expenditure of the central government.[12] This indicates that private investment does depend on public investment in infrastructure and other development activities. Therefore, neglecting these areas of public investments should have an adverse effect on private investment.

$$I_{PC} = 7.28 + \underset{(3.15)}{0.84}\,CE - \underset{(-3.14)}{0.10}\,PLR \tag{3}$$

$$I_{PC} = 16.26 + \underset{(3.37)}{9.23}\,DE - \underset{(-3.84)}{0.13}\,PLR \tag{4}$$

**Note:** $I_{PC}$ = Gross fixed capital formation to GDP for private corporate sector,

$CE$ = Share of capital expenditure to GDP

$DE$ = Share of developmental expenditure to GDP

$PLR$ = Real Prime Lending Rate of term lending institutions

t-statistics are given in the parentheses.

Earlier, we demonstrated that the government resorts to harnessing the fiscal deficit by curtailing the rate of capital expenditure, and not revenue

---

[10] Data are collected from *National Accounts Statistics, CSO*, different issues and *Handbook of Statistics on Indian Economy 2003–04*, RBI.

[11] *PLR* turns out I(0).

[12] Since variables are taken in 'log', coefficients offer elasticity.

expenditure and that this bears an important political connotation. It is obvious that governments consider curtailing the rate of revenue expenditure
as a possible cause of unpopularity and in view of future elections, choose
politically safer alternatives in the form of curtailing the share of capital expenditure. Revenue expenditure reflects the burden of wages, salaries, pen-
sions, subsidies, and funds earmarked for employment guarantee schemes
and many other central/state sponsored schemes. One way to justify such
political strategy is to assume that the poor are either myopic or have a very
high rate of time preference, thus caring only about current consumption.
Given this preference structure, it is clear that the political parties currently
in power and seeking re-election will go for pure redistributive measures.
The standard mechanism by which inequality affects growth presumes that
taxes collected from the rich have no better use than increasing the current
income of the poor. If the government could create more valuable public
goods helping the poor, inequality would not be bad for growth. On the
other hand, models of inequality and credit market imperfection blame it
on the distribution of wealth skewed in favour of the rich. Embedded in a
political economy framework, such models would predict a democracy with
redistribution positively affecting the poor man's ability to borrow. This
should lead to better human capital accumulation and growth. Again, the
use of tax revenue as means for public investment in infrastructure is not
vouched as a theoretical possibility. If redistributive strategy could work
through the increasing possibility of human capital accumulation by the poor,
there would be some relationship between educational attainments in the
lower income groups and increasing access through institutional funding for
education. This has not happened in India; although, according to Burgess
and Pande (2005), a nationalized banking system, possibly at the cost of un-
economical expansion of bank branches in rural areas, does have a positive
impact on poverty alleviation. This will confirm the hypothesis that bank
nationalization was a politically correct strategy to be adopted. In what follows, we construct a simple example to argue why the poor, despite having a
fairly long-term view of life and hence a fairly low rate of time preference,
will still not desire a productive public investment programme that the government may consider. This in turn will mean that the government in its
own selfish electoral interest will be happy to engage in pure redistributive
policies. This will be consistent with a scenario where the benefits of higher
economic growth does not reach the poor and we experience the emergence
of a dualistic pattern of development.

# 4. A Simple Framework

In the following simple framework, we explore the possibility of a fairly rational reaction on the part of the poor that favours a pure redistributive policy package rather than long-term public investment in infrastructure. This reaction is consistent even in the face of substantial future benefits from public investment. The argument runs as follows. Indivisibility of infrastructural investment; poor resource mobilization, such as, inadequate tax revenues; regulatory problems crippling the possibility of private investment or public–private joint ventures in infrastructure and standard history of rampant corruption and false promises all lead up to substantial pessimism. The poor are hardly convinced that current investments will yield substantial benefits for them in future. This does not have anything to do with a high rate of time preference. In fact, even with a subjective discount rate of one, a more attractive policy package for the poor will be that of pure redistribution. In a way, the government cannot credibly pre-commit its intentions of pursuing something, which will be beneficial to the poor over a longer run. If there are two alternatives, one where the government promises to use tax revenue of Rs 100 for investment in major irrigation projects and the other, where the government just pays it to the poor as an unconditional subsidy, the poor will prefer the latter despite the realization that investment in irrigation is a more fruitful strategy. Given the awful track record of public investment in major irrigation projects, the promises of an investment will not be credible and the poor will, therefore, go for the bird in hand.

Some sort of explanation has, thus, been provided for why the 'median voter' would vote for a redistributive package involving taxation of capital income. Growth rate may still be enhanced if the provision for certain public goods through public investment is more efficient than through private investment. If such an argument is not taken care of, one does not know why taxing capital income would be bad for growth. What we try to argue is that despite such a positive role of public investment, the poor may still not favour it. Pure income transfer to the poor is not a substitute for lumpy public investment even if the poor put in that extra income only into investments. Underdeveloped infrastructure itself discourages private investment. All of this tells us that the 'median voter' will naturally be interested in tax-financed public investment. One has to explain why they are still inter-ested in having pure income transfers, subsidies or unemployment benefits. The case is, of course, different when such transfers are necessary for sheer survival.

In our terminology, the poor are those who do not pay taxes and the rich are the ones who do. Also, we have a homogenous rich group earning $Y$ as total income, and a homogenous class of poor people who individually earns $y$. The tax rate is $t$. It is a two period (present and future) framework. In the present period, the poor have per capita income $y_1$ and in the future $y_2$, $y_1 = y_2$, when there is no public investment in infrastructure ($g$). It is by taxing $y$ that $g$ is financed.

$$g = tY \qquad (5)$$

The income generation process is given by:

$$y_2 = y_2(\alpha tY) \qquad (6)$$

where $\alpha \in (0,1)$ represents the fraction of tax revenue actually invested in infrastructure. $(1 - \alpha)tY$ is lost due to various types of leakages, including corruption.

It is a bipartite democracy with the incumbent and the opposition. Both parties look only at the preference of the poor since they are the majority and announce a policy the poor prefer in order to be re-elected.

The fraction of income $tY$ can also be distributed as direct transfer, which the poor will consume in the current period. If there are '$n$' of them, each gets $(\beta tY/n)$, where $\beta \in (0,1)$. Leakages in a pure redistributive programme are represented by $(1 - \beta)$. Since infrastructural investment is indivisible, the poor cannot individually invest in infrastructure. Public investment is essential. Therefore, the typical poor can either choose

$$V_1 = y_1 + \frac{\beta tY}{n} + y_1 \qquad (7)$$

or, $\quad V_2 = y_1 + y_2(\alpha tY) \qquad (8)$

Note that by directly adding income for two periods we have implicitly assumed any subjective rate of time preference. Here, one has to check whether $V_2 > V_1$, that is,

$$y_2(\alpha tY) > y_1 + \frac{\beta tY}{n} \qquad (9)$$

It is logical to assume that if $\alpha t Y$ does not go beyond a critical value, say $\bar{I}$, infrastructural investment will simply not be possible. Therefore, for all tax rates, $t < \bar{t} = (\bar{I}/\alpha Y)$, $y_2 = y_1$, and $V_1$ will be opted for. In other words, if tax revenue is not substantial, the poor will be happy with direct income transfers because they know that the government cannot harness enough resources for investment. Similarly, for given $t$, if the extent of corruption and consequent leakage $(1 - \alpha)$ is very high, the same outcome will follow. The poor, although very much interested in public investment, perceives that the political authorities are incapable of guarantying substantial (effective) funds for infrastructure. Therefore, $V_1$ is the preferred choice.

### FIGURE 8

**Relationship between investment, income and taxation**

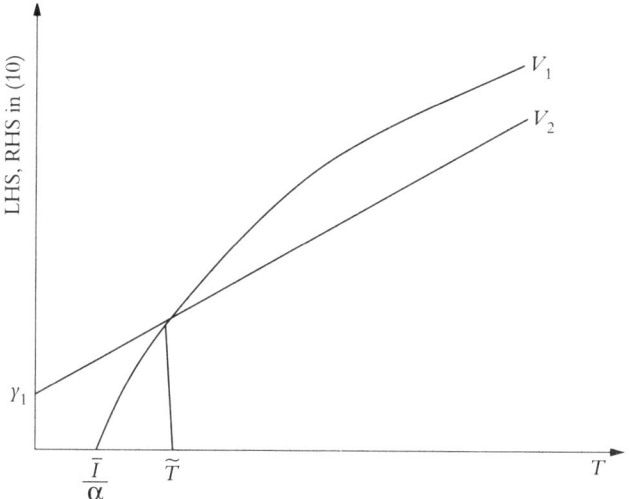

**Source:** Authors' calculations.

Let us look at Figure 8. We simplify by making $tY = T$, a lump-sum tax, $I = \alpha T$ and $y_2(I) = y_1$, for $I \leq \bar{I}$, with $y_2'(I) > 0$, $y_2''(I) < 0$, for $I > \bar{I}$. Now, equation (9) looks like

$$y_2(\alpha T) > y_1 + \frac{\beta T}{n} \tag{10}$$

Let $\quad y_2(\alpha \tilde{T}) = y_1 + \frac{\beta \tilde{T}}{n}$

It is clear that, $\forall T \leq \widetilde{T}$, $V_1$ will be preferred. Lower the $\alpha$ or higher the $\bar{I}$, $\widetilde{T}$ will shift further to the right, making $V_1$ the preferred political outcome. If the extent of infrastructural investment has to cross a threshold limit and the government does not have the means to harness enough resources, the poor will not vote for any public investment programme that promises high return only in the longer run. Coupled with this, there may be a perception of a very low $\alpha$ or a very high $(1 - \alpha)$. People may believe that a lot of promised investment will be lost due to corruption and other leakages. If direct transfers are easier to monitor by the people, then $\beta$ should be greater than $\alpha$, increasing the possibility of a higher $\widetilde{T}$. The ability of the poor to utilize newly created infrastructure, that is, the slope of the $y_2(\cdot)$ function, may be weak and lead will, therefore, to the same outcome. Evidently, the poor do care about the 'future' and are as 'patient' as anybody else, but they may choose to vote for a pure redistributive package. This note is a supplement to the standard 'median voter' theorem and the literature on inequality and growth. As stated earlier, the 'median voter' may be concerned about public investment financed by taxation and this may induce growth. One has to understand why the poor do not care about such investments.

The last exercise we perform in this context is to relate political competition to economic and social performance. We construct a 'political competition index'[13] or 'political sustainability index' by taking the ratio of the number of elections between 1980 and 2001 (Table 9). We correlate this index with some well known economic variables, that is, changes in the share of capital expenditure to NSDP, annual growth in real PCNSDP, annual growth of real capital expenditure by the states and also with changes in the human development index (HDI) (Table 10). We do not find any significant relationship between 'political competition index' and change in HDI as well as other economic variables. Observations suggest that there is reason for a detailed analysis of the economic performance of the state relating to political competition.

---

[13] 'Political competition index' (for a certain state) is defined as the number of actual changes in government (of a particular state) to total number of possible turnarounds. Though state assembly elections do not fall in identical years, attempt is made to cover the political turnaround of a state government from the early 1980s to the early 2000s, which is the concerned period for political turnover of major states, and to figure out the value in formulating an index. By and large, there has been six elections for each state during the above-mentioned period, where the total number of possible turnarounds is five for those six assembly elections.

### TABLE 9

#### Some political and economic variables of major states

| States | PCI | Δ(CE/NSDP) | $\gamma_{PCNSDP}$ | $\gamma_{CE}$ | ΔHDI |
|---|---|---|---|---|---|
| Andhra Pradesh | 0.8 | (–) 0.0157 | 9.91 | 9.61 | 0.45 |
| Assam | 1 | (–) 0.1156 | 4.34 | (–)1.07 | 0.37 |
| Bihar | 0.6 | (–) 0.0639 | 3.54 | (–)1.09 | 0.32 |
| Gujarat | 0.4 | (–) 0.0177 | 7.99 | 7.36 | 0.6 |
| Haryana | 1 | (–) 0.0211 | 6.77 | 7.41 | 0.68 |
| Karnataka | 0.8 | (–) 0.0343 | 10.8 | 4.49 | 0.6 |
| Kerala | 1 | (–) 0.0247 | 9.06 | 3.78 | 1 |
| Madhya Pradesh | 0.6 | (–) 0.0480 | 5.69 | 0.07 | 0.39 |
| Maharastra | 0.2 | (–) 0.0188 | 6.78 | 3.96 | 0.71 |
| Orissa | 0.6 | (–) 0.0233 | 3.54 | 3.56 | 0.42 |
| Punjab | 1 | (–) 0.0139 | 6.35 | 6.63 | 0.75 |
| Rajasthan | 0.6 | (–) 0.0161 | 8.38 | 8.74 | 0.47 |
| Tamil Nadu | 0.8 | (–) 0.0460 | 12.53 | 1.52 | 0.73 |
| Uttar Pradesh | 0.6 | (–) 0.0256 | 3.79 | 2.97 | 0.38 |
| West Bengal | 0 | (–) 0.0055 | 6.15 | 8.76 | 0.59 |

**Source:** *Statistical Report on General Election to Legislative Assembly of States*, Election Commission of India and *Handbook of Statistics on the Indian Economy 2003–04*, RBI.

**Notes:** PCI Political Competition Index (1980–81 to 2000–2001)

Δ(CE/NSDP) Change in share of Capital Expenditure to Net State Domestic Product (1980–81 to 2000–2001)

$\gamma_{PCNSDP}$ Annual Growth of Real Per Capita Net State Domestic Product (1980–81 to 2000–2001)

$\gamma_{CE}$ Annual Growth of Real Capital Expenditure (1980–81 to 2000–2001)

ΔHDI Change in Goalpost Values of Human Development Index (1980–81 to 2000–2001).

### TABLE 10

#### Correlation matrix

| | PCI | Δ(CE/NSDP) | $\gamma_{PCNSDP}$ | $\gamma_{CE}$ | ΔHDI |
|---|---|---|---|---|---|
| PCI | 1 | | | | |
| Δ(CE/NSDP) | (–)0.368 | 1 | | | |
| $\gamma_{PCNSDP}$ | 0.193 | 0.261 | 1 | | |
| $\gamma_{CE}$ | (–)0.196 | 0.798** | 0.352 | 1 | |
| ΔHDI | (–)0.378 | 0.289 | 0.358 | 0.092 | 1 |

**Source:** *Statistical Report on General Election to Legislative Assembly of States*, Election Commission of India and *Handbook of Statistics on the Indian Economy 2003–04*, RBI.

**Notes:** PCI Political Competition Index (1980–81 to 2000–2001)

Δ(CE/NSDP) Change in share of Capital Expenditure to Net State Domestic Product (1980–81 to 2000–2001)

$\gamma_{PCNSDP}$ Annual Growth of Real Per Capita Net State Domestic Product (1980–81 to 2000–2001)

$\gamma_{CE}$ Annual Growth of Real Capital Expenditure (1980–81 to 2000–2001)

ΔHDI Change in Goalpost Values of Human Development Index (1980–81 to 2000–2001).

** Correlation is significant at the 0.01 level (2-tailed)

## 5. Summary and Concluding Observations

The purpose of this section has been to track down recent developments in the quantitative tradition of 'political economy' in general and to identify analytical themes in the context of the Indian economy. The pattern of research that largely dominated the Indian political economy scenario so far has been discursive in nature. Recently, however, India has witnessed considerable development in the more empirically based approaches to the issue. These include, although not limited to, the issues in the federal system of governance, political alignment and centre–state relationship, political business cycles, analytical content of political stability, economic stagnation and interest group. We have devoted a substantial amount of concern to reviewing and highlighting major findings from research in these genres, typically in favour of further initiatives for work in the field.

We have reviewed some of the more influential studies in the area of the discursive traditions in political economy in India; the newer traditions in the quantitative approaches, which include discussions on the federal system of governance, political business cycles, political stability and stagnation. One other area that deserves special attention on account of its importance on purely economic considerations and no less for its deeply entrenched political implications, is the issue of fiscal discipline in India. Here, in particular, we raise the issue of the rationality of decisions made by the poor or the median voter in a poor democracy like India, in relation to their preference for public investments. This issue seems largely neglected in a wide variety of related papers that we have surveyed. We have emphasized that the lack of credibility that inflicts actual implementation of promised public investments and associated provisions in poor countries often influences the median voter to prefer short-run transfers over long-run publicly funded projects. This seems to be completely in agreement with the evidence in India, where the poor prefer unconditional subsidies in the short run to public investments in schools, health services, roads and electricity, knowing fully well that the latter variety of investments could improve their livelihood and quality of life for a longer period than any ad hoc transfers are ever capable of ensuring. We further argue that all political parties, whether at the centre or in the respective states, inculcate this attitude towards populist transfers for their own political stability. We further argue that it may not be the myopic attitude of the poor voter as much as the lack of trust on the government that forces a typical voter towards such decisions, which will turn out to be self-defeating in the long run.

This is, in fact, corroborated by evidence from the immediately preceding sub-sections on the fiscal conditions of the state governments and its implications for corporate investment. We have shown that successive governments strongly preferred reduction in the pace of capital expenditure meant largely for social and infrastructural development, while maintaining the revenue expenditure at its already high levels. The various policy implications associated with such practices in the country have also received due emphasis in the course of this deliberation. We hope that our endeavour will draw further insights and work in this vibrant area of research.

**Sugata Marjit,** Centre for Studies in Social Sciences, Calcutta, R-1, B. P. Township, Kolkata 700 094, India. E-mail: sugata@cssscal.org

**Dibyendu S. Maiti,** Centre for Studies in Social Sciences, Calcutta, R-1, B. P. Township, Kolkata 700 094, India. E-mail: dibyendu@cssscal.org

# References

Alesina, A. and A. Drazen. 1991. 'Why are Stabilisations Delayed?', *American Economic Review*, 81(5): 1170–88.

Alesina, A. and D. Rodrik. 1994. 'Distributive Politics and Economic Growth', *Quarterly Journal of Economics*, 109(2): 465–90.

Alesina, A., G. Cohen and N. Roubini. 1993. 'Electoral Business Cycle in Industrial Democracies', *European Journal of Political Economy*, 9(1): 1–23.

Alesina, A. and G. Tabellini. 1988. 'External Debt, Capital Flight and Political Risk', NBER Working Paper No. 2610, NBER.

Banerjee, A. V. and A. F. Newman. 1993. 'Occupational Choice and the Process of Development', *Journal of Political Economy*, 101(2): 274–98.

Bardhan, P. 1984. *The Political Economy of Development in India*. New Delhi: Oxford University Press.

———. 2003. *Political-Economy and Governance Issues in the Indian Economic Reform Process*. The Australian National University, Canberra: ASARC Publications.

Baron, D. and J. Ferejohn. 1989. 'Bargaining in Legislatures', *American Political Science Review*, 83(4): 1181–206.

Biswas, R. and S. Marjit. 2002. 'Political Lobbying and Fiscal Federalism—Case of Industrial Licensees and Letter Intent', *Economic and Political Weekly*, 37(8): 716–25.

———. 2005. 'Political Lobbying and Discretionary Finance in India: An Aspect of Regional Political Influence in a Representative Democracy', in N. Banerjee and S. Marjit (eds), *Development, Displacement and Disparity*. Delhi: Orient Longman.

Bhaduri, A. 1973. 'A Study in Agricultural Backwardness under Semi-Feudalism', *Economic Journal*, 83(329): 12–37.

Bhat, K. S. and V. Nirmala. 1991. 'Causality between Public Expenditure and National Income in India', *Marjin*, 23(4): 333–41.

Bhattacharya, D. 1999. 'Political Economy of Reforms in India', *Economic and Political Weekly*, 34(23): 1408–10.

Breton, A. and A. Scott. 1978. *The Economic Constitution of Federal States*. Toronto: Toronto University Press.

Burgess, R. and R. Pande. 2005. 'Can Rural Banks Reduce Poverty? Evidence from the Indian Social Banking Experiment', *American Economic Review*, 95(3): 780–95.

Central Statistical Organisation. *National Accounts Statistics*, Government of India, Different Issues.

Chakrabarti, A. and S. Cullenberg. 2003. *Transition and Development in India*. New York and London: Routledge.

Chakraborty, P. 2003. 'Unequal Fiscal Capacities across Indian States: How Corrective is the Fiscal Transfer Mechanism?', WIDER Discussion Paper, United Nations University, Helsinki.

Chaudhuri, K. and S. Dasgupta. 2005. 'The Political Determinants of Central Governments' Economic Policies in India: An Empirical Investigation', *Journal of International Development*, 17(7): 957–78.

———. 2006. 'The Political Determinants of Central Governments' Economic Policies in the States of India: An Empirical Investigation', *Journal of Development Studies*, 42(4): 640–61.

Cukierman, A., E. Edward and G. Tabellini. 1992. 'Seigniorage and Political Instability', *The American Economic Review*, 82(3): 537–55.

Dasgupta, S., A. Dhillon and B. Dutta. 2004. 'Electoral Goals and Centre-State Transfer: A Theoretical Model and Empirical Evidence', www.dur.ac.uk/economics.guestspeakers/2004_05/Dhillon.pdf

Drazen, A. 2001. 'How Does Politics Affect Economic Outcomes? Insights from "New" Political Economy', *The Political Economist*, Winter.

Election Commission of India. *Statistical Report on General Election to Legislative Assembly of States*. Various Issues, Government of India, New Delhi; www.eci.gov.in

Frey, S. F. and F. Schneider. 1978. 'An Empirical Study of Politico-Economic Interactions in the United States', *The Review of Economic and Statistics*, 60(2): 174–83.

Galor, O. and J. Zeira. 1993. 'Income Distribution and Macroeconomics', *Review of Economic Studies*, 60(1): 35–52.

Ghosh, B. and P. De. 2005. *Infrastructure Database*, Vols I and II. Delhi: Blackwell Publishing.

Holmes, J. M. and P. A. Hutton. 1990. 'On the Causal Relation between Government Expenditures and National Income', *The Review of Economics and Statistics*, 72(1): 87–95.

Inman, R. P. and D. L. Rubinfeld. 1997. 'The Political Economy of Federalism', in D. C. Mueller (ed.), *Perspectives on Public Choice: A Handbook*. Cambridge and New York: Cambridge University Press.

International Monetary Fund. *Government Finance Statistics Yearbook*, Different Issues. Washington DC.

Karnik, A. 1996. 'Why Do Structural Adjustment Programs Go Awry? Political Economy Perspective', *Cybernetics and System: An International Journal*, 27(1): 93–103.

———. 2002. 'Overcoming Political Obstacles to Economic Reforms via Redistribution', *Economic and Political Weekly*, 37(21): 2059–64.

Karnik, A. and M. Lalvani. 1996. 'Interest Groups, Subsidies and Public Goods: Farm Lobby in Indian Agriculture', *Economic Political Weekly*, 31(13): 818–20.

———. 1997. 'Interest Groups, Government Size and Growth', in D. M. Nachane and M. J. Manohar Rao (eds), *Macroeconomic Challenges and Development Issues*. Mumbai: Himalaya Publishing House.

Kletzer, K. and N. Singh. 1997. 'The Political Economy of Indian Fiscal Federalism', in S. Mundle (ed.), *Public Finance: Policy Issues for India*. New Delhi: Oxford University Press.

———. 2000. 'Indian Fiscal Federalism: Political Economy and Issues for Reform', in A. Lanyi (ed.), *Institutions, Incentives, and Economic Reforms in India*. New Delhi: Sage Publications.

Krueger, A. O. 1974. 'The Political Economy of Rent-Seeking Society', *American Economic Review*, 64(3): 291–303.

Lalvani, M. 2003a. 'Sounding the Alarm: Impact of Political Instability on Growth and Fiscal Health of the Indian Economy', *Economics of Governance*, 4: 103–14.

———. 2003b. *Political Economy of State Intervention in India—A Public Choice Approach*. Mumbai: Himalaya Publishing House.

Lindbeck, A. 1976. 'Stabilisation Policies in Open Economies with Endogenous Politicians', *American Economic Review*, Papers and Proceedings, 66(2): 1–19.

Marjit, S., S. Ghosh and A. Biswas. 2006. 'Informality, Corruption and Trade Reform', *European Journal of Political Economy* (forthcoming).

Marjit, S. and S. Kar. 2005. 'Pro-Market Reform and Informal Wage—Theory and the Contemporary Indian Perspective', *India Macroeconomics Annual 2004–2005*. Calcutta: Centre for Studies in Social Sciences.

Marjit S. and V. Mukherjee. 2006. 'Poverty, Taxation and Governance', *Journal of International Trade and Economic Development*, 15(3): 325–33.

Marjit, S., V. Mukherjee and M. Kolmar. 2004. 'Redistributive Politics, Corruption and Quality of Public Investment', Working Paper, www.ssrn.com

Mohsin, Md. and K. S. Bhat. 1992. 'Causality between Public Expenditure and National Income in India', *Asian Economic Review*, 34(2): 375–90.

Nordhaus, W. 1975. 'The Political Business Cycle', *Review of Economic Studies*, 42(April): 169–90.

Olson, M. 1982. *The Rise and Decline of Nations*. New Haven: Yale University Press.

Patnaik, U. 1987. *Peasant and Class Differentiation—A Study in Method with Reference to Haryana*. New Delhi: Oxford University Press.

Persson, T. and G. Tabellini. 1990. *Macroeconomic Policy, Credibility and Politics*. Chur: Harwood Academic Publishers.

———. 1994. 'Is Inequality Harmful for Growth?', *American Economic Review*, 84(3): 600–621.

Pindyck, R. S. and A. Solimano. 1993. 'Economic Instability and Aggregate Investment', NBER Working Paper No. 4380, NBER.

Rao, M. and N. Singh. 1998. 'An Analysis of Explicit and Implicit Inter-governmental Transfers in India', University of California at Santa Cruz, http://econ.ucsc.edu/~boxjenk/cre4.pdf

Rao, M. G. and N. Singh. 2001. 'Federalism in India: Political Economy and Reform', Working Paper No. 108, Centre for Research on Economic Development and Policy Reform, Stanford University.

———. 2003. 'The Political Economy of Centre-State Fiscal Transfer in India', in J. McLaren (ed.), *Institutional Elements of Tax Design and Reform*. Washington DC: World Bank.

Reid, B. 1998. 'Endogenous Elections, Electoral Budget Cycles and Canadian Provincial Governments', *Public Choice*, 97(1–2): 35–48.

Reserve Bank of India. 2004. *Handbook of Statistics on the Indian Economy 2003–04*. Mumbai.

———. *Handbook of Statistics on State Government Finances 2004*.

Rogoff, K. 1990. 'Equilibrium Political Budget Cycles', *American Economic Review*, 80(1): 21–36.

Rogoff, K. and A. Sibert. 1988. 'Elections and Macroeconomic Policy Cycles', *Review of Economic Studies*, 55(1): 1–16.

Sarkar, A. 2006. 'Political Economy of West Bengal: A Puzzle and a Hypothesis', *Economic and Political Weekly*, 61(4): 341–48.

Sen, K. and R. R. Vaidya. 1996. 'Political Budget Cycles in India', *Economic and Political Weekly*, 31(30): 2023–27.

Siermann, L. J. 1998. *Politics, Institutions and the Economic Performance of Nations*. New York: Edward Elgar.

Singh, N. and G. Vasistha. 2004. 'Some Patterns in Centre-State Fiscal Transfers in India: An Illustrative Analysis', http://econ.ucsc.edu/faculty/boxjenk/wp/SV_11Sept04.pdf

Tornell, A. and T. Velasco. 1992. 'The Tragedy of Commons and Economic Growth: Why Does Capital Flow from Poor to Rich Countries', *Journal of Political Economy*, 100(4): 1208–31.

Tullock, G. 1967. 'The Welfare Costs of Tariffs, Monopolies and Theft', *Western Economic Journal*, 5: 224–32.

Venieris, Y. P. and D. K. Gupta. 1986. 'Income Distribution and Socio-political Instability as Determinants of Savings: A Cross-Sectional Model', *Journal of Political Economy*, 94(4): 873–83.

Wagner, R. E. 1976. 'Revenue Structure, Fiscal Illusion and Budgetary Choice', *Public Choice*, 25(Spring): 45–61.

Wagner, R. E. and W. E. Weber. 1977. 'Wagner's Law, Fiscal Institutions, and Growth of Government', *National Tax Journal*, 30(1): 59–68.

# Section II

# Employment as an Objective*

AMITAVA BOSE
Indian Institute of Management Calcutta

This article discusses some macro effects of direct creation of jobs by the government in the government sector. In particular, we are interested in the effects of such action on aggregate employment. We show that if in the government sector employment is given an independent weight, maximizing social income may well end up in reducing aggregate employment.

**JEL Classification:** E10, J21, O11, O33
**Keywords:** Unemployment, Job creation, Choice of techniques, Productivity

## 1. Introduction

This article raises some questions about interventions by the government in the name of employment generation. It is not about the status of employment as a social objective. That full employment is among the best desired of social goals is simply taken for granted. What is also taken for granted, notwithstanding assertions to the contrary, is that the market is a notoriously imperfect institution when it comes to employment generation. Unemployment is a fact of life in every market economy. In India, liberalization may have improved GDP growth, but it hasn't helped the cause of employment generation. Not only did employment growth fall in the 1990s, it fell so sharply that unemployment actually went up. This being the case, it is quite natural to prescribe government intervention in preference to *laissez-faire* when it

* Earlier versions of this article were presented at seminars in Calcutta University in 2005 and Jawaharlal Nehru University in 2006. Some of the comments received on these occasions, including disagreements, have been stimulating. I should like to thank Sugata Marjit, Amiya Bagchi, Anjan Mukherjee, Gita Sen and S. Subramanian for their feedback in these seminars. I am also grateful to Kaushik Basu, Amit Bhaduri, Dipankar Dasgupta and Mukul Majumdar for encouraging written comments on the first, skeletal version of this article.

comes to employment generation. However, we need to be aware of certain problems. This article discusses some macro effects of the direct creation of jobs by the government in the government sector. In particular, we are interested in the effects of such action on aggregate employment. It is useful to carry out the analysis in the context of the well-known 'choice of techniques' framework of early development economics (Sen 1968, the introduction, in particular). Employment policy consists of selecting appropriate labour-capital ratios at the micro level. In what follows, that framework is extended so that technology, work environment and capital allocation get linked up.[1]

## 2. Technology and Employment: Choice of Techniques

In the literature on choice of techniques and social cost-benefit analysis (especially Sen 1968 and UNIDO 1972), government policy is driven by an aggregate social objective function that is reducible to a weighted sum of basic societal goals such as aggregate consumption, distribution of consumption, employment, health and so on. For the sake of brevity, we may refer to this reduced form of the objective as 'societal income'. The government uses different instruments to maximize societal income, one instrument being the micro-level project choice. This instrument induces choice of labour intensity at the micro level.

To see how project choice is used as an instrument of government policy, think of replacing profit maximization with the maximization of societal income as the appropriate decentralized objective for government units. The standard way to proceed is to say that if the government wishes to raise aggregate employment above what it would otherwise, then it should assign higher weightage to the employment component of the aggregate societal objective function.[2] Assuming that this decision is communicated down the line, the decentralized objective at project level would also increase the weight on

---

[1] We are going to ignore effective demand problems; the Kahn-Keynes multiplier can be superimposed on the present analysis. That multiplier has, if anything, been overworked. Our concern here is less with a definitive result-oriented theorem than with suggesting the need for a richer framework of analysis.

[2] In terms of market objectives, employment does not receive any independent weightage. It is valued only for the output produced and income generated. If employment is valuable *per se*, then that calls for an additional weightage. That weight has to be devised as a 'national parameter'. See UNIDO (1972) for details.

employment. Clearly, that amounts to giving preference to projects that are, *ceteris paribus*, more labour intensive.

It is necessary first of all to establish precisely the link between micro choices—involving labour intensity at the project level—and the macro effect of such choices on aggregate employment. The choice of techniques literature takes this link pretty much for granted. This actually amounts to slipping in a number of implicit assumptions that make the link appear to be obvious. However, some of these assumptions are, in fact, questionable, and we shall have occasion to abandon them.

We now spell out the two steps that are required to go from the micro to the macro. Although obvious though these steps may appear to be, spelling them out helps uncover certain hidden assumptions. Once these assumptions are relaxed, the link is snapped and, consequently, one finds that selecting more labour-intensive techniques at the micro level does not necessarily raise aggregate employment.

## 2.1 Step I: The Economy's Average Labour Intensity

Consider the relation between 'labour intensity' and 'employment' to be more or less as it would be in Sen (1968). To expose the micro-macro details, it is convenient to pose the question in an activity analysis framework. The aggregate production function can be derived from this framework in a familiar linear programming manner of which Koopmans' (1951) analysis is a classic example. So this paper, in fact, takes a peep into the derivation of the production function, viewing the construct as more than just simply given.

There are a countable number of production activities that make up the technological blue print of what is possible. Each production activity $j$ is associated with three variables: output, fixed capital and labour. These variables are well defined and all activities, when operated, produce the same kind of output good and employ the same kind of capital and labour. All activities require positive amounts of labour but may not require any capital and may not produce any output. Given constant returns to scale, each activity can be normalized by setting the level of labour input at unity. So each activity $j$ is characterized by an output-labour ratio $y_j$, a capital-labour ratio $k_j$, and an 'intensity level' $L_j$ denoting how much labour is being used. Thus, the employment level of activity $j$ acts as the scale variable while the other two variables together make up the input-output vector that fully identifies the $j$th basic activity.

Divide all activities into two mutually exclusive and collectively exhaustive sets. Let $A$ denote the set of positive integers, and $B$ that of negative integers.

If $j \in A$, then $k_j > 0$. For $j \in A$, we define the associated labour-capital ratio $l_j = (1/k_j)$ and this is a finite, positive number. We shall also write $K_j = L_j k_j$. Let $\theta_j = (K_j/K), j \in A$ with $\Sigma_{j \in A} \theta_j = 1$. Then, summing up $j \in A \cup B$, aggregate employment $L$ can be defined as:

$$L = \Sigma_j L_j = \Sigma_{j \in A}(K_j l_j) + \Sigma_{j \in B}(L_j) = K(\Sigma_{j \in A} \theta_j l_j) + \Sigma_{j \in B}(L_j)$$

In the above, the micro-level choice variables are the $\theta_j$s which are the capital allocation factors. Dividing through by $K$, it is seen that the economy's 'macro labour intensity' or the average labour capital ratio $(L/K)$ is the sum of two things: (a) the weighted average of activity level 'micro' labour intensities in the A-sector, the weights being the capital allocation factors; and (b) the sum of employment across B-sector activities divided by the aggregate capital stock. If a higher weight is placed on relatively more labour intensive activities at the micro level, that is, if a given amount of capital is reallocated in favour of more labour intensive activities, then that increases overall labour intensity. In this scheme, giving a higher weight to an activity is equivalent to allocating more capital to it.

Second, directly increasing employment $L_j$ in the pure-labour activities—those in the B-sector—also raises the average labour-capital ratio. In particular, it may be noted that one can always raise $(L/K)$ by adding a new pure-labour activity. On the other hand, introduction of a new activity in the A sector would affect the allocation of capital. Third, if some of the micro-level labour intensities $l_j$s were increased, that would raise the average labour intensity *ceteris paribus*. This operation can be seen as the combination of two things: (a) introduction of some new activities and (b) discontinuation of some existing activities. The former involves raising the capital allocation coefficient of hitherto 'dormant' activities for which $\theta_j$ had been 0; the latter involves changing the $\theta_j$ associated with an existing activity from something positive to 0. This case is therefore covered by the device of weight-changes discussed above. This concludes the first step.

## 2.2 Step II: The Aggregate Capital Stock

The second step is a very short one. It consists of going from average labour intensity to aggregate employment. Now, one assumption of the choice of techniques literature is that the aggregate stock of capital $K$ is given in the short run. Given this assumption an increase in the average labour intensity is equivalent to an increase in aggregate employment.

Breaking down the argument into two steps brings into focus two crucial assumptions, one behind each step. These are:

(*i*) the *ceteris paribus* clause: when some allocations are changed or some new techniques introduced, productivity levels in other activities are unaffected;[3] and

(*ii*) the capital immobility clause: when current indicators change, investors are slow to respond.

These two assumptions correspond to the requirements of the two steps in the argument. If the first assumption is violated, then an increase in labour intensity on some units does not imply an increase in average labour intensity. If the second assumption is violated, an increase in average labour intensity need not be accompanied by an increase in aggregate employment.

There are reasons to question both assumptions.

# 3. Productivity Effects

Let us suppose that the government creates some extra jobs that absorb some of those who were previously unemployed.[4] However there is not much work for them to do since their employment was not driven by market demand in the first place. The government action can be seen as the introduction of a new activity in the government sector. At the cost of sounding extreme, this kind of new activity may even be a zero output activity. If that is the case, it is to be located in the B-sector. The introduction of this activity certainly raises labour intensity in that particular organization, but does it increase *aggregate* employment? That depends on the validity of the *ceteris paribus* clause, to which one's attention must be drawn.

## 3.1 Work Norms

The fact that some people are given employment but not assigned enough work actually affects others who do have work to do. One desirable organizational goal is an equitable distribution of workload. In reality, work assignments are not divisible; this hampers redistribution of workload across activities. Organizational structures are fairly rigid too. Thus, it may not be

---

[3] Thus labour intensities in other activities are assumed to remain unchanged in the choice of techniques literature.

[4] They need not have been unemployed.

possible or feasible to equitably redistribute workload once the *status quo* has been disrupted by an act of deliberate job creation.[5] Therefore, 'disguised unemployment' is sometimes accompanied by blatant inequalities in distribution of workload. Once that happens, work norms get redefined *de facto*— perhaps informally—to reduce inequality of work effort. This is an exercise of effort equalization in which most people take the least work activity as the benchmark. Such exercises earn legitimacy and gain a measure of organizational acceptance precisely because they are seen as seeking to redress something that is not acceptable, viz., an unbalanced distribution of workload.

Thus, 'authorized' consumption of leisure in the work place by some individuals inevitably leads to increased consumption of leisure by other individuals, many of whom were not fortunate in the first place to be blessed with low demand for their services. In an entirely predictable manner, the average productivity level for the organization as a whole falls. Whether authorized or not, work norms get redefined *ex post* for such organizations.

### 3.1.1 *Digging Holes and Filling Them Up: Effort and Productivity*

One may refer, in this context, to Keynesian-style 'digging-holes-and-filling-them-up' strategies putatively designed to maintain work norms. An example of this could be to hire a person and ask him to copy out each day's newspaper, ending the day by destroying what has been copied. Will this help overcome the work-norms problem posed in the previous paragraph? It may or it may not. That would seem to depend on whether the belief in the illusion that this wholly artificial activity is a worthwhile thing to do can be kept up for any length of time. The internal motivation to apply adequate effort in assigned tasks depends, among other things, on credibility: the credibility of the assignment being useful to the organization and to the worker's self esteem. It is possible, of course, that a task is not really useful but we still believe—or are made to believe through deliberate brain-washing—that it is so. It is not that everyone has to be brainwashed. Only some people may need to be and then 'herd behaviour' can take care of the rest. I start believing that what I am doing is useful because others doing the same thing believe that it is so. Consider round-about methods, red-tapism and needless paperwork, especially in government administration. The creation of additional

---

[5] Of course to recognize this here is not to say that such rigidities are not relevant for other questions. In particular, absorption of technological change—to the extent that such change is not wholly predictable—requires a certain degree of flexibility in organization structure.

posts may simply lengthen the tape without tangible increase in output and with no apparent flagging of worker motivation or morale in the organization. However, the net result is a slowing down of production. The net result is a growing belief that the consumer is unimportant.

We need to distinguish between application of effort and productivity. Effort may not fall—at least not immediately—but productivity does. More-over, attitudes about the quality of output and relevance of work, change. These attitudinal changes have far-reaching consequences.

### 3.1.2 *The Leisure Epidemic and the Social Multiplier*

There is no reason to believe that the redesigning of work norms and the re-labelling of what is useless for the client as useful are things that stay confined to any particular organization in the government sector. There is fairly close communication between employees of different units within the state sector, especially on issues related to discrimination, rights and receivables. Second, there is social interaction outside the work place involving employees of different organizations. Third, the work environment of an organization is observed by customers and other agents who are themselves employees of other organizations. As a result, any erosion of work norms in one organiza-tion gets transmitted to several other organizations falling within a certain domain of contact and communication. Much of the recent work in diverse areas of macroeconomics emphasizes the 'social multiplier' that results from social interaction and 'herd behaviour'.[6] What we are emphasizing is that employment generation methods are not immune to these phenomena.

It should be stressed that the above issues of work norms are relevant for several categories of salaried employees. That includes not only workers and clerical staff but equally, if not more, officers, managers, professors and others. The impulse effects of deliberate employment generation on prod-uctivity spread out in concentric circles, engulfing one activity neighbour-hood after another. This kind of social multiplier may be referred to as the *leisure-at-work epidemic*.

The ultimate effect of this multiplier is a deterioration of 'work culture' over an entire region. It is possible to conceptualize work culture as an en-vironment good that enters individual and organization-level production functions as a shift parameter, affecting activity input-output coefficients. The deterioration of work culture is then like pollution. Deliberate job cre-ation has effects that are the opposite of investing in public infrastructure.

---

[6] See Banerjee (1992) and Glaeser and Scheinkman (2002), as samples.

It is stressed here that the epidemic is not confined to the government sector. It affects the expectations of both workers and employers. Thereby norms of work are affected across entire regions and they engulf the organized private sector as well. The difference is that in the private sector, the consumer is important. An activity is useful not because you are told that it is but because consumers are willing to pay for it.[7] Choices in the private sector are sensitive to commercial profits and the response to the pollution of productivity is pretty swift. We turn to these effects now.

# 4. Work Pollution and Employment

The effect that we wish to emphasize is the downward shift of the production function in the organized private sector as a result of the deterioration in the work culture good, work culture good being denoted as G. We can now work with the production function which is $Y = F(L, K, G)$. To begin with, $K$ is taken as given and effects of a fall in G on productivity, employment and profits are noted.

The impact effect on employment is ambiguous. That depends on how changes in G affect the marginal product of labour at different levels of employment. If work pollution reduces the *marginal* productivity of labour at the existing level of employment, then there must be a fall in the level of employment that maximizes profit at the existing wage rate. However it is not axiomatic that the marginal productivity of labour should fall. If it rises employment goes up, and if it is unchanged, employment is unchanged.[8]

For concreteness, assume G is labour augmenting in the manner of Harrod-neutral technical progress. Then, of course, a fall in G reduces the demand for labour at the prevailing wage rate. It also reduces output and profits. These effects are obvious.

## 4.1 Capital Mobility

There is a less ambiguous effect of work pollution. This can be uncovered by removing the capital immobility clause. The development literature takes the aggregate stock of capital as given for the short run. This is appropriate for the closed economy. However, when questions of 'regional' or 'sectoral'

---

[7] That market demand may reflect whims and fancies and itself be induced by herd behaviour is not relevant here.
[8] The reader is encouraged to explore these possibilities in terms of an activity analysis framework.

employment are at issue, it is better to allow cross-sectional mobility of capital. Additionally, contemporary economic reality has to reckon with global mobility of capital.

Once the assumption that the aggregate capital stock is fixed gets jettisoned, the question of what determines that variable has to be faced. In a general way, the aggregate capital stock $K$ will depend on the discounted stream of prospective returns (after taking into account opportunity costs including interest).[9] These prospective returns are, however, not that visible, since they belong to the future. Investors will, therefore, fall back upon certain currently observable 'economic signals' that they interpret as legitimate proxies for the real thing. The work environment is one such signal. Other things being equal, comparatively low marks for work environment—here represented by $G$—will reduce the regional $K$. A fall in $G$ will tend to reduce investments to the region. The precise rate at which the capital stock changes—the degree of capital mobility—depends on a host of factors that need not be spelled out here. Taking a large enough interval for the unit period, we may write:

$$K = K(G, r),$$

where $r$ is the current rate of profit and where an increase in $G$ and/or $r$ increases $K$.

Reverting to the exercise of this article, it is now immediate that a deliberate increase in government employment, in so far as it reduces $G$, leads to a fall in $K$. The effect of that is an unambiguous reduction in private sector employment.

It may be noted that if we shorten the unit time interval, the reaction to the fall in $G$ would show up as an impact effect reduction of the level of domestic investment. In the short run, the reduction in the aggregate demand for labour may usefully be seen in terms of a reduction of *effective demand*.

## 5. The Policy Dilemma

For the policy maker striving to abide by the social objective of generating more employment, the market presents a vexing problem. If in the

---

[9] Under imperfect capital mobility, it would be better to deal with changes in $K$ rather than its level. The change in the capital stock would depend on net imports of capital goods and domestic production of investment. The latter would have an effective demand effect on employment in the current period.

government sector employment is given an independent weightage, maximizing social income may well end up in reducing aggregate employment. This happens through adverse effects on the market demand for labour as argued earlier. So what should the policy maker do? It seems ludicrous to suggest that if the sincere policy maker wants to maximize employment then he should act as if he were trying to do the opposite. Chances are that he would be evicted from office in the next round of elections.

The point is that even if employment is an end in itself, it does not follow that giving employment only for the sake of giving employment is a good thing for aggregate employment. Disregarding what is produced and how continue to be relevant questions to ask. As productivity and output effects have a habit of quickly spilling over, it is risky to assume that when some extra jobs are created, the effects are only local. At one level, this may be seen as a challenge to the problem of decentralizability of national objectives: *other things are far from unchanged*.

**Amitava Bose,** Indian Institute of Management Calcutta, Diamond Harbour Road, Joka, Kolkata 700 104, India. E-mail: abose@iimcal.ac.in

# References

Banerjee, A. 1992. 'A Simple Model of Herd Behaviour', *Quarterly Journal of Economics*, 107(3): 797–818.
Glaeser, E. and J. A. Scheinkman. 2002. 'Non-Market Interactions', in M. Dewatripont, L. P. Hansen and S. Turnovsky (eds), *Advances in Economics and Econometrics: Theory and Applications, Eighth World Congress*. Cambridge: Cambridge University Press.
Koopmans, T. C. 1951. 'Analysis of Production as an Efficient Combination of Activities', in *Activity Analysis of Production and Allocation*, Cowes Commission Monograph 13. New York: Wiley.
Sen, Amartya. 1968. *Choice of Techniques*, 3rd Edition. Oxford: Blackwell Publishing.
UNIDO. 1972. *Guidelines for Project Evaluation*. New York: United Nations.

# Technology as a Channel of Economic Growth in India

SUPARNA CHAKRABORTY*
Baruch College, City University of New York

After decades of slow growth since independence from the British Raj, Indian economy registered its own small miracle, when growth rate of GDP per capita surpassed the long-term growth rate of many advanced economies. What caused this miracle? This article searches for an answer in the neoclassical growth model. Productivity as measured by Solow residual is used as the exogenous shock. The idea is to quantitatively measure to what extent fluctuations in productivity can account for observed fluctuations in macroeconomic aggregates in India. We find that exogenous fluctuations in productivity can well account for fluctuations in output during the boom periods of 1982–88 and 1993–2002. However, fluctuations in productivity alone result in a much worse drop in output during the period between 1988 to 1993 than observed in the economy.

**JEL Classification**: E10, O11, O14, O33
**Keywords**: GDP growth, Growth accounting, Transition dynamics, India

## 1. Introduction

Since the 1980s the Indian economy has rapidly transformed itself from a poor economy that at best earned the label of a 'developing' economy to an economy viewed by many as the new miracle. A brief look at the growth rate of GDP per capita bears testimony to this fact. During the period between 1960 and 1979, the growth rate of GDP per capita stood at 1.1 per cent. Since 1980, the growth rate has increased to 3.8 per cent, which is higher

* I am thankful to Sugata Marjit, an anonymous referee and other seminar participants for their comments. I gratefully acknowledge the support of the RBI Endowment at the Centre for Studies in Social Sciences, Calcutta for hosting me as a visiting scholar during this project. All errors are mine.

than the long-term growth rate of 2 per cent observed in many industrialized countries, like the United States.

In this article, I ask the question 'To what extent can changes in productivity quantitatively account for the observed changes in output per capita?' The common understanding is that the Indian economy saw an unprecedented spurt of software development, which, coupled with drastic changes in policy encouraging free markets and liberalization, led to a rapid growth in productivity. This development, coupled with the fact that India is traditionally a cheap labour market, which now became a source of skilled labour, at least in the software arena, led to increases in output per capita.

Literature in this area has been comparatively sparse, though much debate has ensued as to what caused India's small miracle? There are quite a few papers which agree with the contribution of Indian IT sector as the catalyst of economic growth. On the one hand we have Singh (2004) who argues in favour of the important role played by the Indian IT sector in promoting growth. This view, perhaps not surprisingly, finds great support among the IT pioneers of India. N.R. Narayan Murthy, Chief Mentor of Infosys, one of the fastest growing IT companies that originated in India, hails the changing climate in India by arguing at the Indian Economy Conference at Cornell University (2002) that '... the economic reforms of 1991 changed the Indian business context from one of state-centred, control orientation, to a free, open market orientation—especially for hi-tech companies. It allowed Indian companies to start competing effectively on a global scale'. On the other end of the spectrum, we have Subramanian and Rodrick (2004) who investigate '... a number of hypotheses about the causes of this growth—favourable external environment, fiscal stimulus, trade liberalization, internal liberalization, the green revolution, public investment—and find them wanting'. They argue that '... growth was triggered by an attitudinal shift on the part of the national government towards a pro-business (as opposed to pro-liberalization) approach'. So, it is probably safe to surmise that the debate as to the cause of growth is very much alive.

I take an alternative approach to the entire question by trying to quantitatively account for the extent to which the growth rate of GDP per capita can be explained by growth in aggregate productivity. To this end, I use a dynamic general equilibrium model with exogenous productivity as representative of the Indian economy. My objective is to see how output per capita, investment per capita and labour respond to an exogenous change in productivity.

My approach is the neoclassical approach of business cycle accounting popularized by Kydland and Prescott (1982). The economy is modelled as a dynamic general equilibrium where the only source of exogenous shocks is changes in productivity. The neoclassical approach of Kydland and Prescott considers productivity in the simplest form: changes in Total Factor Productivity (TFP) as the residual of output after accounting for capital and labour contributions. In this sense, the approach does not provide any insight as to the sources of productivity growth or sectors where the growth might have originated. It is simply meant to capture if such exogenous changes in TFP can substantially explain changes in macroeconomic aggregates if TFP is the only exogenous shock to hit the economy.

The rest of the article is organized as follows. In Section 2, I provide an outline of the Indian economy from 1960 to 2004. In Section 3, I provide an outline of the model. In this section, I also describe the methodology that I apply to solve the model for the policy variables, including the calibration technique to solve for the model parameters. Section 4 provides a summary of the results. Section 5 concludes the article.

# 2. The Indian Economy

Let us begin our analysis with an examination of the National Income Accounts of India from 1960 to 2004. The variables of interest to us are output per capita, investment per capita and the evolution of labour throughout the period. In keeping with the tradition of neoclassical analysis, our population is the working age population, that is, population aged between 15 and 64 years. Further, we are interested in seeing how the macro aggregates of the Indian economy diverged from the balanced growth path values of these aggregates. One of the problems that we encounter is that data available on labour hours pertains to1982 onwards. Consequently, we summarized the period between 1960 and 1982 in figures and plot the evolution of the economy since 1982. We assume, like Prescott and Hayashi (2002), that the long-term growth rate of an economy poised to be on the balanced growth path is 2 per cent. We detrend output per capita, investment per capita and government expenditure per capita by 2 per cent and report the results. We further report the observed labour hours.

## 2.1 Output and Investment Per Capita

GDP per capita grew well below trend during the period between 1960 and 1980 and it grew progressively worse between this period. Since 1980, the GDP per capita has started growing. Since 1994, the per capita growth rate of GDP has consistently been above 2 per cent till the present period. Figure 1 shows GDP per capita with respect to a 2 per cent trend between 1982 and 2002.

**FIGURE 1**

**Observed output per capita**

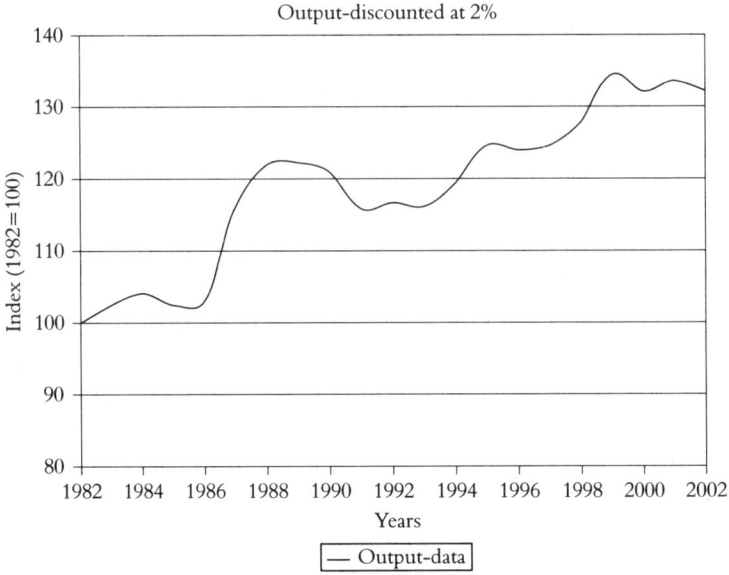

Output-discounted at 2%

**Source:** Author's calculations.

A similar trend of growth is observed when we look at investment per capita after accounting for the long-term trend. The difference is that while growth rate of output per capita worsened from 1960 to 1980, we do not see such an experience for investment per capita. It remained pretty stable till 1980 but has substantially picked up since then. So during the period between 1960 and 1980, if increased investment did not translate into increased output, the problem might be in productivity. Figure 2 captures investment trend since 1982.

## 2.2 Share of Government Expenditure in GDP

What is also interesting in the Indian context is the observed ratio of Government expenditure to GDP. We find that the share of government expenditure in GDP increased since 1960 and throughout the 1980s. The share fell briefly during the early part of the 1990s. Government has played a major role in Indian development since the planning period and fiscal policy was a big part of it. The problem was that increased government expenditure could not translate to increased economic growth. The trend in government expenditure since 1982 is captured in Figure 3.

**FIGURE 2**

**Observed investment per capita**

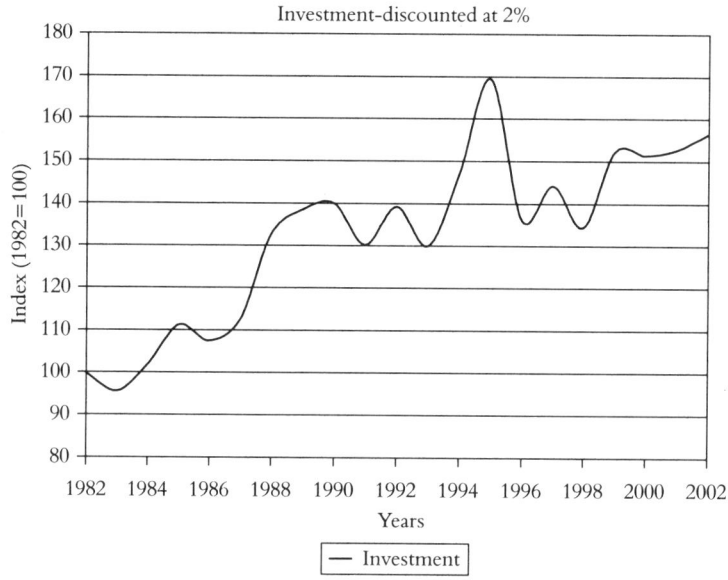

**Source:** Author's calculations.

**FIGURE 3**

**Share of government expenditure in output**

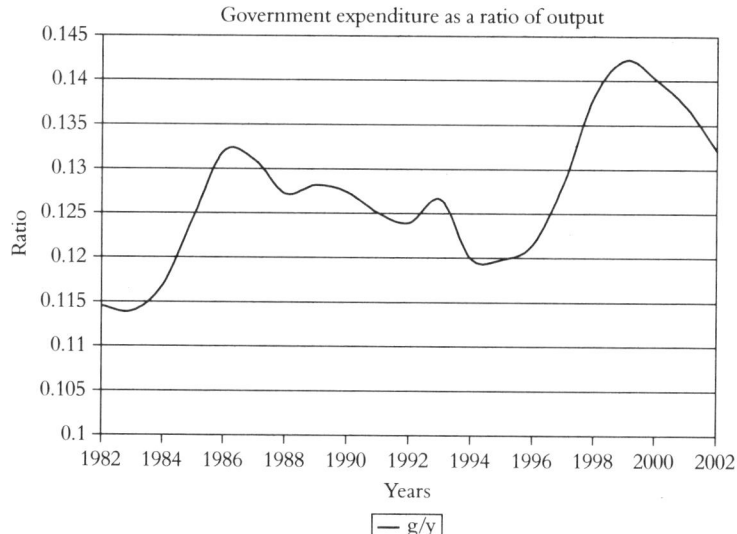

**Source:** Author's calculations.

## 2.3 Employment and Labour Hours

Tracing the evolution of employment and labour hours in India is a unique challenge. The data on employment is available only from the organized sector and in India, a large proportion of the population is either self-employed or employed in the unorganized sector. Similarly, data on labour hours is only restricted to the organized sector. We can gather data on working population as a percentage of total population from Bureau of Labour Statistics. The years for which data is available are from 1982 onwards. Our definition of working population is population aged between 15 and 64 years. Further, we have data on the percentage of population unemployed. We calculate employment by subtracting, the unemployed population from the working population. As for labour hours, we assume that any labour has 100 hours a week at his or her disposal. For our analysis, hours worked is taken as hours worked in manufacturing.

We denote labour as:

$$l(t) = \frac{E(t) * H(t)}{N(t) * 100}$$

where $\dfrac{E(t)}{N(t)}$ : employment as a fraction of working population; and

$\dfrac{H(t)}{100}$ : labour hours as a fraction of total hours.

From our analysis, we find that $l(t)$ increases from .4 to .44 between 1982 to 2002. This is depicted in Figure 4.

# 3. Indian Economy from a Growth Theory Perspective

## 3.1 Model Description

Our economy consists of a continuum of infinitely lived identical agents who have one unit of time endowment. They value consumption and leisure and earn wage and rental income. They spend their after-tax income on consumption and save the rest in the form of capital used for future production. We assume taxes to be lump-sum. Further, we assume that there is just one good that is used for consumption and investment. The consumer maximizes the present discounted value of lifetime utility subject to the budget constraint. Therefore, the representative consumer's problem can be written as:

**FIGURE 4**

**Labour hours**

Labour (I)

**Source:** Author's calculations.

$$Max \sum_{t=0}^{\infty} \beta^t u(c_t, 1-l_t)$$

subject to:

1. $c_t + k_{t+1} - (1 - \delta)k_t \leq w_t l_t + r k_t - t_t \ \forall t$
2. nonnegativity constraints

where $c_t$ is the consumption in period $t$, $l_t$ is labour in period $t$, $k_t$ is capital in period $t$, $t_t$ is the per capita lump-sum taxes charged by the government, $w_t$ is the wage rate in period $t$, and $r_t$ is rental rate in period $t$. We further denote the rate of time preference as $\beta$. The rate of depreciation of capital stock is denoted by $\delta$.

The economy also consists of an infinite number of identical firms that own the production technology and maximizes profits every period. The firm's problem can be written as:

$$Max \ y_t - w_t l_t - r k_t$$

subject to:

$$y_t \leq F(k_t, l_t, z_t) \ \forall t$$

where $y_t$ denotes output in period $t$, and $z_t$ denotes productivity.

Apart from consumers and the representative firm, the economy also has a government that balances budget every period so that the aggregate government expenditure every period $G_t$ is equal to the aggregate lump-sum taxes, $T_t$ Further, the resource constraint of the economy every period is given by:

$$c_t + k_{t+1} - (1 - \delta)k_t + g_t \leq y_t$$

where $g_t$ denotes per capita government expenditure. The equilibrium in the economy can be summarized as consisting of a set of allocations, $\{c_t, l_t, k_{t+1}, y_t\}_{t=0}^{\infty}$ and a set of prices $\{w_t, r_t\}_{t=0}^{\infty}$ such that the representative consumer maximizes present discounted value of lifetime utility subject to budget and non-negativity constraints as outlined in the consumer's problem; the representative firm maximizes profits every period subject to the technology constraint. Further, every period the government balances the budget and resource constraint is satisfied.

## 3.2  Solution Procedure

To solve the model, we first have to decide on the functional forms. For purposes of our analysis we assume that the utility function is of the form:

$$u(c_t, l_t) = \log c_t + \alpha_1 \log(1 - l_t)$$

We assume the production function to be Cobb-Douglas with labour augmented technology:

$$F(k_t, l_t) = k_t^{\theta} (z_t l_t)^{1-\theta}$$

We solve for the first order conditions using the functional forms specified above. Further, we also allow for population growth and assume that population grows every period at a constant rate $\eta$.

Now the representative consumer's problem reduces to:

$$Max \sum_{t=0}^{\infty} (\beta\eta)^t (\log c_t + \alpha_1 \log(1 - l_t))$$

Subject to:

1. $ct + \eta k_{t+1} - (1 - \delta)k_t \leq w_t l_t + r_t k_t - t_t \ \forall t$
2. nonnegativity constraints

The firm's problem reduces to:

$$Max \ y_t - wl_t - rk_t$$

Subject to:

$$y_t \leq k_t^\theta \ (zl_t)^{1-\theta} \ \forall t$$

and government's problem remains the same. The resource constraint reduces to:

$$c_t + \eta k_{t+1} - (1 - \delta)k_t + g_t \leq y_t$$

We want to solve the model using the technique of log linearization around the steady state. So we have to transform the model variables by discounting them with the long-term growth rate $g_z$. The model can be summarized by the following first order conditions, where hat denotes a variable discounted by the long-term growth rate, for example $\hat{x}_t = x_t / (1 + g_z)^t$

$$\frac{\alpha}{1-\theta} = \frac{\hat{w}_t(1-l_t)}{\hat{c}_t} \tag{1}$$

$$\beta E_t \frac{\hat{c}_t}{\hat{c}_{t+1}} \left\{ \hat{r}_{t+1} + 1 - \delta \right\} = (1 + g_z) \tag{2}$$

$$(1-\theta) = \frac{\hat{w}_t \, l_t}{\hat{y}_t} \tag{3}$$

$$\theta = \frac{\hat{r}_t \, k_t}{\hat{y}_t} \tag{4}$$

$$\hat{y}t \leq \hat{k}_t^\theta (\hat{z}_t l_t)^{1-\theta} \tag{5}$$

$$\hat{c}_t + \eta(1 + g_z) \hat{k}_{t+1} - (1 - \delta) \hat{k}_t + \hat{g}_t \leq \hat{y}_t \tag{6}$$

For our model solution, we first need to calibrate the model parameters such that the moments of the model match the moments of the data.

## 3.3 Data Description and Model Calibration
The data is collected from the World Bank database of World Development Indicators. We need data on output per capita, investment per capita and labour to solve for the model parameters. Data on output per capita and

investment per capita is available from World Development Indicators. Note that we are assuming a closed economy, hence we add net exports to consumption to account for net exports in a closed economy set-up. We collect the labour data from the Bureau of Labour Statistics. The data for India is only available from 1982 onwards. One problem that we encounter is the unavailability of capital stock data for the economy. To derive capital stock data, we assume a depreciation rate of 25 per cent as used in the Indian tax code and, given the data on investment, we use the perpetual inventory method to generate the time series of capital stock. The share of output going to labour presents another difficulty as India has a large self-employed sector for which data is limited. We, therefore, assume the share of labour to be .69 as given in literature. We can conduct the robustness test for our results with different parameter combinations. Given the data restrictions, we restrict the data analysis to the period between 1982 and 2002.

TABLE 1

**Moments of the data
(taking averages of the period 1982–2002)**

| | | |
|---|---|---|
| $c/y$ | = | .69 |
| $x/y$ | = | .19 |
| $wl/y$ | = | .64 |
| $l$ | = | .433 |
| $\eta$ | = | .0235 |
| $g_z$ | = | .02 |

**Source:** Author's calculations.

I am assuming that the long-run growth rate of the economy is 2 per cent which is the long-run growth rate of the United States. As for depreciation, we pick the depreciation rate $\delta$ to be 25 per cent, the rate allowed by the Indian tax code on physical capital. One other problem is calculating the share of GDP going to labour. We assume the value from growth literature. We can conduct the robustness check for different values of theta. The calibrated parameters of the model reduces to:

TABLE 2

**Calibrated value of model parameters**

| | | |
|---|---|---|
| $\theta$ | = | .36 |
| $\alpha$ | = | 1.22 |
| $\beta$ | = | .77 |
| $\delta$ | = | .25 |

**Source:** Author's calculations.

Once we calibrate the parameters of the model, we can find the steady state values which enables us to log-linearize the model. We want to use King et al.'s (1988) technique to solve for the policy parameters. When we log-linearize the equations, our system reduces to:

$$\widetilde{y}_t - \theta * \widetilde{k}_t - (1-\theta)*(\widetilde{z}_t + \widetilde{l}_t) = 0 \tag{7}$$

$$\widetilde{y}_t - \left(\frac{c}{y}\right)*\widetilde{c}_t - \eta*(1+g_z)\frac{k}{y}\widetilde{k}_{t+1} + (1-\delta)*\frac{k}{y}\widetilde{k}_t - \frac{g}{y}\widetilde{g}_t = 0 \tag{8}$$

$$\frac{\alpha}{1-\theta}\widetilde{y}_t - \frac{\alpha}{1-\theta}\widetilde{c}_t - \frac{y}{cl}\widetilde{l}_t = 0 \tag{9}$$

$$\theta\frac{y}{k}E_t(\widetilde{y}_{t+1} - \widetilde{k}_{t+1}) + \frac{1+g_z}{\beta}E_t(\widetilde{c}_t - \widetilde{c}_{t+1}) = 0 \tag{10}$$

The solution procedure is to use the Method of Undetermined Coefficients. In equations (7) to (10) there are three control variables: $\{\widetilde{y}_t, \widetilde{c}_t, \widetilde{l}_t\}$, one endogenous state variable, $\widetilde{k}_t$ and two exogenous state variables, $\widetilde{z}_t$ and $\widetilde{g}_t$. For our analysis, we assume that log deviations of productivity from its steady state value $\widetilde{z}_t$ and log deviation of government expenditure from its steady state value, $\widetilde{g}_t$ follow a vector autoregressive process of order one, such that:

$$\widetilde{z}_{t+1} = \rho_z * \widetilde{z}_t + \epsilon_{zt+1}, \ \epsilon_{zt+1} \sim n(\epsilon_z, \sigma_z^2) \tag{11}$$

$$\widetilde{g}_{t+1} = \rho_g * \widetilde{g}_t + \epsilon_{gt+1}, \ \epsilon_{gt+1} \sim n(\epsilon_g, \sigma_g^2) \tag{12}$$

The solutions to our unknowns will take the form:

$$\widetilde{y}_t = \widetilde{y}(\widetilde{s}_t, \widetilde{k}_t) \tag{13}$$

$$\widetilde{c}_t = \widetilde{c}(\widetilde{s}_t, \widetilde{k}_t) \tag{14}$$

$$\widetilde{l}_t = \widetilde{l}(\widetilde{s}_t, \widetilde{k}_t) \tag{15}$$

$$\widetilde{k}_{t+1} = \widetilde{k}(\widetilde{s}_t, \widetilde{k}_t) \tag{16}$$

where

$$\widetilde{s_t} = \left( \widetilde{z_t}, \widetilde{g_t} \right)$$

Or translating in matrix form:

$$\widetilde{v_t} = RR * \widetilde{k_t} + SS * \widetilde{s_t}$$

where

$$\widetilde{v_t} = \left( \widetilde{y_t}, \widetilde{c_t}, \widetilde{l_t} \right)$$

$$\widetilde{k}_{t+1} = PP * \widetilde{k_t} + QQ * \widetilde{s_t}$$

For our analysis, we first calculate the productivity $z_t$, where

$$z_t = \frac{y_t^{(1/1-\theta)}}{k_t^{(\theta/1-\theta)} l_t}$$

As Figure 5 indicates, productivity discounted for a long-term trend of 2 per cent shows an initial increase from 1985 to 1988 and thereby registers a decline till 1993 after which it starts increasing once again.

**FIGURE 5**

**Total factor productivity**

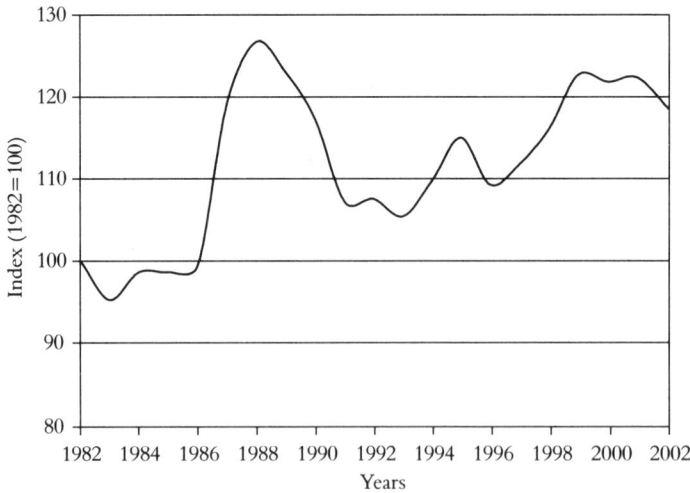

**Source:** Author's calculations.

# 4. Solution

## 4.1  Growth Accounting

We start by analyzing the results of a simple growth accounting exercise. We can use the production function and employ a little mathematical manipulation to decompose growth rate in output into three parts:

$$y_t = k_t^\theta \, (z_t * l_t)^{1-\theta}$$

$$\Rightarrow y_t^{1-\theta} = \left(\frac{k_t}{y_t}\right)^\theta (z_t * l_t)^{1-\theta}$$

$$\Rightarrow y_t = \left(\frac{k_t}{y_t}\right)^{\frac{\theta}{1-\theta}} (z_t * l_t)$$

where

$\dfrac{k_t}{y_t}$ : capital intensity factor

$z_t$: TFP factor

$l_t$: labour factor

Given the trend in productivity, we can divide the time period in three parts: 1982–88, 1988–93, and 1993–2002.

**TABLE 3**

**Growth rate in variables and their decomposition**

| Year | 1982–88 | 1988–93 | 1993–2002 |
|---|---|---|---|
| Output | 21.96 | −4.73 | 13.76 |
| Capital intensity factor | −12.2 | 14.83 | −.4 |
| TFP factor | 26.83 | −16.83 | 12.63 |
| Labour factor | 9.53 | −.24 | 1.4 |

Table 3 showcases a rather interesting phenomenon. It appears like growth in output has been primarily driven by growth in TFP factor along with growth in labour. Capital intensity factor has moved in the direction opposite to output. We, therefore, next trace the transition dynamics with respect to TFP factor. For our analysis, we take $\rho_z = \rho_g = .95$. We have already solved for parameter values and calculated TFP as a Solow Residual. We solve for the policy functions using the standard Uhlig toolkit, which gives us the relevant coefficients. We now feed in the TFP process in our model and estimate the model's estimation of output per capita, capital-output ratio and labour.

The policy functions are summarized by the matrices as listed in Table 4:

TABLE 4

**Coefficients of policy functions as calculated by Uhlig toolkit**

| | | |
|---|---|---|
| $PP$ | = | 0.6169 |
| $QQ$ | = | [0.5125, –0.0376] |
| $RR$ | = | [0.2789, .5024, –.1267] |
| | | 0.7021  0.0463 |
| $SS$ | = | 0.5310 –0.0813 |
| | | 0.0970  0.0724 |

## 4.2 Transition Dynamics

The objective of our analysis is to quantitatively estimate the impact of productivity shocks on the Indian economy. We further use our analysis to account for the evolution of GDP per capita in the Indian economy since 1982 using TFP as the only exogenous factor. In other words, during the years 1982–2002, if TFP was the only exogenous factor that deviated from its balanced growth path value, how would GDP per capita, capital-output ratio and labour evolve? To what extent would it quantitatively trace the evolution of GDP per capita, capital-output ratio and labour as observed in data?

In our analysis, we divide the period of study into three sub periods as we did for growth accounting: 1982–88, 1988–93, 1993–2002. Data for the period 1982–88 shows that output per capita increased by 21.96 per cent as compared to a 2 per cent long-term trend. During the same period, capital intensity factor went down by 12.2 per cent and labour increased by 9.53 per cent. Feeding in exogenous TFP shocks in our model, we find that output per capita increased by 22.01 per cent, accompanied by a 7.28 per cent fall in capital intensity factor and a 3.76 per cent increase in labour.

The performance during the 'slow period' of 1988–93 is also traced similarly. Data shows a fall in output per capita by 4.73 per cent and a fall in labour by .24 per cent. Capital-intensity factor actually registered an increase by 14.83 per cent. Feeding in exogenous TFP shocks, we find that output per capita declines by 11.07 per cent accompanied by a 2.79 per cent fall in labour and a 10 per cent increase in capital intensity factor.

Model results of the 'booming period' of 1993–2002 also yield some interesting insights. During this period, output per capita increased by 13.76 per cent.

It was a period of growth all around. Labour increased by 1.4 per cent and capital-intensity factor only declined slightly by −.4 per cent. The model with exogenous TFP shocks shows an increase in output per capita by 12.17 per cent, and an increase in labour by 1.34 per cent. The model also registers a fall in capital-intensity factor by 1.72 per cent.

In summarizing the results of all the three sub periods, we can deduce that productivity did play an important role in the evolution of the Indian economy, especially during the earlier years between 1982 and 1988 and then later during the booming period between 1993 and 2002. However, the performance of TFP shocks in accounting for macro aggregates during the slowdown from 1988 to 1993 is not very satisfactory. Though the direction of movement of the variables generated by the model match the direction of movement from the data, the magnitude of fluctuations in the model is far more than the magnitude of fluctuations in the data. This begs the question, if only TFP shocks would have spelt even more disaster for the economy during the slowdown, what kept the economy from further deterioration? The present paper cannot answer that question and leaves this observation as an interesting puzzle for future researchers.

**FIGURE 6**

**Output (observed and model outcome)**

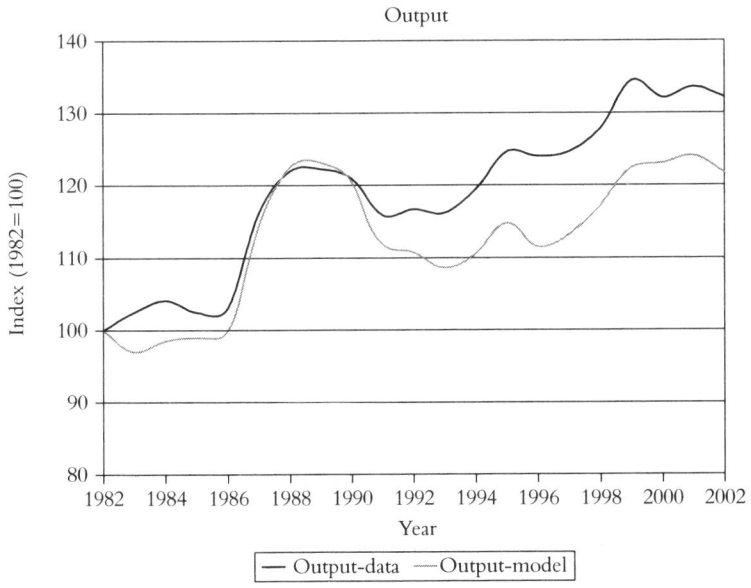

**Source:** Author's calculations.

**FIGURE 7**

**Capital-intensity factor (Observed and model outcome)**

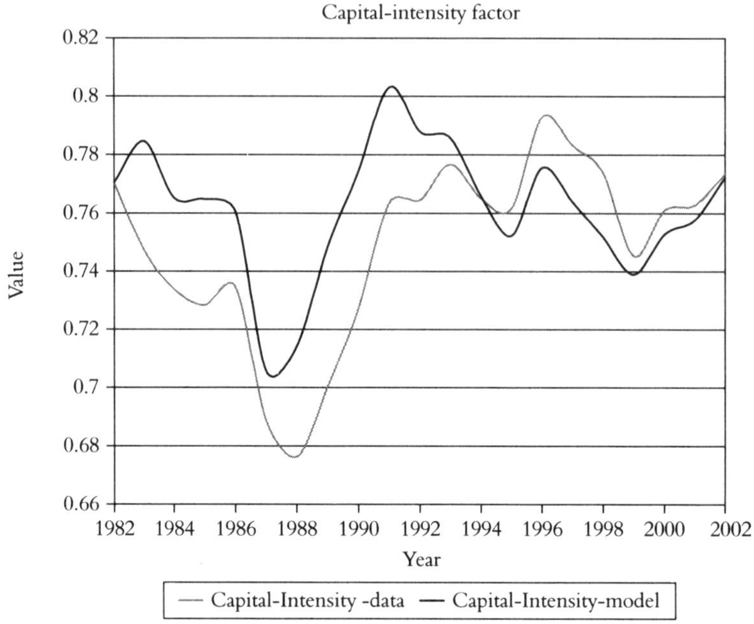

Capital-intensity factor

**Source:** Author's calculations.

# 5. Conclusion

The performance of the Indian economy since independence from the British in 1947 has been dubbed by Dani Rodrick as 'Hindu growth'. The term highlights an economy that is not a miracle, neither a debacle. But since the early 1980s Rodrick was proved wrong as the Indian economy started booming and the growth rate of GDP per capita registered an average 3.8 per cent increase between 1982 and 2002 which surpassed the long-term growth rate of 2 per cent of the developed economies.

This article aims at quantitatively accounting for the performance of the Indian economy since 1982 from a growth theory perspective. The technique of growth accounting pioneered by Kydland and Prescott (1982), who feed in exogenous technical shocks to a growth model after calibrating the model parameters to match moments of the data, was employed. At the crux of the analysis is the idea that if there was no deviation of technology from its steady state path, economy would be at equilibrium. As technology deviates from

**FIGURE 8**

**Labour (Observed and model outcome)**

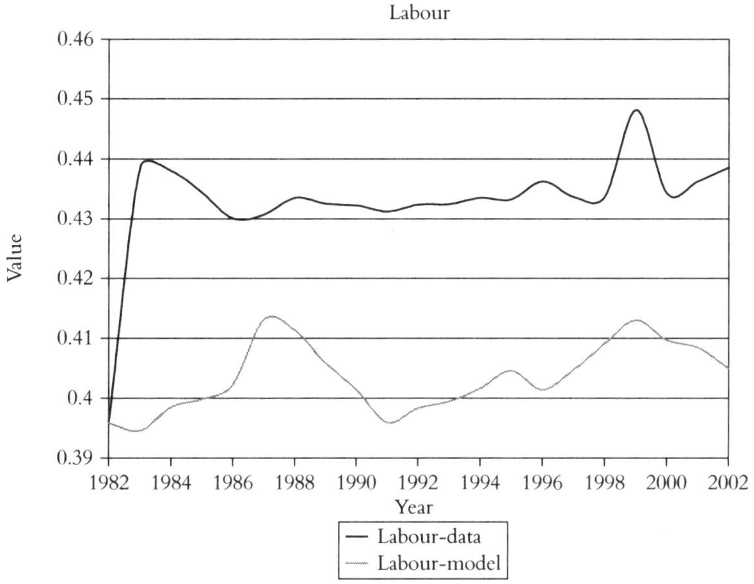

Labour

**Source:** Author's calculations.

steady state value, macroeconomic aggregates also respond to technical deviations by deviating from their steady state values. To what extent can technical deviations alone account for movements in macro aggregates?

We applied this technique to India during the period 1982–2002. The period restriction is because of the data on the availability of employment and hours was available only from 1982 onwards.

Our results indicate that productivity as measured by TFP did play an important role in the Indian economy especially during the booms. However, during 1988–93, the Indian economy experienced a sharp drop in productivity which was not reflected to the same degree in output per capita. Simple growth accounting shows that capital intensity increased during this period which might be a factor in preventing a sharp output drop.

This article opens up many interesting questions, as it looks at the Indian economy from the growth theory perspective. This article is not designed to investigate the primitives behind a fluctuating TFP. It might be that TFP is picking up fluctuations in capacity utilization, or increasing returns to scale. As the Indian economy started its process of liberalization, increases in international operations could well result in the utilization of hitherto unused capacity as well as lead to the development of new technology. Firm-level micro data would provide us a better look at the primitives and would be the direction of future research in this area. Growth theory, as used in this article, is also limited in that it also does not include other channels of shocks like financial frictions or labour market frictions. An extended model like Business Cycle Accounting of Chari et al. (2002) would provide richer answers.

**Suparna Chakraborty,** Department of Economics and Finance, Zicklin School of Business, Baruch College, City University of New York, One Bernard Baruch Way, New York, NY 10010. E-Mail: Suparna_Chakraborty@baruch.cuny.edu

# References

Amaral, P. and J. Macgee. 2002. 'The Great Depression in Canada and the United States: A Neoclassical Perspective', *Review of Economic Dynamics*, 5(1): 45–72.

Bergoeing, R., P. J. Kehoe, T. J. Kehoe and R. Soto. 2002. 'A Decade Lost and Found: Mexico and Chile in the 1980s', *Review of Economic Dynamics*, 5(1): 45–72.

Chari, V. V., P. J. Kehoe and E. R. McGrattan. 2000. 'Accounting for the Great Depression', *American Economic Review Papers and Proceedings*, 92(2).

———. 2002. 'Accounting for the Great Depression', *Federal Reserve Bank of Minneapolis Quarterly Review*, 27(2): 2–8.

———. 2005. 'Business Cycle Accounting' Revision (2005), Federal Reserve Bank of Minneapolis Staff Report. Minneapolis.

Cole, H. L. and L. E. Ohanian. 1999. 'The Great Depression in the United States from a Neoclassical Perspective', *Federal Reserve Bank of Minneapolis Quarterly Review*, 23(Winter): 2–24.

Fischer, J. 2004. 'Technology Shocks Matter', Working Paper Series WP–02–14, Federal Reserve Bank of Chicago.

Gali, J. 1999. 'Technology, Employment, and the Business Cycle: Do Technology Shocks Explain Aggregate Fluctuations?', *American Economic Review*, 89(1): 249–71.

Gali, J. and P. Rabanal. 2004. 'Technology Shocks and Aggregate Fluctuations: How Well Does the RBC Model Fit Postwar U.S. Data?', *NBER Macroeconomics Annual*, Forthcoming.

Kehoe, T. J. and K. J. Ruhl. 2003. 'Recent Great Depressions: Aggregate Growth in New Zealand and Switzerland 1973–2000', *New Zealand Economic Papers*, 37(1): 5–40.

King, R., C. Plosser and S. Rebelo. 1988. 'Production, Growth, and Business Cycles: The Basic Neoclassical Model', *Journal of Monetary Economics*, 21(2): 195–232.

Kydland, F. E. and E. C. Prescott. 1982. 'Time to Build and Aggregate Fluctuations', *Econometrica*, 50(6): 1345–70.

Narayan Murthy, N. R. 2002. 'The Impact of Economic Reforms on the Hi-Tech Industry in India: A Case Study of Infosys', The Indian Economy Conference, Cornell University, April 19–20.

Prescott, E. C. 1999. 'Theory Ahead of Business Cycle Measurement', *Federal Reserve Bank of Minneapolis Quarterly Review*, 10 (Fall): 9–22.

Prescott, E. C. and F. Hayashi. 2002. 'The 1990s in Japan: A Lost Decade', *Review of Economic Dynamics*, 5(1): 206–35.

Sachs, J. 2002. 'Growth Prospects of the Indian Economy', The Indian Economy Conference, Cornell University, April 19–20.

Singh, N. 2004. 'Information Technology as an Engine of Broad-Based Growth in India', Development and Comp Systems 0412012, Economics Working Paper Archive, Washington University, Seattle.

Singh, N. and T. N. Srinivasan. 2004. 'Indian Federalism, Economic Reform and Globalization', Public Economics 0412007, Economics Working Paper Archive, Washington University, Seattle.

Subramanian, A. and D. Rodrick. 2004. 'From "Hindu Growth" to Productivity Surge: The Mystery of the Indian Growth Transition', CEPR Discussion Paper 4371, CEPR, London.

# School Dropout and Informal Apprenticeship

Padmini Dasgupta
Indira Gandhi Institute of Development Research, Mumbai

Bibhas Saha
University of East Anglia, Norwich and
Indira Gandhi Institute of Development Research, Mumbai

Rudra Sensarma*
University of Birmingham

This article draws attention to the issue of school dropout for 'adolescent' children in a typical developing country and extends the Basu-Van (1998) model to allow for informal apprenticeship. The major findings of the article include: a comprehensive ban on child labour can sufficiently raise the equilibrium wage resulting in the permanent elimination of child labour; and when children (belonging to poor families) are truly low performers in the academic sector and their performance measure determines their formal sector earnings, many of them may benefit by working as child labour. Such work experience may enhance their adult-age earnings. A ban on child labour is self-liquidating in the first case and likely to hurt future earnings in the second. We offer empirical evidence from India in support of our hypotheses.

**JEL Classification:** D81, J24, J82, J88
**Keywords:** Child labour, School dropout, Public policy, India

* We thank seminar participants at the Centre for Studies in Social Sciences, Calcutta where an earlier version of this article was presented. The remaining errors, if any, are our responsibility.

# 1. Introduction

## 1.1 The Problem

Nothing is more distressful than the sight of a child working to make a living for himself or for his family. Yet people in developing countries are used to this horrible sight, just as they are to disease, destitution and poverty. The latest ILO estimates suggest that around 246 million children worldwide have suffered this misfortune and India's share, according to some estimates, is a staggering 44 million or nearly 20 per cent.

By now there is a fairly adequate documentation of child labour in India, thanks to some remarkable contributions such as Weiner (1991) and Burra (1995). Several factors that are often cited as causes of child labour are: (*i*) paucity of schooling opportunities, (*ii*) abject poverty, (*iii*) lack of parental awareness, (*iv*) poor enforcement of minimum wage laws, (*v*) preference for children for certain types of work (the nimble finger argument) (*vi*) fraudulent money-lending practice[1] and (*vii*) coercion, kidnapping and use of physical force.[2] Many researchers have highlighted the importance of these factors, and political scientists and sociologists have criticized the Indian government for the lack of political will to ban child labour.

Though the Indian constitution promised to eradicate child labour, the Indian government had moved away in the past from the goal of eradication of child labour and endorsed a strategy to improve the working conditions of the child workers.[3] Finally, on 10 October 2006, child labour was banned in India. On the education side, however, some progress has been made in terms of expansion of schooling facilities and the recent provision of mid-day meals. The school attendance rate is likely to improve, and one hopes that with such measures the worst form of child labour—children under the age of 10 working—will come down.

---

[1] Pledging child's and other family members' labour against loans has been well documented by researchers (see Burra [1995] for example). This is strictly illegal. Other types of frauds include simply wrong calculations of interest obligations. This is deliberate and victims are typically illiterate.

[2] Burra (1995: 18–21) provided an account of how children from some parts of Bihar were kidnapped and made to work in the carpet industry of UP. Times of India (Mumbai) reports on 21 April 2005 that *zari* workshops of Mumbai employ a large number of child workers, some as young as eight, brought from far away places in Bihar, Uttar Pradesh and Jharkhand. Separated from their families these children are made to work in inhuman conditions and for long hours, sometimes as long as 20 hours a day. The recent death of a twelve-year-old child worker was attributed to mistreatment at workplace and malnutrition.

[3] A major shift occurred in the government's policy in 1986 when a new law, The Child Labour (Prohibition and Regulation) Act was passed to replace the Employment of Children Act, 1938.

In this article, we do not question the merits of such measures. Instead, we wish to draw attention to a relatively unnoticed problem that can very well be a significant factor for child labour and that may not be countered by the 'supply-side' measures that we discussed earlier.

Our argument primarily applies to what we may call 'adolescent labour' instead of child labour. The age group to which we would like to restrict our attention ranges roughly from 11 to 16. Though the legal age of working as a non-child worker is 14, there is no doubt that the formative age of a child goes beyond the age of 14. Children ought to complete 10 years of education, which is probably necessary for some reasonable amount of human capital acquisition. However, data suggests that dropout at the later stage of high school is a chronic problem.[4] Since the factors causing dropout either at an age of 11 or at an age of 16 are similar, we need to review some of the well-known causes of child labour.

To economists, child labour is a manifestation of several problems, which usually occur elsewhere in the economy, such as the credit or the labour market, technology and firm regulation, industrial policy and opportunities for training. In some cases, there may be serious problems even within the household viz., the distribution of family resources, which is often found to be discriminatory against girl child. We, however, will not go into the discussion of such intra-household resource allocation.

The most well-known economic model of child labour has been given by Basu and Van (1998), where it is argued that the labour market in low income economies is often characterized by multiple equilibria, which has, as constituents, low wages and the participation of children in the labour market. Basu and Van call it a 'bad equilibrium'. Another equilibrium, which is referred to as a good equilibrium, involves high wages and the participation of only adult workers. Unfortunately, both the good and bad equilibria can be stable. Therefore, forcing the market to operate in a good equilibrium requires some sort of intervention, such as banning child labour, or a facilitating a big shift in labour demand, thus making the bad equilibrium inoperative (assuming that the ban is perfectly enforced). However, the authors caution that other types of interventions such as boycotting the products made by child labour (causing a loss in labour demand) will only increase poverty and will not help the affected children; nor will it eliminate child labour.

---

[4] For the age group 11–14, gross enrolment ratio in 1989–90 was 59.1 per cent (girls 44.6 per cent and boys 73 per cent). This improved to 67.7 per cent in 1992–93 (girls 55.2 per cent and boys 79.3 per cent). For the age group 14–17, this rate was merely 22.2 per cent in 1987 (girls 14.5 per cent and boys 29.4 per cent).

By this model, Basu and Van made a formal counterpoint to an old Western argument, which emphasizes parental exploitation of children. They have shown that it is not the lack of altruism on the part of the parents, but the lack of income to meet subsistence consumption that drives parents to send their children to work. Thus, poverty has been brought back as the prime cause of child labour. Once the connection between poverty and child labour is recognized, one can trace the factors in the labour and credit markets that cause low wage and low parental investments on children, and that would be a natural starting point for policy formulation.

## 1.2  Our Hypothesis

In this article, we propose a new argument. Even when the parents are able to meet the subsistence consumption and wish to see their children educated (assuming schooling costs are insignificant), they may wonder how long they would keep them at school. The child's human capital acquisition is essentially a result of the investment decision made by his parents. It may very well be that under a variety of constraints a poor parent optimizes on his investment on a child that turns out to be extremely low, and the major constraints may not necessarily be on the supply side (such as the lack of schooling opportunities).

Before we spell out the exact nature of the constraint that forms the core of our argument, we should note that one constraint, namely the credit constraint has been amply highlighted. Ranjan (2001) has argued that credit constraint does not allow a poor parent to finance his child's education by pledging the child's future earnings, even when the child is academically bright (and hence his future earnings are more predictable). Unable to provide good education and meet family's consumption needs, a poor parent sends his child to work. An empirical support to this argument is found in Dehejia and Gatti (2002) who studied cross-country data on financial development and child labour. Sociological literature provides many telling accounts of permanent indebtedness and labour bondage (Burra 1995). Lack of insurance at work place, accidents and alcoholism are other factors.

We would like to focus on yet another factor—the training constraint— that is, the lack of vocational training programmes. Vocational training opportunities are neither a part of high school curriculum, nor are they provided through formal institutions. There are very few formal training institutions run by the government that aim at moderately educated youth. The few institutions that are accessible demand a high school degree. The Industrial Training Institutes, for example, require high school completion. Being in great demand, such institutions create another problem by restricting admission only to candidates with better academic records. Once again, poorly performing students are pushed out of competition.

The high school curriculum has also remained unchanged in its orientation. It is designed to be a foundation course for future college graduates and professionals; but it offers very little to those who do not wish to go to college. The government's promise to offer vocational training has remained unfulfilled. High school graduation does not add much to a student's credential in terms of any occupational skill. His chances of getting a government job or formal sector employment are also few, considering the large pool of applicants for such vacancies. In fact, for very poor households, sending a child for higher education can be a risky choice. The more educated one is, the higher will be one's reservation wage, and more importantly, the less willing one will be to take up a menial job. This implies a great deal of risk for a low-income household.

Labour market has solved the problem of missing training market by creating what we may call informal apprenticeship. One can access it only by being a worker first. It is also self-financing, because the worker pays for it by accepting a lower wage. How low this wage should be and how long it will continue to be so, will depend on a host of factors: the nature of skill (how valuable it is), the speed of learning and the method of learning. The process is further complicated by the fact that this system of training is embedded in a relationship of hierarchy, often coloured by social rules, religion and customs. A young apprentice will fit into this hierarchy with less friction.

If a parent decides to send his child to work with this objective in mind, we may think that he is pursuing an *insurance strategy*, a strategy to reduce uncertainty to his child's future earnings. Not only is he ensuring a sure income for the child when he grows up, howsoever low it is, but he is also giving the child the opportunity to learn some occupational skills that can help him to become self-employed one day. With a bit of luck he can find his way out of poverty. This strategy is a clear winner against the risky choice of school completion, especially when the child's academic performance is not strong enough to make him competitive in the formal labour market and when the parents lack the resources to support self-employment.[5]

---

[5] Here we are aware that this calculation differs between boys and girls. For girls other factors come into play, and we do not want to get into the gender dimension of this problem. It is well known that unless economic compulsions are overwhelming, adolescent girls are not sent out to the labour market. This also means in some cases that young male members of the household must work harder. However, girls are also not sent to school after an age for the same reason of insecurity and for the risk of not finding a bridegroom for an 'over-educated' girl.

The insurance strategy is different from the 'survival strategy' of a very poor household which has to send even a five year old to work. The Basu-Van model articulated the survival strategy, and abundantly many field studies have documented it. The infamous match factories of Sivakasi, glass factories of Firozabad, carpet weavers of Uttar Pradesh and the pottery industry of Khurja are examples of such survival strategy.[6] But by no means are these cases of child employment exhaustive. Motor garages, lathe factories, tailoring shops, electrical suppliers and service providers and construction work, especially masonry, are some of the examples where workers begin at an early age and learn their way through; eventually many of them do become self-employed. These occupations are skill-dependent and such skills are acquired over time. Given the hierarchy-driven method of apprenticeship, late entry into the workforce can be a disadvantage.

We may quote a paragraph from Weiner (1991: 22) describing the story of an engineering workshop manager in the city of Bangalore:

> The manager of the Globe Engineering Works, a grand name for a small 20 foot by 20 foot workshop across the road from the central city market, said he began work as a helper in the workshop when he was only seven. He was uneducated and he was paid four annas a day. Today, he said with pride, he earns 1,500 rupees a month, and has a printed card with his name as manager. He taught himself to read and write and to do numbers. The shop is clean and the machinery used for threading pipes is well-polished. He employs two boys, both Muslims like himself. The older boy, Said, age thirteen, is paid 200 rupees per month and is being taught how to use the equipment. The younger boy, age eleven, is paid 5 rupees a day to keep the shop clean and run errands. Neither boy has been to school. Until he was twelve, Said stayed at home helping his mother care for his three younger sisters. The manager is particularly keen on helping Said learn the trade.

It may be argued that the skill acquired through such pre-mature employment is of minor nature and it can be acquired at a later age much more quickly. Indeed that would be the case, if there were enough formal institutions to impart this training; but in their absence, workplace apprentice is

---

[6] Each of these cases shows some additional dimensions as well. In case of Sivakasi protection of backward technology has been responsible for perpetuating child labour, though official excuses are always of drought and poor agriculture. In Firozabad and also in Khurja, child employment is task-specific. Certain tasks along the chain of work (again traditional technology dependent) are so unskilled that employing adult workers is unprofitable.

the only way out. A somewhat more compelling objection to our argument can be that a large number of such apprentices do not end up with self-employment or significant improvement in their earnings. Nor is the process of informal training always different from mere exploitation and hardship. Casual observations certainly favour this argument. Here, our response is that the process of learning is uncertain, as it is with any other learning activity; success is not guaranteed. Moreover, the workplace is unregulated, having no checks on hazards and exploitative behaviour. An apprentice will be at the mercy of his employer and may experience more abuse and hardship than real training; but that does not negate the objective of the parents, and casual observations do not rule out this possibility either.

We are going to pose this hypothesis as an explanation of school dropout and adolescent workers. Our argument is developed in two stages. First, we carry out a theoretical analysis to argue that this type of child labour (informal apprentice) can be welfare improving from the point of view of the child. We do so by extending the Basu-Van model to a dynamic set-up allowing for the child's future to enter into consideration, and to show that under certain circumstances withdrawing a 'low ability' child from the school is optimal. Several issues such as the mid-day meal, consumption loan and an improvement in the ability of the child are then allowed to vary to see how they would affect the parental decision.

In the second stage of our analysis we look at the census data and carry out an empirical analysis to determine what factors are important determinants of child work. The methodology used in our model is standard. Our data corresponds to state-level child labour figures and an array of economic variables. While we consider standard variables such as state domestic product and poverty rate, we introduce two new variables which are proxies for potential employment accessibility, namely the urban job opportunity (measured by employment exchange figures) and vocational training opportunities (measured by government initiative on training). While poverty and education variables seem to have strong effects on child labour, our variables of interest do show the desired relationship. In other words, employment accessibility variables have a negative relationship with child labour.

There are several studies that have echoed similar views and emphasized the labour market conditions. Almost in an identical vein, Mendelievich (1979) and Bonnet(1993) have argued that child workers can be seen as apprentices learning the trade, and not necessarily as an exploited lot. Most recently, Ersado (2005) has examined cross-country data on child labour and schooling for both rural and urban regions and concluded that while poverty seems to be the main cause of child labour in rural areas, it does not appear to be so in urban areas. Cain and Mozumder (1980) have argued that the structure of the labour market needs to be taken into account before deciding the economic value of the children. Grooteart and Kanbur (1995b) have pointed out that relative importance of the informal sector in the labour market is a determinant of the demand for child labour. In an interesting formulation, Gupta (2000) uses bargaining between employer and parent to determine the wage of the child worker. The child wage has a cash and a kind component. The kind component goes to the child usually in the form of meals at workplace and the cash to the parent of the child. One of the main conclusions of this model is that the total child wage would be an average of the marginal product and the average product of the child worker, while the kind component is only an efficiency wage. Therefore, going by the wage received by the child, the child's work should not be viewed as exploitative; but the parental selfishness can be blamed for the child's participation.

## 1.3   Policy Implications

Our analysis is not complete without a discussion of policy. As promised in our constitution, the ultimate goal is to eliminate child labour. What policy can achieve this goal? Western scholars and a school of Indian researchers have always insisted on the outright ban of child labour in all industries. Government's reluctance and the lack of political will to do so have been severely criticized by scholars like Weiner and Burra. But the majority view on this is that a ban is hardly going to be effective because the government is not in a position to enforce it, and more importantly, a ban, if it is fully enforced, will make the conditions of the families worse. This view, regarded by the hardliners as a tacit approval of child labour, is based on certain aspects of ground reality. This line of thinking has led to the new child Labour Act of 1986, and it is also worth remembering that the 1938 Act did not place a comprehensive ban. It banned child labour only in hazardous industries. The focus of the 1986 law and the thrust of activism since then centred on the general recognition of child workers' rights, and specifically on the improvement of the working condition of children and providing education at workplace. Various programmes are in place to achieve this objective; but the scale of the problem is too large to be tackled by such small scale efforts.

The biggest problem with both the government approach and the position taken by various NGOs is that there is no plan to phase out child labour. While trying to improve the condition of a child worker is very noble, the policies and programmes do not aim at stopping the inflow in future. Another problem is the failure to distinguish between the worst form of child labour from other types of child labour. There is a big difference between an eight-year-old child worker and a 12-year-old child worker. The former is absolutely vulnerable to exploitation of worst kind, and being away from home for a long time will be extremely traumatic to him. There should be a hardline stand on insisting that a child of such tender age should not be allowed to work under any circumstances. In other words, a realistic policy should take a middle ground by placing a comprehensive ban below a certain age, while allowing relaxation for 'older' children. This must vary between industries depending on the severity of hardship.

It is also well known that an anti-child-labour policy is not effective without a compulsory primary schooling policy. The Indian Constitution has advocated for free and compulsory education up to the eighth grade; but the state governments have been reluctant to implement it for a variety of reasons. The recent Supreme Court ruling requiring all states to provide mid-day meal in state-run primary schools has been producing encouraging results in terms of children's school participation. In addition to the provision of schooling, two other factors are to be paid attention to: first, an improvement in the minimum adult wage (and its enforcement) and availability of work, and second, credit market access of poor households. Thus, an anti-child-labour policy must have four prongs: targeting the child and adult labour markets, schooling and credit market accessibility of the poor.

The specific policy recommendations that emerge from our analysis are as follows. First, high school curriculum must have a vocational component, effective and useful for low income families. Some basic training imparting introductory skills of, say, carpentry, electrical repairing, plumbing, tailoring, allied agricultural activities such as horticulture and so on, can be imparted from the age twelve onward. Second, the number of formal training institutions, which can admit students above the age of fourteen must increase and should be subsidized. Third, factories using child workers should be regulated in some form at least for the child employment, and they should be classified in terms of the type of work children are engaged in. If an establishment provides on-the-job training in a fair manner, it should receive encouragement in the form of grants, certification and tax exemption. But as argued before, employment of children below a certain age (say 10) should not be tolerated.

To sum up, the general focus of our recommendation is restricted only to urban and semi-urban areas and mostly with respect to male children. As girl children and rural areas present different complexities, we have kept them out of the purview of our analysis. We have no specific recommendation for them.

Our article is organized as follows. The next section presents an extension of the Basu-Van model to delineate our theoretical argument. Section 3 presents an empirical analysis based on census data and discusses possible determinants of child labour. Finally, in the concluding section, we discuss policy prescriptions on how to reduce or eliminate child labour based on insights gained from our analysis.

## 2. Theoretical Argument: An Extension of the Basu-Van Model

In this section, we will extend the Basu-Van (1998) model to allow for informal apprenticeship. Our key objective is to modify the crucial backward-bending labour supply curve and generate some additional equilibria, which may show that informal apprenticeship can sometimes be a welfare improving choice.

Following Basu and Van (1998), we consider an economy with $N$ identical households, each of which consists of a parent and a child. The parent always works and earns an adult wage of $w_A$ in the first period. The child can either go to school or work or do both based on what the parent decides. The child's labour is denoted as $e$, which can be at the most one. There are two time periods, present and future. In future the child grows up and, we assume, faces a dualistic labour market. The formal labour market will offer $y_F = aw_F$, but will require full schooling. Here, $a$ refers to some broad measure of 'ability' which is exogenous and random. Suppose $a$ can take two values: $a_L$ and $a_H$, $a_L < a_H$. The proportion of $a_H$ type in the population is $\lambda$ and the proportion of $a_L$ type is $(1 - \lambda)$. We may refer to them as low and high ability individuals; however, as we discuss later, the interpretation of ability can be very broad.

The informal labour market, on the other hand, does not care about schooling; and, moreover, it rewards prior informal labour market experience, which comes at the expense of schooling.

These labour market features are summarized in the earnings (or wage) function of the formal and informal sector respectively:

$$y_F = aw_F \text{ if } e = 0$$
$$= 0 \text{ otherwise}; \ a \in \{a_L, a_H\}.$$
$$y_I = w_I (1 + e).$$

We can say that earnings in the formal sector is determined by an individual's ability $a$ and an average wage in the formal sector $w_F$. Here, the ability parameter *a* can mean a range of things. First, it may refer to the 'innate' ability that a person is born with. We can presume that ability to learn a particular subject varies between individuals, even when they are exposed to identical teaching inputs. While some students have stronger aptitude in mathematics, others may hold an edge in science or literature. So in our model, ability may indicate an overall capability over a basket of subjects that are typically taught in school. Exam scores or IQ may reflect such abilities.

Second, we can also permit a different interpretation in which all children are born with equal innate ability to learn (a given set of subjects), but they begin to perform differently because of different schooling quality and different household investment in education. This interpretation may not allow the variable *a* to be completely random. It can be influenced by household investment (such as private tutoring) and schooling choice. Here, we do not take this approach, though admittedly it is an interesting approach. To keep our analysis simple, we may assume that schooling quality is random and the household does not make additional investment on children. With these assumptions, we can allow *a* to be fully random.

Third, yet another possible interpretation is that *a* reflects the subjective probability of getting a formal sector job, provided *a* is restricted below one. Here, the chance of getting the job is entirely a subjective assessment of the parent, which may depend on his own labour market experience and perception of the employment practices of the formal sector. Such perception may vary across individuals and we can treat these variations as random.

Our model can easily adapt to any of the three interpretations, though the third one particularly suits our assumption that the parent learns his child's ability quite early on. In fact, we make the parent decide how long to keep his child at school right at the beginning, based on his knowledge or perception about *a*. This is not always satisfactory, especially when parents gradually learn and discover their children's abilities through repeated performance measures. In such cases, we clearly need to model the dynamic process of learning; but that will make our analysis far more formal than what we have attempted here. A compromise has been made by granting the parent the full knowledge of *a* beforehand.

In Figure 1 we illustrate the difference between the two earnings functions, and show how ability affects formal sector earnings. As long as schooling is less than one, formal sector earnings are zero. But when schooling equals to one, formal sector earnings will be high or low, described by two solid dots, depending on the values of *a*. In contrast, for the informal sector, work experience counts much more. The earnings function of this sector is a declining function of schooling. In particular, when schooling is zero, the earnings from this sector are as high as $2w_I$, and on the other extreme, when schooling is full, it drops to $w_I$. We have drawn this figure with the assumption that for a 'low ability' child, zero schooling generates greater adult-age income, while for a 'high ability' child, full schooling generates greater income.

**FIGURE 1**

**Earnings functions**

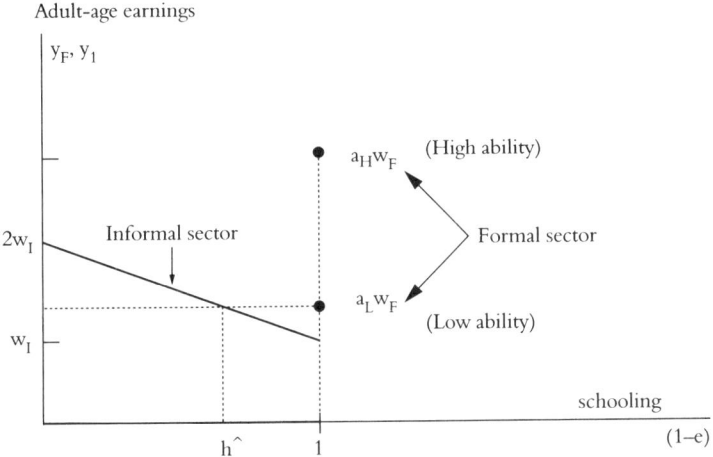

**Source:** Authors' calculations.

The difference between the two sectors can very well reflect a well-known dichotomy in the market for training. As is the case in India and many other developing countries, the formal sector values education because it imparts general training to potential workers. On the foundation of general training, specific skills can be built. But the informal sector generally depends on workers trained within the industry. Here, the general skill of the workers may be inadequate, but their specific skills and low-level specializations can be very profitable for repetitive tasks and operations that such firms are typically engaged in.

The parent has full knowledge about these two markets, and while deciding on the child's schooling, he must also decide which labour market he wishes to send his child to. This is captured in the household's objective function, which is the sum of its current utility and the future utility of child, which in turn depends on his future income. To allow for future considerations, we need to modify the well-known 'luxury axiom' of Basu and Van. However, we retain their 'substitution axiom' as it is.

*Modified luxury axiom*: A family will send its children to the labour market if the family cannot ensure subsistence consumption today from its adult income alone, or if the family's lifetime utility increases from doing so.

*Substitution axiom*: A firm takes the adult and child labour as substitutes.

## 2.1  Supply Curve of Child Labour

The household tries to maximize

$$U = (c - s)(1 - e) + \theta y \ \text{ if } c \geq s \tag{1}$$
$$= (c - s) \ \text{ if } c < s \tag{2}$$

subject to the budget constraint

$$w_A + ew_C \geq c(1 + \beta),$$

where $e$ belongs to $[0, 1]$ and $(1 - e)$ represents the child's education. $\beta < 1$ is the child's consumption equivalence term, and $\theta$ represents a weight on the child's future income. This weight represents the parental concern for their children's future, $\theta \in [0, \infty)$. Depending on the value of $\theta$, we can interpret parental concern. If $\theta$ is very large, it indicates that the household (or the parent) is solely concerned about the future of the child. However, if $\theta$ takes a value $< 1$ we can also interpret it as the rate at which the household discounts the future. Here, $c$ and $s$ denote the current and the subsistence consumption of the individuals, and $w_A$ and $w_C$ denote the wages earned by the adult and the child in the first period in the labour market respectively.

Now that the child's future income can vary depending on whether he will be working in the formal or informal sector, the household must choose the optimal $e$ to maximize its utility depending on which sector it is aiming at, provided that its consumption $c$ is above the subsistence level $s$.

So when $c \geq s$, the household chooses one of the following:

$$Max \ U = (c - s)(1 - e) + \theta(1 + e)w_I \tag{3}$$

with respect to $(c, e)$ subject to

$$w_A + ew_C \geq c(1 + \beta)$$

or, set $e = 0$ and choose to solve the problem

$$Max \ U = (c - s) + \theta aw_F \tag{4}$$

subject to

$$w_A \geq c(1 + \beta).$$

Comparing the total utility that the household receives from the two alternative choices, it decides on which labour market to target in the second period.

First, consider the case of the household that decides to send the child to the labour market. The optimal labour supply of the child will be given by the labour supply curve as shown in Figure 2.

**FIGURE 2**

**Child labour supply (informal sector)**

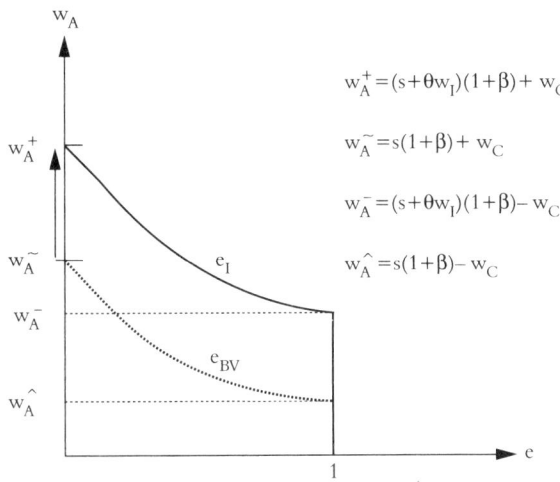

**Source:** Authors' calculations.

Here the solid convex curve represents the child's labour supply as predicted by our model. It shows an inverse relationship between adult wage and the time the child is ready to spend in the labour market (according to his parent's decision). If the adult wage is very high, the child does not work, which is an implication of the luxury axiom. But as the wage falls below a critical level, the child is withdrawn from school after some education. This process continues, until the wage drops to another critical level below which the child devotes full time to the labour market, or becomes a full time informal apprentice. The labour supply curve of the child is vertical at this point with $e = 1$.

Why does it happen? There are two reasons: the first one has to do with meeting subsistence consumption of the household, which is evident from the term $s(1 + \beta)$. The second reason is parental concern for the child's future earnings, which is reflected in the term $\theta w_1(1 + \beta)$. If the informal apprenticeship helps to increase the child's adult-age earnings, the parent will be inclined to impart this apprenticeship at the cost of schooling, even when there is no compulsion for meeting subsistence consumption.

This is made clearer by the broken curve labelled $e_{BV}$. This curve represents the child labour supply curve of the Basu-Van model. Since our model differs from that only in terms of future concerns, the difference between the intercepts of the two curves represents the range of wages at which the child is withdrawn from the school, entirely because informal training is imparted. The intercept of the $e_{BV}$ curve gives the critical wage below which the child drops out for both apprenticeship and meeting the subsistence consumption. We provide the mathematical expression of the supply curve in the appendix.

Now we consider the case where the household aims at the formal labour market, which requires full time schooling by the child. Here, the household keeps the child full time in school as long as the adult wage is large enough to support the subsistence consumption; but when the subsistence consumption cannot be met by the adult alone, the child needs to work. So in this case, the child's labour supply will vary between two extremes from zero to full, as shown in Figure 3. If the adult wage is below $s(1 + \beta)$, the subsistence

**FIGURE 3**

**Child labour supply (formal sector)**

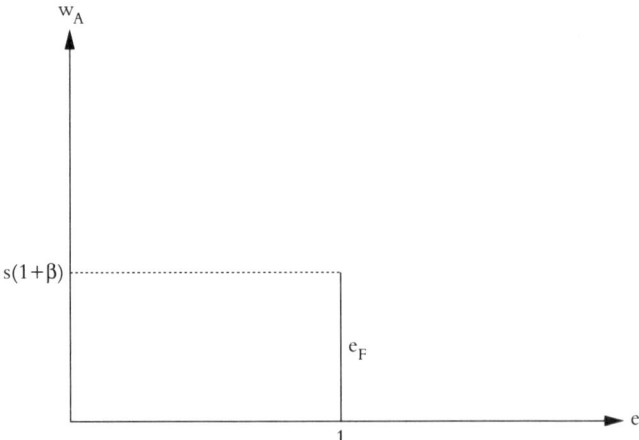

**Source:** Authors' calculations.

consumption can no longer be met. Here, the child drops out completely. Once again, details of this case are shown in appendix.

Our next task is to determine the final choice of the parent and the resulting individual as well as aggregate child labour supply curve. Since all households are identical, considering one is just sufficient. The parent's final choice depends on a comparison of the resulting utility (or indirect utility) levels from the two alternative choices: targeting the formal sector or the informal sector as the future work place of his child. The most interesting situation arises when targeting the formal sector is preferable at all wages above $s(1 + \beta)$, if the child is 'high ability' type; but targeting the informal sector is preferable at all wages between $w_A^-$ and $w_A^+$ if the child is the 'low ability' type.[7] Further, we may assume that $s(1 + \beta) < w_A^-$.

Next, by combining Figures 2 and 3 and using the above information on parental choice, we can deduce aggregate child labour supply curve as shown in Figure 4. At (adult) wages above $w_A^+$ all children remain in school. As the wage begins to fall below $w_A^+$, low ability children are made to divide their time between school and work according to the $e_I$ curve as shown in Figure 2. The high ability children, however, are still full time at school, because $s(1 + \beta)$ is much below $w_A^-$ (see Figure 3). When the wage reaches $w_A^-$, all low ability children devote their entire time to the labour market; but the high ability children are still in school for the full time. So between $w_A^-$ and $w_A^+$ total child labour supply in the economy is $(1 - \lambda)e_I N$. Here, note that because of our normalization, that $e \in [0, 1]$, $e_I$ is also the fraction of the child's time spent at work. At all wages between $w_A^-$ and $s(1 + \beta)$ the supply curve is vertical until the wage drops to $s(1 + \beta)$ when even the high ability children also drop out and work full time. Here, the child labour supply curve is completely vertical and assumes a value of $N$.

## 2.2  Labour Demand Curve

So far we have not said much about the firms that hire child or adult workers. Though we treat child's work as apprenticeship, which enhances his future informal sector earnings, from the firm's point of view, it is simply labour input. The firm values the child's work as long as it is profitable to do so. Here, we invoke our Substitution Axiom to say that work performed by a child and work performed by an adult are substitutable, but they are imperfect substitutes. One child labour unit is equivalent to $\gamma$ unit of adult labour ($\gamma < 1$). That is to say, the combined labour of one child and one adult is $(1 + \gamma)$ adult labour unit, which is strictly less than 2 units.

---

[7] Many other possibilities exist, but most of them are not as interesting.

**FIGURE 4**

**Total child labour supply**

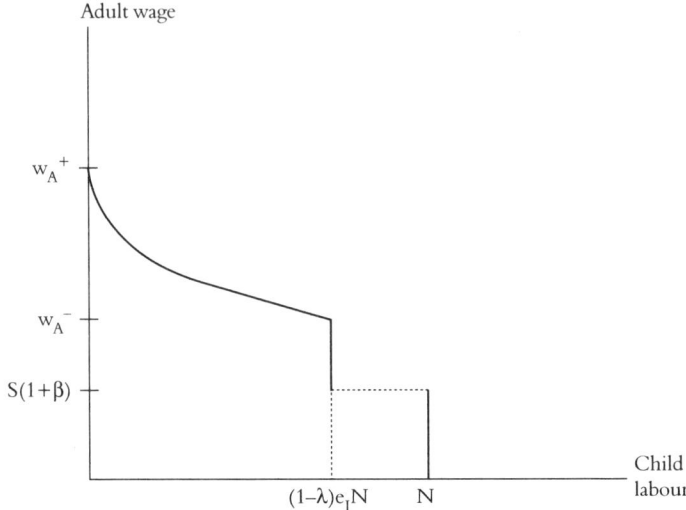

**Source:** Authors' calculations.

With this consideration we write the representative firm's profit function as:

$$\pi = pf(L_A + \gamma L_C) - w_C L_C - w_A L_A$$

The first term is the revenue of the firm, with $p$ representing price, which we assume constant in the spirit of perfect competition, and $f(\cdot)$ is a standard, strictly concave production function with labour as the main input. The remaining two terms are the wage cost for two types of labour.

By maximizing profit we can derive the firm's demand for adult and child labour, which can then be aggregated over the number of firms operating in the economy. Regardless of the number of firms, which we assume to be too many, and the specific form of the production function, it can be taken for granted (given the concavity of the production function) that the labour demand curve will be downward sloping against the wage.

However, the most important thing to notice here is that the Substitution Axiom implies that if the relative cost of hiring adult workers exceeds that of hiring child labour, the firm will completely switch to child labour, and vice versa. So to hire both types of workers, the wage costs must be comparable in a way that the firm becomes indifferent between the two types. If $w_A > w_C/\gamma$ the firm will hire only child workers, and if $w_A < w_C/\gamma$ the firm will hire only adult workers. In the intermediate case of $w_A = w_C/\gamma$, the firm may hire both types of workers. This particular point is crucial for our discussion of market equilibrium in the next section.

## 2.3  Labour Market Equilibrium

If the labour market equilibrium is to be presented in terms of adult labour unit and its corresponding adult wage rate, then we need to re-express the child labour supply curve of Figure 4 into adult labour units. As we have already specified, each child labour unit is just $\gamma$ times the adult labour unit; the conversion is straight forward. However, we also have to take into account the fact that the firms hire both types of labour only if two wages are balanced, that is, if $w_A = w_C/\gamma$. Since our interest is to study equilibria involving both types of labour, we need to restrict our attention to the set of all wages that maintain such a balance. In formal terms, this will require us to present our aggregate labour demand and supply curves against a 'ridge line' wage representing the balance specified above. This, in turn, will require modifying the critical wages such as $w_A^+$ and $w_A^-$. The modified values of the critical wages are derived and given in the appendix, and they are denoted as $\omega_A^+$ and $\omega_A^-$ respectively.

In Figure 5, we finally combine the labour demand and labour supply curves expressed in adult units aggregating over all adults and all children of the economy. Note that the aggregate labour supply curve takes into account $N$ units of adult labour (of the parents) that is inelastically supplied. Thus, the combined supply curve represents a simple shift of origin, when compared to Figure 3. Of course, our wage axis is now actually a ridge line, instead of just representing the wage. As is shown $\omega_A^+$ and $\omega_A^-$ replaces $w_A^+$ and $w_A^-$ respectively, and the behaviour of the supply curve remains unchanged from Figure 4. Below the ridge line wage $s(1 + \beta)$, all children and parents work full time giving rise to a total labour of $N(1 + \gamma)$, and above $\omega_A^+$, only parents work, but the children remain at school. Between $\omega_A^-$ and $s(1 + \beta)$, all parents and 'low ability' children work full time, while the 'high ability' children remain at school. The labour demand curve is drawn simplistically as linear; but that need not be the case. Any downward sloping continuous curve may very well serve the purpose.

First, we draw the reader's attention to multiple equilibria. This is, of course, not inevitable. It can have a unique equilibrium, to which we turn shortly;

**FIGURE 5**

**Labour market equilibria**

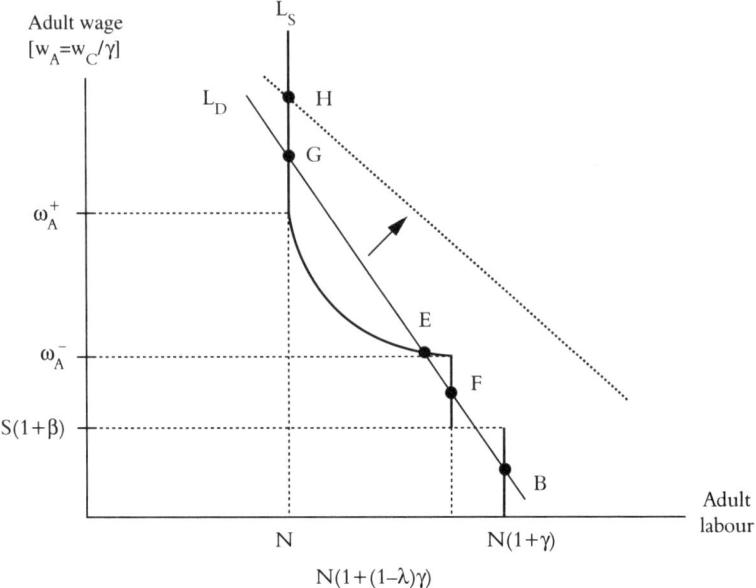

**Source:** Authors' calculations.

but multiple equilibria gives rise to interesting scenarios. Note that there are four equilibria, points *G, E, F* and *B*. Of these, three are stable, *G, F* and *B*, meaning that any of these three can emerge (and stay put) as equilibrium. Out of the three, *G* is a 'good' equilibrium, because it does not involve child labour, and *B* is a 'bad' equilibrium for children never go to school. While the first one is associated with high wage, the second one with very low wage, thus emphasizing poverty as the underlying cause of child labour.

This was primarily the Basu-Van argument. We put forward a new equilibrium, point *F*, in which high ability children remain in school, while low ability children work. Furthermore, this equilibrium is not driven by poverty (or subsistence needs), but by the parental concern for the child's adult-age earnings. In this equilibrium, some children never go to school, because they want to be in informal apprenticeship. Interestingly enough, both types will end up in future with their highest income (in respective sectors). Therefore, even though such an equilibrium involves full time child labour, its welfare implication is different.

### 2.3.1 *Ban on Child Labour*

To understand how different policies work in this environment, we first consider the case of a comprehensive ban on the use of child labour. It does not matter on whom the ban is imposed—the household or the firm. If the ban is perfectly enforced, then, in our environment, only point $G$ can survive as the unique equilibrium. This is indeed a good outcome, because the household welfare is likely to be higher and once this equilibrium is achieved, the parent will not send his child to work, and this will be repeated over periods. In this sense, the ban is self-liquidating; in all subsequent periods, there is no need to repeat the ban.

The same effect can, however, be achieved if the labour demand curve shifts out resulting in a unique equilibrium like $H$. Child labour disappears in this case too; but this time it is the market force, not a legislative intervention, that eliminates child labour. So, growth in the economy can also help to eliminate child labour.

Now we argue that even when the ban helps to eliminate child labour, a question can be raised about the child's future earnings. We wish to ask: does a ban always improve the child's future earnings? The answer we find is 'no', particularly for 'low ability' children.

Suppose initially we are at equilibrium $F$. The 'low ability' children are going to earn in future $2W_I$ (please refer to Figure 1). After a ban, the economy is pushed to point $G$, and the low ability children's future earnings become $a_L w_F$. If $a_L w_F > 2w_I$, that is, if $a_L > (2w_I/w_F)$, the ban will surely benefit them. But if $a_L < (2w_I/w_F)$, then clearly the ban reduces their adult-age earnings. There is more to this argument. After the ban, the 'low ability' children still have the option to work in the informal sector in their adult life. They will do that if $a_L w_F < w_I$. This will exhibit a pattern where the formal and informal sector workers have the same schooling history.

We can generalize this argument to any pre-ban equilibrium that occurs between $G$ and $F$. For example, consider Figure 6, where a stable equilibrium occurs at point $K$. Here all the parents work, and all the 'low ability' children drop out after some amount of schooling. Here, they will be earning $(1 + e^*)w_I$ in their adult age. Now if a ban is imposed, the labour supply curve will be completely vertical at $N$ (indicated by the dark broken line), and the new equilibrium will be given by point $M$ with a slightly higher wage.

Now suppose $(w_I/w_F) < a_L < 2(w_I/w_F)$, which implies that having acquired full education the low ability children will prefer to work in the formal sector and earn $a_L w_F$. Clearly, this will be smaller than in the pre-ban case (namely equilibrium $K$), if $a_L w_F < (1 + e^*)w_I$. Then we can argue that there exists a

**FIGURE 6**

**Labour market equilibria**

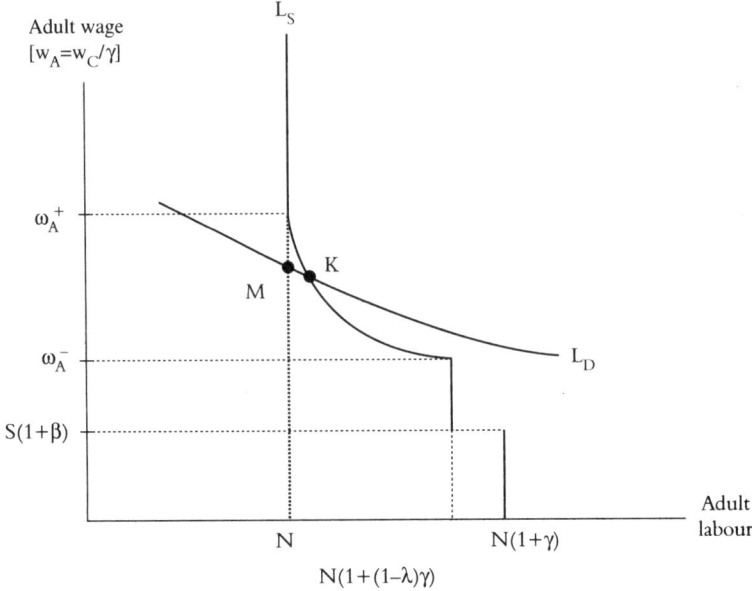

**Source:** Authors' calculations.

critical level of apprenticeship $\hat{e} = \dfrac{a_L w_F - w_I}{w_I}$ such that any pre-ban equilibrium that involves greater apprenticeship than $\hat{e}$ will generate greater adult-age earnings of these children than any post-ban equilibrium. In other words, a ban reduces the 'low ability' children's future earnings under these conditions. We may refer to Figure 1, where $\hat{h}$ refers to this critical level of schooling, and $\hat{h} = 1 - \hat{e}$.

There are several policies that have been carried out in an attempt to improve the school participation of low income children. One example is mid-day school. It can be shown in terms of our model that such a provision would indeed reduce the child's labour market participation, and will, in turn, increase their school attendance. Another policy suggested by many economists is to provide cheaper consumption loan to poor parents so that poverty induced desperation would be reduced. Here, the results are unclear as far as our model is concerned. It seems to be beneficial in the context of 'high ability' children, but for 'low ability' children it seems to be useless. We do not go into the details of these issues in this article.

*Main Results*

The main results may be listed out in the following way:

(*i*) A comprehensive ban on child labour can sufficiently raise the equilibrium wage resulting in the permanent elimination of child labour. A ban in such cases is self-liquidating.

(*ii*) A similar outcome can be achieved if there is big surge in labour demand resulting in a similar wage increase. This indicates that favourable market forces can substitute for state intervention.

(*iii*) A ban on child labour can also cause distress and loss in household welfare (see Figure 6).

(*iv*) It is quite plausible that poor families want their children to drop out of school and acquire informal training, especially when they feel that their children will not be able to compete in the formal job market, and when the school does not offer vocational courses.

(*v*) When children (belonging to poor families) are truly low performers in the academic sector and their performance measure determines their formal sector earnings, many of them may benefit by working as child labour. Such work experience may enhance their adult-age earnings. A ban on child labour will be most likely to hurt their future earnings.

# 3. Empirical Analysis: Determinants of Child Labour

In this section, we conduct an exploratory analysis of the determinants of child labour in India. While the literature has focused on various socio-economic variables, the role of the labour market has been hitherto neglected. In this work, we try to fill this lacuna. Hence, our main focus of interest would be to look into whether the employment or training opportunities in the formal sector has any role to play in the prevalence of child labour. We explore trends in the data and then perform two-variable regression analysis to examine the association between child labour and other relevant variables. Finally, we do a principal components analysis to study the relative importance of the variables.

## 3.1 Existing Evidence from India

Due to the paucity of child labour data in India, the empirical literature analysing the determinants of child labour is very sparse. Using various census data, studies have observed that the main factors associated with child labour in India are poverty, lack of child education and low adult literacy rates (Chaudhuri 1997; Duraisamy 1997; Singh 1997). Studies based on various primary surveys have confirmed that the above factors are indeed responsible for child labour (Gupta and Mitra 1997; Sharma and Sharma 1997; Swaminathan 1997; Usha and Devi 1997). Thus, there appears to be a consensus in the empirical literature regarding the importance of poverty and education as the main determinants of child labour in India. However, some studies done for other developing countries have shown that poverty is not always a determinant of child labour (Ahmed 1999; Ersado 2005).

As stated before, our attempt, in this article, is to look at some other determinants of child labour in India apart from poverty and education. What we are trying to study is whether the existence of employment or training opportunities has any significant impact on child labour. There can be two channels through which employment opportunities in the formal sector labour market can affect child labour. Not being able to get a job has a direct and an indirect effect on the decision of the household to send their children to work. The immediate effect translates itself into the family not being able to meet the subsistence consumption which forces the family to send the children to work in order to augment the income stream of the households. This is the standard poverty argument or the modified luxury axiom of Section 2. The indirect effect of unemployment is that the future returns from education become more uncertain and less attractive to the poor households who then prefer to send their children to work from an early age so that they can get used to the job and can start earning early. This was referred to as the insurance strategy of the parents in Section 2. As pointed out by Duraisamy (1997), even if education is free, cost has to be incurred in getting books and other accompaniments. Coupled with uncertainty, education in such cases is not at all an attractive option. Therefore, the worsening of the accessibility to the job market could lead to an increase in child labour. Since the decision of dropping out of school and opting for child labour can also be viewed as informal apprenticeship, the availability of formal training opportunities can also be a deterrent to child labour. This is another aspect of the labour market that we analyse in order to ascertain its relationship with child labour.

## 3.2 Description of the Data and Preliminary Trends

The data used in this exercise has been taken from Government of India (1991c) and the annual reports of the ministry of Labour and Ministry of Education. Using this data, a cross-section analysis at the state level has been performed. Government of India's Census provides data on child work participation every 10 years. However, there are certain problems associated with using census data across years. One problem is that there could have been substantial changes within the 10-year periods and hence any analysis based on data across Census years may not be reliable. Another major problem is the change in definition of workers across the Census years, which may lead to inconsistencies in estimation. To identify a worker, both the 1961 and the 1971 Census use a dual approach (usual status and current status) with a reference period of one year (seasonal) and one fortnight or one week for the 1961 and the 1971 Census respectively. However, in the 1981 Census, the usual status approach is adopted uniformly for all work. Further, in 1981, the workers have been divided into two categories, viz., main workers (who worked at least 183 days in the last year) and marginal workers (who worked sometimes during last year) to include more people than in the earlier years. The 1991 Census further tried to reduce the under-enumeration of workers by specifically instructing the enumerators to include unpaid workers in farms or in family enterprises as workers. This was mainly done to cover the hitherto ignored children and women engaged in unpaid household work. Similarly, there is no uniformity in the definition of the child worker as well, across Census years. Consequently, it would be misleading to use data from different Census years in the same analysis. Hence we use data from the latest available Census at the time of doing this study, that is, 1991, for the present analysis.

Before going on to the analysis, we provide a brief discussion of the variables that have been used in the empirical exercise. Our main variable of interest is child work participation rate (henceforth denoted as CL) which is defined as the ratio of the total child workers[8] to total number of children in the population.[9] While discussing the factors responsible for child labour we will first briefly discuss the explanatory variables which have been used in the ensuing exercise following the literature and then talk about the variables that we have introduced. As discussed before, to determine the causes of child labour, the variables that are most cited by literature are the poverty rate, the enrolment ratio and the literacy rates. The poverty rate gives the percentage of population below the poverty line. We have taken the poverty rate of 1993–94 as a proxy (henceforth denoted as POV),[10] since the poverty rate for the year under consideration is not available. The female literacy rate

---

[8] This includes the main and the marginal workers.

[9] Persons up to age 14 years are considered as child workers.

[10] The exercise was also done with the poverty rates of 1987–88 as well as the average poverty rate calculated as the average of the rates for 1987–88 and 1993–94. The results remain qualitatively unchanged.

(henceforth denoted as FEM) is the ratio of the total number of educated females to the total number of females in the age group greater than 15 years. We also use the total literacy rate (henceforth denoted as TLR) to consider overall parental literacy. The primary enrolment rate[11] (henceforth denoted as ENR) is a ratio of the total number of children enrolled in school to the total number of children in that age group. Female work participation rate (henceforth denoted as FWPR) is also considered as one of the possible determinants of child labour. This variable denotes the ratio of total females working to total females in the specified population. Two other variables considered are the per capita net state domestic product (henceforth denoted as PCNSDP) and the proportion of scheduled castes and tribes in the total population (denoted as SC/STs).[12]

Finally we discuss our main variables of interest. The existence of a dual structure (viz., formal and informal) of the labour market has implications for child labour. Our objective is to capture this segmentation through the employment situation in the formal sector. We consider two different variables for this purpose. Our first employment variable is the total number of people who get placed in the formal sector in a particular year. A better employment situation can be interpreted as the existence of higher chances of the child getting a job if he goes through formal education. This was captured by the ability parameter $a$ in Section 2. Low ability translates into lower possibilities of getting a job which would also happen when job opportunities are fewer in the formal sector. In such cases, the parents would rather send the child to work. Another way of looking at the decision of sending the child to work is to look at child labour as informal training. Therefore, if training opportunities exist which can substitute for the informal apprenticeship, then child labour would be lower. Thus our second employment variable is the vocational training opportunities available.

For the first employment variable, we use data published by the Government of India (1991b) in the Annual Report of the Ministry of Labour on the number of people who had been placed in that particular year as shown from the records of the Employment Exchanges. We give a brief overview of how the data is compiled by the Employment Exchanges. The National Employment Service consisted of a network of 851 Employment Exchanges in the country at the end of 1990–91, the period of analysis. Registration of job seekers and their placement against vacancies notified by employers is

---

[11] It considers the enrolment rate up to class five.

[12] Duraisamy (1997) noted that an increase in the proportion of SCs/STs in the population leads to a significant increase in child labour.

one of the main activities of the Employment Exchanges. The Employment Exchanges (Compulsory Notification of Vacancies) Act, 1959 applies to all establishments in the public sector and those establishments in the private sector which are engaged in non-agricultural activities and employ 25 or more workers. Under the Act, it is obligatory for the employers to notify vacancies (other than those exempted in the Act) occurring in their establishments to the prescribed Employment Exchanges and to render certain periodical returns on employment and vacancies in their establishments. The Act covered 189,000 establishments at the end of March 1989 (144,000 in the public sector and 45,000 in the private sector). Enforcement of the Act is the responsibility of the states and union territories, and a majority of them have special enforcement machinery for this purpose.

We were able to collect data on the number of people placed through the Employment Exchanges in 1990–91 to proxy for formal sector job opportunities. To reduce the heterogeneity arising due to the different size of states and union territories we take the formal sector placement data in per capita terms. Therefore, per capita placement (henceforth denoted as PCP) is the first variable capturing the formal sector employment scenario.

For the second employment variable, we use number of seats available for vocational training. The craftsmen training scheme was introduced in 1950, mainly with the purpose of providing training in 'various vocational trades to meet the technical manpower requirements for technological developments and industrial growth of our country' (Government of India 1991b). The number of seats and institutions have been steadily increasing due to an increased demand for manpower. The educational qualification required for entering these institutes varies from the eighth standard to the twelfth standard. We can, therefore, construct a proxy for employment accessibility as the per capita total seats of the training institutes and the centres provided under the craftsmen-training scheme (henceforth called PCTS).

Since we perform a cross-section analysis, it would be instructive to first look at how the states and the union territories differ in their behaviour with respect to certain important variables (see Table 1).[13] While the first column of Table 1 reports the child work participation rates, in the subsequent columns we rank the states according to their performance with respect to some of the important variables.

---

[13] Out of 32 states and union territories, we include, here, those 27 that have complete data on all variables considered. Note that henceforth we shall refer to both states and union territories simply as states.

**TABLE 1**

**A comparison of states with respect to the main variables**

| States | CL | CL$_{RANK}$ | PCP$_{RANK}$ | POV$_{RANK}$ | ENR$_{RANK}$ | FEM$_{RANK}$ |
|---|---|---|---|---|---|---|
| Andaman and Nicobar Islands | 1.8% | 5 | 2 | 15 | 5 | 8 |
| Andhra Pradesh | 10.0% | 27 | 19 | 5 | 23 | 23 |
| Assam | 5.5% | 19 | 21 | 24 | 18 | 19 |
| Bihar | 4.0% | 13 | 22 | 27 | 27 | 27 |
| Chandigarh | 1.4% | 3 | 4 | 1 | 4 | 3 |
| Delhi | 3.9% | 12 | 3 | 3 | 9 | 5 |
| Goa | 2.0% | 6 | 8 | 4 | 2 | 6 |
| Gujarat | 5.3% | 17 | 11 | 6 | 17 | 18 |
| Harayana | 2.6% | 8 | 10 | 8 | 13 | 21 |
| Himachal Pradesh | 4.6% | 15 | 6 | 12 | 6 | 13 |
| Karnataka | 8.8% | 25 | 23 | 13 | 19 | 20 |
| Kerala | 0.6% | 2 | 9 | 9 | 1 | 1 |
| Lakshadweep | 0.3% | 1 | 1 | 7 | 3 | 4 |
| Madhya Pradesh | 8.1% | 24 | 17 | 25 | 21 | 24 |
| Maharashtra | 5.7% | 20 | 14 | 18 | 10 | 10 |
| Manipur | 3.7% | 10 | 25 | 14 | 15 | 17 |
| Meghalaya | 7.4% | 23 | 15 | 20 | 24 | 16 |
| Mizoram | 9.4% | 26 | 5 | 10 | 8 | 2 |
| Nagaland | 5.3% | 18 | 16 | 21 | 16 | 9 |
| Orissa | 5.9% | 21 | 12 | 26 | 22 | 22 |
| Pondicherry | 1.5% | 4 | 13 | 19 | 7 | 7 |
| Punjab | 3.0% | 9 | 20 | 2 | 11 | 14 |
| Rajasthan | 6.5% | 22 | 24 | 11 | 25 | 27 |
| Tamil Nadu | 4.8% | 16 | 7 | 16 | 14 | 12 |
| Tripura | 2.3% | 7 | 18 | 22 | 12 | 11 |
| Uttar Pradesh | 3.8% | 11 | 26 | 23 | 26 | 25 |
| West Bengal | 4.2% | 14 | 27 | 17 | 20 | 15 |

**Source:** Authors' calculations.

Depending on performance we have assigned ranks to the states ranging from 1 to 27. The best performer with respect to a particular variable has been assigned rank 1 and the worst performer rank 27.[14] A study of the above table reveals that many states which are performing well in terms of child labour are also performing well with respect to the other variables. Andhra Pradesh is at one end of the spectrum having the largest child participation in the work force with Lakshadweep and Kerala at the other end of the spectrum having the least child work participation rate. We can observe from the table that Kerala, Chandigarh and Goa are among the better performance states.

---

[14] For example the state with the highest female literacy rate has been assigned rank 1 and the state with the highest child labour has been assigned rank 27.

In fact, these states have consistently performed well with respect to all the variables. On the other hand, there are states, which have performed poorly with respect to child labour and also fare badly in terms of other variables. Some of the poor performing states are Uttar Pradesh, Rajasthan and Madhya Pradesh. Some authors (Chaudhuri 1997; Duraisamy 1997) have also found a similar pattern in the inter-state variation showing that the above mentioned states have always been poor performers. Hence, there is reason to suspect that a relationship exists between child labour and the other variables. Not all states, however, conform to this pattern. To give an example, Bihar which has performed badly with respect to all the variables has done moderately well with respect to child labour. On the other hand, Delhi, which has fared well in terms of the other variables has performed poorly with respect to child labour. Therefore, from a simple examination of the ranks we cannot conclude whether the pattern of behaviour mentioned above is statistically significant. To probe deeper into the relationship between child labour and other variables we need to conduct a formal analysis of the determinants of child labour.

From the scatter plots of the data, we can form an idea of the type of relationship that exists between child work participation rate and some of the important variables under consideration. Figure 7 shows the scatter plot between child work participation rate and per capita placement rate. We can clearly detect the existence of a negative relationship between the two. On the other hand, even though we can discern a positive relation between poverty and child labour, but the relation is not very pronounced as seen from Figure 8. Per capita seats also affects child labour negatively which appears to be the case from Figure 9. Therefore, a quick visual analysis indicates that there could be a negative relationship between child work participation rate and the employment scenario.

From the table as well as the graphs it can be deduced that not all states conform to any given relation in a consistent way. The question that now arises is what type of relationship exists between child work participation rate and the other variables and whether the relationship is significant.

## 3.3 Empirical Analysis

We conduct a cross-section analysis of the determinants of child labour using state-level data from the 1991 Census. Since the explanatory variables are such that they could be correlated, a battery of tests are conducted to determine the presence of multicollinearity.[15] The tests revealed that there exists

---

[15] Results are not reported to save space.

FIGURE 7

**Scatter plot showing the relation between child labour
and per capita placement**

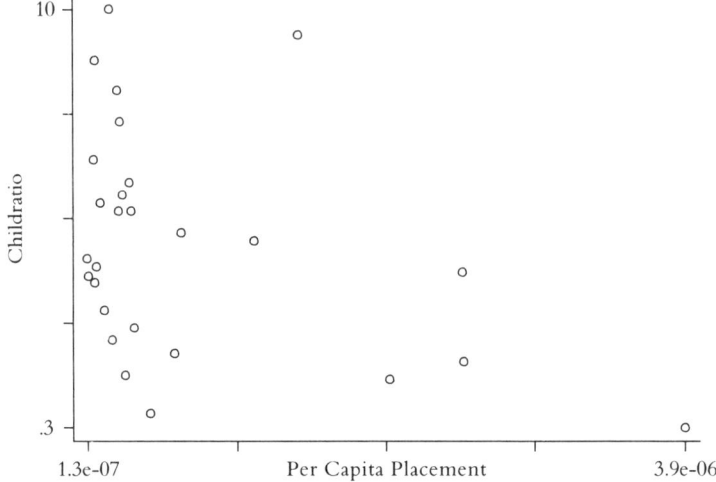

**Source:** Authors' calculations.

FIGURE 8

**Scatter plot showing the relation between
child labour and poverty**

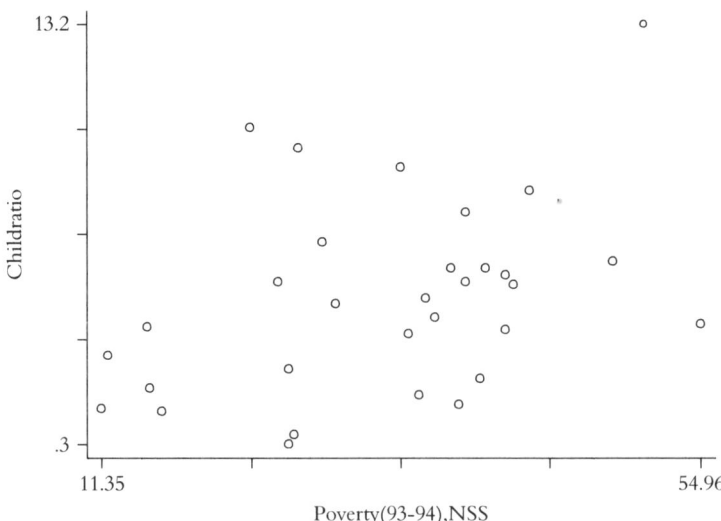

**Source:** Authors' calculations.

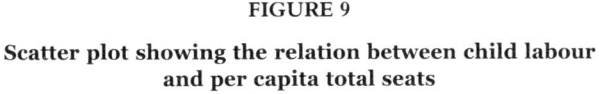

**FIGURE 9**

**Scatter plot showing the relation between child labour
and per capita total seats**

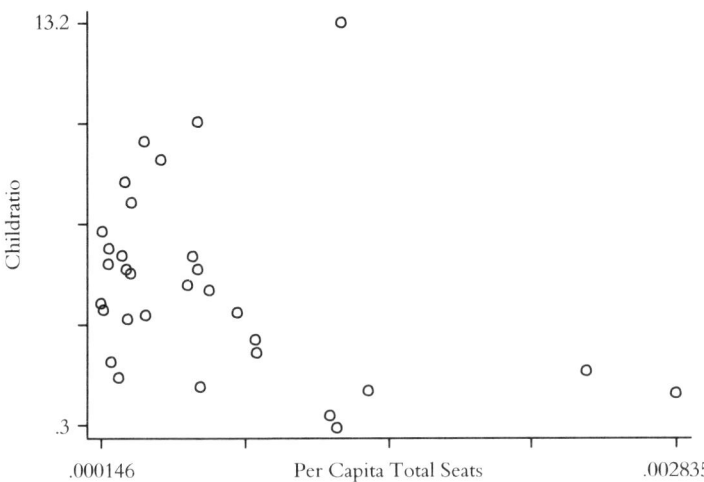

**Source:** Authors' calculations.

collinearity between the variables. In such a situation, if multiple regression is still carried out then there can be serious problems in the signs of the regression coefficients, their magnitudes and standard errors. To avoid the problem of multicollinearity, we perform a series of two-variable regressions and interpret the coefficients accordingly. The basic equation to be estimated is

$$CL = \alpha + \beta Z_i + u_i \qquad\qquad (5)$$

where $CL$ stands for the dependent variable representing child labour and $Z_i$ stands for the different explanatory variables which have been used in the regression analysis. $\alpha$, the intercept term and $\beta$, the slope term are the parameters to be estimated with $u_i$ which represents the random disturbance term. The method of ordinary least squares is used to estimate the equations after checking for heteroscedasticity.[16] Child work participation rate is regressed on each variable separately and the regression estimates along with the t-statistics are reported below.

---

[16] Both the White's test and the Breushe-Pagan test did not reject the null of homoscedasticity.

TABLE 2

**Summary of the regression results**

| Variables | Coefficients | t-statistic | Adj R-square in % |
|-----------|-------------|-------------|-------------------|
| PCP | –0.4115 | –2.72** | 20.0 |
| PCTS | –0.4639 | –2.80** | 19.0 |
| ENR | –3.1108 | –5.30*** | 48.0 |
| TLR | –2.0229 | –4.48*** | 39.0 |
| FEM | –1.1152 | –3.77*** | 30.0 |
| SC/ST | 0.3291 | 1.76* | 7.0 |
| PCNSDP | –0.3998 | –1.26 | 4.5 |
| FWPR | 0.9196 | 4.53*** | 40.0 |
| POV | 0.7792 | 2.29** | 12.4 |

**Source:** Authors' calculations.
**Note:**   ***, **, * represent significance at 1%, 5% and 10% respectively.

The results summarized in Table 2 indicate that all the variables, except per capita net state domestic product, are significantly associated with child labour.[17] In line with the empirical literature, an increase in enrolment rates, female literacy and total parental literacy are found to have negative and significant impact on child labour. Our main variables of interest are per capita placements and the per capita seats. From the table we infer that both the above variables have negative and significant effects on child labour. This is quite intuitive, since, as we argued earlier, an increase in the job or training opportunities in the formal sector will deter the prevalence of child labour. Further we also observe that, conforming to the literature, an increase in female work participation rate and an increase in the scheduled castes and tribes in the population lead to a decrease in child labour. Finally, we observe that child labour is positively associated with poverty.

However the above partial analysis does not tell us the relative importance of a variable in affecting child labour. Since multiple regression is not possible because of multicollinearity, we try to analyse the relative importance of each explanatory variable using principal components analysis, which is a multivariate statistical technique for examining relationships among several quantitative variables. The principal components are uncorrelated linear combinations of the original variables[18] with the weights equal to the eigen vectors of the correlation or the covariance matrix. The first principal component by

---

[17] Since the variables are taken in log terms, the coefficients (β) can be interpreted as the partial elasticities.

[18] The maximum number of components formed will be equal to the number of original variables used.

construction explains the maximum variation in the original data with the others explaining the remaining variation in the data. The contribution of each original variable to the first principal component will determine the importance of the original variables in the total variation of the data. In conducting the principal components analysis we have used only those variables whose coefficients are statistically significant in the two-variable regression. So, we have left out PCNSDP while carrying out the principal component analysis.[19]

Table 3 shows that the first principal component explains around 51 per cent of the variance in the data. A look at the first principal component shows that there is no single variable that dominates its formation. In fact out of the six variables considered, four of them, including per capita placement, have almost equal representation in the first principal component.

TABLE 3

**The first principal component**

| Variable | PC1 |
| --- | --- |
| PCP | 0.45572 |
| SC/ST | −0.20261 |
| POV | −0.41150 |
| FWPR | −0.26892 |
| ENR | 0.52227 |
| FEM | 0.48662 |
| Proportion of the variance explained | 0.5106 |

**Source:** Authors' calculations.

To analyze the relative importance of the different variables in the first principal component, we compute the correlation coefficients (known as factor loadings) of each explanatory variable with the first principal component. A higher correlation value can be interpreted as a greater influence of a particular variable in forming the principal component. We find that no one variable is the most important in forming the first principal component and PCP is no less important as compared to the rest of the variables. In fact, the correlation value for PCP lies right after those for ENR and FEM.[20]

---

[19] We have reported results with PCP as the variable for employment accessibility and female literacy as the proxy for adult literacy. The results remain qualitatively unchanged with PCTS in place of PCP and total literacy in place of female literacy. The results are not reported to save space.

[20] The results are not reported to save space.

Finally regressing child work participation rate on the first principal component, we observe that the coefficient of the first principal component is negative and significant, that is, the first principal component is significant in explaining child labour.[21] Based on the fact that PCP is important in influencing the first principal component, we conclude that even though educational and other factors may have a very strong influence on child labour, the effect of employment accessibility is no less important. Since the lack of employment opportunities might make itself felt indirectly through the socioeconomic factors, in a multivariate framework the effect of PCP will not appear to be individually stronger as it might be acting indirectly through the socioeconomic factors as well. But in a two-variable framework as well as in the principal components framework, the employment variables have a significant association with child labour. Therefore this suggests that employment and training opportunities may influence parents' decision to send their child to work. These findings can be interpreted as follows. First, employment prospect has a significant bearing on the parents' decision to send a child to work. Therefore, a child with lower employment potential may be sent to work at an early age. Second, training opportunities are found to substituting child labour. In other words, in the absence of training opportunities child labour can be looked at as informal apprenticeship that improves the future earnings of the child. The empirical evidence, therefore, supports the insurance strategy of the parent suggested in Section 2.

## 4. Policy Prescription and Conclusion

In this section, we first summarize the policy prescriptions that are usually adduced to address the problem of child labour. Then we try to collate the policy prescriptions emerging out of our analysis.

Policy prescriptions have mainly centred around the banning of child labour. One example of a policy to ban child labour is the Harkins Bill (1992) that wanted to ban the entry of those goods into the US which used child labour. Basu (1999) points out that a ban may not be an optimal way to eliminate child labour as that might consequently result in some people being worse off. In fact, it has been seen that banning child labour has led to other serious problems like children getting employed in more hazardous clandestine jobs and the employers not revealing the existence of child employees due to fear of the law.

---

[21] Even if we take the first three components together, only the first component appears to be statistically significant.

Pigou (1962) (as cited in Basu 1999) talks about providing social welfare to the poor families as the ban can result in a fall in income of the poor families. According to Grooteart and Kanbur (1995a), the ideal policy would be to increase the returns to education. Dessy (2000) suggests that universalization of education with sufficient employment opportunities in the labour market would help to eliminate the problem of child labour. According to the Public Report on Basic Education (PROBE) in India, the lack of proper educational facilities is an important reason for the prevalence of child labour, as total earnings are positively correlated with not only the quantity of education, but also the quality of education (De and Drèze 1999).

Our theoretical analysis revealed that when children are of 'low ability type' parents prefer to send them to work so that they can acquire some training, which will increase their future income. We also studied the effects of a ban on child labour and some incentive-based instruments like providing mid-day meals to the children as well as providing consumption loans to the parents. While for the 'high ability' children, all the instruments are helpful as it increases their future income, for the 'low ability' children it need not necessarily make them better off if their ability is below a critical level.

However, the fact that low ability children might have to stay in the labour market may not be interpreted as exploitation of child labour (Bonnet 1993). For example, a ban may not be able to increase the second period income of the 'low ability' children and they would prefer to work instead of going to school. Therefore, one way of looking at child labour is that, as long as the work is non-hazardous and light, the child works as an apprentice which leads to the passing on of knowledge and expertise, which helps the child to earn a better living in future. In fact, our empirical analysis reveals that employment accessibility (proxied by placement through employment exchanges and seats in craftsmen training schemes) has a significant and negative relationship with child labour. Hence, lack of employment opportunities may lead the parents to retain the child in the labour market rather than sending him to school. Yet again, the issue of child labour boils down to how best one can provide training/apprenticeship under healthy conditions while the child is being sent to work by the parents. So, providing vocational or on-the-job training supplemented with elementary education can be an effective policy of helping underprivileged children who are forced to work.

In sum, this article recognizes the importance of the formal sector employment factors in causing child labour, and observes that using some sort of an instrument to abolish child labour will not necessarily favour all households. We are faced with a trade-off and a total ban on child labour may worsen the situation. In this article, we have argued that child labour can be looked upon as training in disguise, especially in the adolescent age. Therefore, it may be prudent to provide better working conditions for the working children (while banning the worst form of child labour pertaining to children of tender age) along with vocational or on-the-job training and elementary education. This appears to be a more practical solution at least in the short–medium term, while broader objectives of poverty reduction would be successful in reducing child labour in the long term.

# Appendix

## Derivation of the Child Labour Supply Curve

### The Case of the Informal Sector

The parent maximizes problem given by ($Max\ u = (c - s)(1 - e) + \theta(1 + e)w_I$ with respect to $e_I$. Solving the f.o.c. conditions we get the labour supply of the child as:

$$
\begin{aligned}
e_I &= 0 \text{ if } w_A \geq w_A^+, \\
&= \frac{w_C - w_A + (s + \theta w_I)(1 + \beta)}{2w_C} \text{ if } w_A^- \leq w_A \leq w_A^+, \\
&= 1 \text{ if } w_A \leq w_A^-.
\end{aligned}
\tag{A1}
$$

where $w_A^+ = w_C + (s + \theta w_I)(1 + \beta)$, and $w_A^- = (s + \theta w_I)(1 + \beta) - w_C$. Note that because of $\theta > 0$, which is the main differentiating factor between our model and that of Basu and Van, the supply of child labour in our model is greater.[22] This is shown in Figure 2.

With this supply curve, we derive the household's indirect utility:

$$
V_I = \frac{[w_A - s(1 + \beta)]}{(1 + \beta)} + \theta a w_F \text{ if } w_A \geq w_A
\tag{A2}
$$

$$
= \frac{[(w_A - w_A^-) + \theta w_I(1 + \beta)](w_A - w_A^-)}{4w_C(1 + \beta)} +
$$

$$
\frac{[2w_C + (w_A^+ - w_A)]}{2w_c} \theta w_I \text{ if } w_A^- \leq w_A \leq w_A^+
\tag{A3}
$$

---

[22] When $\theta$ becomes 0 our supply curve collapses to the Basu-Van supply curve.

$$= 2\theta w_I \text{ if } s(1 + \beta) - w_C \leq w_A < w_A^-$$

$$= \frac{w_A + w_C - s(1+\beta)}{(1+\beta)} \text{, otherwise.}$$

# Derivation of the Child Labour Supply Curve

## The Case of the Formal Sector

Now the household aims at the formal labour market and accordingly sets

$$e_F = 0, \text{ if } w_A \geq s(1 + \beta) \tag{A4}$$
$$= 1, \text{ otherwise.}$$

The above supply decision partly depends on an assumption that $s(1 + \beta)$ $< w_A^-$. This ensures that the child will have to work full time. Associated indirect utility of the parent is

$$V_F = \frac{w_A - s(1+\beta)}{(1+\beta)} + \theta a w_F \text{ if } w_A \geq s(1+\beta) \tag{A5}$$

$$= 0 \text{ otherwise.}$$

# Derivation of the Aggregate Child Labour Supply Curve

Now, the household's choice of targeting the formal or the informal sector will depend on whether $V_F$ exceeds $V_I$ or not. Assuming $V_F(w_A; a_H) > V_I(w_A)$ at all $w_A \geq s(1 + \beta)$, and conversely $V_I(w_A) > V_F(W_A; a_L)$ at all $w_A \in [w_A^-, w_A^+]$, we determine the aggregate child labour supply in the economy:

$$L_C = N \text{ if } w_A \geq w_A^+ \tag{A6}$$
$$= e_I(1 - \lambda)N \text{ if } w_A^- \leq w_A < w_A^+$$
$$= (1 - \lambda)N \text{ if } s(1 + \beta) \leq w_A < w_A^-$$
$$= N \text{ otherwise.}$$

This child labour supply curve is shown in Figure 4.

Further, to convert the child labour into adult labour unit, we need to write aggregate labour (combining both adult and child labour) as $L = L_A + \gamma L_C$. Further, to restrict our attention to the ridge line wage, $w_A = w_C/\gamma$, we need to modify $w_A^+$, $w_A^-$ and $e_I$ as $\omega_A^+ = \dfrac{(s + \theta w_I)(1 + \beta)}{1 - \gamma}$, $\omega_A^- = \dfrac{(s + \theta w_I)(1 + \beta)}{1 + \gamma}$ and $\widetilde{e}_I = \dfrac{(s + \theta w_I)(1 + \beta) - w_A(1 + \gamma)}{2\gamma w_A}$, respectively.

With the help of these expressions, we can write the combined labour supply curve in adult unit and against the ridge line wage as:

$$
\begin{aligned}
L &= N \ \text{ if } \ w_A \geq \omega_A^+ \\
&= (\widetilde{e}_I(1 - \lambda)\gamma + 1)N \ \text{ if } \ \omega_A^- \leq w_A < \omega_A^+ \\
&= ((1 - \lambda)\gamma + 1)N \ \text{ if } \ s(1 + \beta) \leq w_A < \omega_A^- \\
&= (1 + \gamma)N \ \text{ otherwise.}
\end{aligned}
\tag{A6}
$$

This labour supply curve is shown in Figure 5.

**Padmini Dasgupta,** Indira Gandhi Institute of Development Research, Gen. A.K. Vaidya Marg, Goregaon(E), Mumbai 400 065. E-mail: padmini.dasgupta@gmail.com

**Bibhas Saha,** Department of Economics, University of East Anglia, Norwich, NR4 7TJ UK and Indira Gandhi Institute of Development Research. E-mail: B.Saha@uea.ac.uk

**Rudra Sensarma,** Birmingham Business School, University of Birmingham, University House, Edgbaston Park Road, Birmingham B15 2TT. E-mail: r.sensarma@bham.ac.uk

# References

Ahmed, I. 1999. 'Getting Rid of Child Labour', *Economic and Political Weekly*, 34(3 July): 1815–22.

Basu, K. 1999. 'Child Labour: Cause, Consequence, and Cure, with Remarks on International Labour Standards', *Journal of Economic Literature*, 37(3): 1083–119.

Basu, K. and P. H. Van. 1998. 'The Economics of Child Labor', *American Economic Review*, 88(3): 412–27.

———. 1999. 'The Economics of Child Labor: Reply', *American Economic Review*, 89(3): 1386–88.

Bonnet, M. 1993. 'Child Labour in Africa', *International Labour Review*, 132: 371–89.

Burra, N. 1995. *Born to Work: Child Labour in India*. New Delhi: Oxford University Press.

Cain, M. and A.B.M. Mozumder. 1980. 'Labour Market Structure, Child Employment and Reproductive Behaviour in Rural South Asia', World Employment Programme Research, Population and Labour Policies Working Paper No. 89. Geneva: ILO.

Chaudhuri, D. P. 1997. 'A Policy Perspective on Child Labour in India with Pervasive Gender and Urban Bias in School Education', *Indian Journal of Labour Economics*, 40(4): 789–808.

De, A. and J. Drèze. 1999. *Public Report on Basic Education in India*. New Delhi: Oxford University Press.

Dehejia, R. and R. Gatti. 2002. 'Child Labor: The Role of Income Variability and Access to Credit Across Countries', National Bureau of Economic Research Working Paper No. 9018, Cambridge, Massachusetts: National Bureau of Economic Research.

Dessy, S. E. 2000. 'A Defense of Compulsory Measures against Child Labour', *Journal of Development Economics*, 62: 261–75.

Duraisamy, M. 1997. 'Changes in Child Labour over Space and Time in India', *Indian Journal of Labour Economics*, 40(4): 809–18.

Ersado, L. 2005. 'Child Labor and Schooling Decisions in Urban and Rural Areas: Comparative Evidence from Nepal, Peru and Zimbabwe', *World Development*, 33(3): 455–80.

Government of India. 1991a. *Annual Report*. New Delhi: Ministry of Education.

———. 1991b. *Annual Report*. New Delhi: Ministry of Labour.

———. 1991c. *Census of India*. New Delhi.

Grooteart, C. and R. Kanbur. 1995a. 'Child Labour: An Economic Perspective', *International Labour Review*, 134(2): 187–203.

———. 1995b. 'Child Labour: A Review', Policy Research Working Paper, Washington DC: World Bank.

Gupta, I. and A. Mitra. 1997. 'Child Labour: A Profile of Delhi Slums', *Indian Journal of Labour Economics*, 40(4): 841–47.

Gupta, M. R. 2000. 'Wage Determination of a Child Worker: A Theoretical Analysis', *Review of Development Economics*, 4(2): 219–28.

www.indiastat.com

Institute of Applied Manpower Research. 1999. *Manpower Profile India Yearbook*. New Delhi: IMAR.

Mendelievich, E. 1979. *Children at Work*. Geneva: ILO.

Pigou, A. C. 1962. *The Economics of Welfare*. London: Macmillan.

Ranjan, P. 2001. 'Credit Constraints and the Phenomenon of Child Labour', *Journal of Development Economics*, 64(1): 81–102.

Sharma, R. and R. K. Sharma. 1997. 'Education and Child Labour: The Case of Glass Bangle Industry of Firozabad', *Indian Journal of Labour Economics*, 40(4): 869–75.

Singh, S. 1997. 'Some Aspects of Child Labour in Rajasthan', Working Paper WP-095, Institute of Development Studies, Jaipur.

Swaminathan, M. 1997. 'Do Child Workers Acquire Specialised Skills? A Case Study of Teenage Workers in Bhavnagar', *Indian Journal of Labour Economics*, 40(4): 829–39.

Usha, S. and D. R. Devi. 1997. 'Causes and Earnings of Child Labour in Beedi and Agarbathi Industries', *Indian Journal of Labour Economics*, 40(4): 849–57.

Weiner, M. 1991. *The Child and the State in India: Child Labor and Education Policy in Comparative Perspective*. Princeton: Princeton University Press.

# Did Agricultural Growth Trickle Down in India? What Do We Really-Really Know?

Richard Palmer-Jones
School of Development Studies, University of East Anglia, UK

Kunal Sen[*]
The School of Environment and Development, University of Manchester, UK

The relationship between agricultural growth and poverty has been a contested area of policy studies for more than 30 years. This paper assesses what we know about the agricultural growth–rural poverty relationship, with particular emphasis on the Indian evidence. While the trickle-down hypothesis seems to have strong support in the Indian case, the nature and significance of its role is seen to vary according to initial conditions. Recent empirical studies that make an argument for public investments in research and development and in the less favoured regions as a means to reduce rural poverty remain suspect in terms of the robustness of their methodology, and it is not clear that agriculture-led poverty reduction can be transferred to these regions. The debate on whether agricultural growth and rural non-farm output growth are substitutes or complements in their effects on rural

* Both are corresponding authors and comments are welcome to r.palmer-jones@uea.ac.uk and kunal.sen@manchester.ac.uk. Our work in this area has been partly funded by the Social Science Research Committee of the Department for International Development of the UK Government, in which Dr Amaresh Dubey, of the North-East Hill University, Shillong, India, and Professor Ashok Parikh of the University of East Anglia were sometime collaborators in this project. In our empirical work data from the 38th, 43rd and 50th Rounds of the NSS were made available by NSSO under the collaborative agreement between the Overseas Development Group and the NSSO. We have also used official price data provided by Officials at the Labour Bureau, Shimla. We gratefully acknowledge their support. The views put forward here are not necessarily endorsed either by DFID or the NSSO, or indeed our collaborators.

poverty does not seem to be settled. Finally, we question whether the money-metric measures of poverty that have conventionally been used in the empirical analysis of trickle-down are valid comparable indicators of ill-being.

**JEL Classification:** I38, Q10, R11, O13
**Keywords:** Agriculture, Economic growth, Poverty, Government expenditures, India

# 1. Introduction

There is a view that agriculture went out of favour with development strategists from the mid-1980s, partly as a result of doubts about the success of the green revolution in terms of poverty reduction (Lipton and Longhurst 1989; but also see Osmani 1993), disillusion with post-green revolution agricultural interventions and the main policy analyses of the 'Washington Consensus' (Kydd and Dorward 2001; Timmer 2005). Recently, however, there has been renewed enthusiasm for agriculture as a key component of pro-poor growth (IFAD 2001; DFID 2005; World Bank 2005a; Byerlee et al. 2005).[1] Timmer (2005) identifies three sources of this renewed interest. The most important one is the revolution in understanding the determinants of poverty, recognizing that economic growth is the main vehicle for reducing poverty and that 'in many circumstances, growth in the agricultural sector has been an important ingredient in the formula that connects economic growth to the poor' (ibid.: 4).[2] Much of the evidence on which this shift is based comes from the works that we will review in this article, especially those on India by Datt and Ravallion (1998b and 2002 among others), Ravallion and Datt (1996) and by Shengen Fan and Peter Hazell with co-authors.[3] While the Datt–Ravallion works claim that agricultural growth, especially when associated with non-farm employment (Ravallion and Datt 2002), is conducive to poverty reduction, and that agricultural growth and poverty reduction are conditional on initial conditions (including irrigation), the Fan–Hazell studies claim to establish strong connections between public investments, especially

---

[1] This recent work tends to have a focus on sub-Saharan Africa, and other less developed regions rather than India, but much of it purports to learn from what is portrayed as Indian success with poverty reduction through agricultural growth.

[2] He also lists new genetic technologies that can raise agricultural productivity especially in neglected crops many of which characterize less favoured regions, and new vertically integrated food supply chains which enable farmers to diversify out of low return staple crops. There is as much contestation about both these arenas of policy, into which we do not go here, as there is with regard to trickle-down from agricultural growth.

[3] For an extensive bibliography, see Fan's publications on the IFPRI Website—www.ifpri.org. Selected references are provided in this article.

in roads and agricultural research and poverty reduction, and that marginal returns to public investments are higher in less favoured areas (with less irrigation). Palmer-Jones and Sen (2003, 2006), on the other hand, argue that initial conditions for agricultural growth which has been pro-poor in India include, crucially, agro-ecological conditions in which irrigation is possible and feasible. In a recent paper, Besley et al. (2004), suggest that the elasticity of poverty reduction was higher from secondary and tertiary sectors, while Foster and Rosenzweig (2005) suggest that non-farm employment growth, which is crucial to the trickle-down mechanisms, is higher in areas which have not experienced high crop productivity growth. In their earlier work, which is also rehearsed in the paper just refered to, Besley and Burgess (2002) argue there are important political preconditions for agricultural growth and associated poverty reduction.

Clearly, although nearly all this recent work accepts both the connection between growth and poverty reduction, and the crucial role of agricultural growth in pro-poor growth in India, there is considerable confusion as to what the Indian experience actually has been. Further, there are questions with regard to whether the connections found between agricultural growth and poverty reduction can be legitimately generalized, or whether it is important to take account of circumstances which are able to not only facilitate agricultural growth but also enable the transformation of agricultural growth into improvements in well-being especially of the poor.

Of course, over the years there has been much criticism of 'trickle-down' in relation to agricultural productivity growth, generally, and specifically in the paradigmatic Indian case. At the end of the 1980s an exhaustive assessment argued that the Green Revolution fulfilled the conditions for it to be pro-poor, but that there was a significant 'adding-up' problem which obstructed widespread and sustained poverty reduction (Lipton and Longhurst 1989; but see also Singh 1990, Osmani 1993). This literature emphasized that growth may not be necessary for poverty reduction (Drèze and Sen 1989), or, even, sufficient. This position was argued not only in relation to recent development experiences, but has also recently been made in relation to the original development experience in England in the 18th and 19th centuries, which, as Szreter (2004) argues, has been highly influential in establishing and supporting the idea that economic growth is good for the poor (see for example, the discussion of the English case in World Bank, 2005a).

Moreover, there are other concerns which have not, as far as we are aware, been brought to bear on the agricultural growth-poverty debate. First, concerns about poverty trends since the reforms in India have identified a number of problems with Indian poverty measurements (see Deaton and Kozel 2005, for an overview and rehearsal of many of the arguments; see also Sen and Himanshu 2004a, 2004b). Thus, the criticisms of the consumer price indexes used to calculate poverty lines from the late 1980s, raised by Deaton and Tarrozi (1999) would also, *prima facie*, apply to earlier poverty lines which have been used extensively in all the econometric work on the Indian data referred to above. Further, it is not clear that the sort of money-metric poverty that is used as the welfare indicator in these works has a close relationship with a common, constant, level of well-being, or standard of living, for populations living in different domains, for example, geographical locations characterized by different cultures, or in the same location over time. This is, of course, part of the criticism of GDP and such monetary aggregates as indicators of progress, as discussed, for example, under the notion of human development (Sen 1985b; UNDP 1990). It also, however, rises acutely in the attempt to use household consumption surveys and consumer price indexes to make poverty comparisons which do not take account of 'environmental' goods that are crucial to the translation of commodities into well-being (Dubey and Palmer-Jones 2005b).[4]

This article reviews these issues. It is neither comprehensive nor is it exhaustive, but it reflects the authors' interests and views with regard to the topics that are important for economists to consider. In the next section we review some of the debates about economic and agricultural growth and poverty. In section 3, we review the key econometric works that use Indian data, focussing especially on the contributions of Datt and Ravallion. We also introduce our own work which elaborates the idea of initial conditions. In section 4, we discuss an extensive body of work, which we refer to as the Fan–Hazell (F-H) oeuvre, emanating mainly from authors associated with the International Food Policy Research Institute (IFPRI). The Fan–Hazell papers provide a quantification of the rates of return to public expenditures with respect to poverty reduction and agricultural growth, and have had a significant influence on development thinking in the relatively short time that they have appeared in the public domain. First, we discuss the econometric specification and some data problems in the F-H oeuvre; then we focus specifically on the claim that marginal returns to public investment in

---

[4] We follow the Cost of Living Index literature in using the term 'environmental' in this context to refer to public goods, the environment as usually understood, and 'culture' in so far as it affects the translation of commodities into functionings, capabilities, well-being or what have you.

terms of poverty reduction are higher in less favoured regions. Misunderstanding the agroecological conditions, under which agricultural productivity growth came to be associated with poverty reduction, could lead to relatively fruitless attempts to learn from the Indian Green Revolution for other, less favoured, regions, as certainly appears to be the case in some naïve interpretations of the F-H oeuvre.

While all these works use data derived from the National Sample Survey (NSS) Consumer Expenditure Surveys (CES), most make use of the data made available by Özler et al. 1996. The rest use the Indian census data. In section 5, we discuss and raise some questions about the recent work of Foster and Rosenzweig (2003, 2005). These works suggest a considerable need to revise 'conventional' trickle-down arguments which consider non-farm employment as complementary to farm employment in multiplying the effects of farm productivity growth. Foster and Rosenzweig use a different data set to argue that, as a general equilibrium approach might lead one to expect, farm and non-farm employment growth may be substitutes, rather than complements. They find that for the data they use, non-farm employment growth was faster in areas of low agricultural productivity growth.

In section 6, we question whether money-metric poverty, as calculated from the NSS CES, can be considered a suitable, spatially and temporally comparable measure of welfare which would enable conclusions to be drawn about patterns and trends of welfare. It may be possible to replicate some of the analyses at the state level using other welfare indicators such as mortality and literacy rates, and this would provide other assessments of whether and under what circumstances agricultural growth trickles down.

Finally, we conclude by providing an assessment of the state of debate on trickle-down in rural India, and we draw some conclusions both for the practice of policy analysis and priorities for future work.

## 2. Recent Debates about Economic Growth, Agriculture and Poverty

Strong theoretical reasons to think that agricultural growth will reduce poverty have been a characteristic of much, but not all, development thought. Lewis' classic dual sector model of economic development did not see much opportunity for agricultural growth in traditional agriculture to benefit the poor, who were mainly supposed to benefit in the long run through withdrawal of labourers and the food required to feed them into the modern urban, industrial or large modern farm sectors, and that there was little scope for modernizing traditional agriculture (Lewis 1954). The focus of agrarian policies in India after independence was on promoting agricultural production through investments in large-scale surface irrigation and redistributive land reforms, without otherwise improving agricultural productivity through use of modern inputs. However, by the end of the 1950s and especially in the drought years of the mid-1960s when India experienced food insecurity, it was apparent that these approaches were inadequate. Agricultural policies then shifted to what became known as the Green Revolution. The dual sector approach was superseded in the late 1950s by an understanding of interlinkages between the modern, industrial and urban sectors and agriculture; in this model the upstream demand by farmers for agricultural inputs and services, on the one hand, and downstream enterprises of marketing and processing agricultural products, on the other, generate investments and employment. This indicates that growing agricultural productivity generated 'agricultural growth multipliers' significantly draws on understandings of Japanese and Taiwanese development experiences (Johnston and Mellor 1961; Mellor 1966, 1976). Rejecting both the structuralist thinking underlying the Congress Plan for Agriculture and the modernizationist view of tradition-bound conservative farmers, a new approach developed. This new approach drew on the experiences of the Intensive Agricultural Development Areas where agricultural intensification was promoted through use of modern inputs of fertilizers and experiments with new high yielding varieties of wheat and, later, rice that had been developed in Mexico and the Philippines respectively. Following the conditions of drought and famine in the mid-1960s, India imported large quantities of new high yielding varieties seeds and set in place agricultural input subsidy and price support regimes to support adoption of these seeds as these are also necessary for the intensification of agriculture through the use of chemical fertilizers and other requirements of high input agriculture (Lele and Bumb 1994; for a critical approach, see Byres 1981).

From the start, critics of this approach, drawing on a Leninist tradition of analysis of the development of capitalism in agriculture,[5] spied unequal adoption and benefits in the new approach (Bhaduri 1968; Bardhan 1970; Griffin 1974; Ladejinsky 1969a, 1969b, 1977). They foresaw that it would not benefit the poor, since the benefits would accumulate mainly with the larger farmers and businesses supplying finance and inputs to and using outputs from modern agriculture. The concentration of landownership would

---

[5] For a classic expression, see Byres 1979; Harriss and Harriss 1989.

result in growing landlessness as smaller farmers and tenants were thrown into the labour market, which would be unable to absorb them resulting in stagnant or falling real wages.

A common argument was that to the extent that agriculture grew as rapidly as it did in many areas of India which came to be seen as 'favoured', it would not benefit the poor who were seen as increasingly concentrated in those areas which were not 'favoured' (Chambers 1983). Others, however, like John Mellor and associates, building on the populist traditions of American Land Grant Colleges and the development experiences of East Asia, especially in Japan and Taiwan,[6] promulgated the view that agricultural growth would not lead to the impoverishment of some (Johnston and Mellor 1961; Mellor 1966, 1976). This model, also known as 'the new economics of growth' (Mellor 1976) or the 'agricultural growth linkages model' (Stewart 1987), asserted several routes whereby the poor would benefit from agricultural growth. The most important of these routes would be increased demand for labour as well as increased agricultural incomes, especially in areas where the poor are very small farmers or landless labourers, as in much of India. Demand for labour in general would increase, provided mechanization was not inappropriately subsidized. It would occur in agriculture automatically, and in enterprises supplying inputs to agriculture. Moreover, it would happen through marketing or processing of increased agricultural output, or in employments spawned by demand multiplier effects of the increased incomes. They would also benefit from reduced food prices (absolutely, and in comparison with what they otherwise would have been) which constitutes an important route whereby increased agricultural productivity has potential to reduce both rural and urban poverty.[7]

These models provide the theoretical underpinning of trickle-down benefits of agricultural growth to the poor. Much empirical effort was applied to estimating the sizes of growth-linkages supporting large institutional agendas, especially that of the Consultative Group on International Agricultural Research (CGIAR) institutions. This effort often involved large-scale surveys

---

[6] but also Denmark and New Zealand as cases of agriculture-led modernization (Johnston and Mellor 1961).

[7] See Irz et al. (2001) and Thirtle et al. (2004) for recent summaries of the mechanism suggested as linking agricultural growth with poverty reduction. The role of food prices in mediating the relationship between agricultural growth and poverty has been contentious. Dharam Narain drew attention to the negative effect of rising food prices in increasing poverty. Critics of the Green Revolution had drawn attention to the role of output price supports in facilitating the adoption of cash intensive new agricultural technologies. As Narain and others pointed out, this was not good for the poor (Mellor and Desai 1985).

and cross section analyses (Bell et al. 1982; Hazell and Röell 1983; Hazell and Ramasamy 1991). Many aspects of these methods and results have been, however, disputed (Harriss 1987; Hart 1989).[8] However, much effort has been devoted to assessing the role and value of agricultural research and support in relation to the putative benefits of agricultural growth (Evenson et al. 1999). Nevertheless, as noted in the introduction, towards the end of the 1980s agriculture-led development went out of favour in mainstream development policy.[9]

To some extent, even critics of the Green Revolution came to accept that in areas where it occurred, the Green Revolution had reduced poverty. But they and indeed many of those who take a more favourable view of the Green Revolution alike accepted that there were limits to these processes, for example in the areas which experienced an absence of agricultural growth; and many suggested that there were complex conditions as well as necessary limitations to the Green Revolution. But many did agree that in the absence of assured irrigation or abundant and well-spread rainfall, the Green Revolution model was inappropriate (Chambers 1983; Lipton and Longhurst 1989). Further, many authors argued that the Green Revolution required massive state support which in the first instance was contingent on a particular combination of political and economic circumstances, but which then developed a momentum of its own as the farmers who benefited became politically articulate and powerful and able to induce subsidies for themselves, to some extent to the detriment of other areas that were yet to benefit from the Green Revolution. These authors have spent much effort attempting to learn from the Green Revolution in India, and in establishing its potential in other areas—in semi-arid India and, in particular, in sub-Saharan Africa. They emphasize the role of agricultural research, infrastructure, state support, and so on, in the Green Revolution (Delgado et al. 1998) and often argue directly, or imply, that a similar concentration of resources can similarly bear fruit in these areas.

Yet, others have consistently drawn attention to presumed or actual differences between the areas favoured by the Green Revolution and those

---

[8] See Hart (1993) for a more recent critique of the Muda and related studies. As she argues, most of these studies did not consider that the surplus generated in agriculture through growth is more likely to be channelled out of rural areas into the urban sector (for example, into the construction of residential buildings) and may, therefore, have weak linkages with the rest of the rural economy.

[9] Timmer (2005) suggests that this partly reflected the rise of alternative (to growth) development fashions (such as basic needs, human development, gender and environment) and single issue advocacy (NGOs), jockeying and grandstanding for attention and funding.

that were not, and consistently point out that the 'Green Revolution largely by-passed sub-Saharan Africa' (Barrett et al. 2006).

While the growth-linkages model has been the main framework for interpreting the effects of the Green Revolution on poverty, other routes by which agricultural growth can benefit the poor, particularly the raising of real income and food entitlements, have also been emphasized. An increase in food production in relation to population (and work effort), whether through increased production and incomes of farmers or through increased real wages of labourers, is not only directly beneficial to these groups as consumers, but may also raise their productivity. This has been emphasized by Fogel (1991, 1994) in his account of the English Industrial Revolution. Fogel draws attention to the low availability of food in relation to population and the poor anthropometric status of the majority of the population before the Industrial Revolution. An increase in food production in relation to population in the 18th century improved health and nutrition and enabled a greater work effort and productivity. While less emphasized in discussions of the Green Revolution (to our knowledge), Irz et al. (2001) list this as one of the benefits of agricultural growth (see also Timmer 2005).

However, Fogel's account of the benefits of growth on poverty in the Industrial Revolution has been disputed in favour of an account that draws attention to the harmful effects of industrialization on health (Szreter 1997, 2004). Szreter argues that McKeown (1976, 1979) misinterprets the epidemiological evidence (Szreter 1988, 1994, 2004; Guha 1994; Johansson 1994), and argues, instead, that industrialization had a deteriorating effect on the environment causing bad health, especially in urban areas. Further, the increased movement of goods and populations gave rise to greater exposure to disease. Eventually, public action was induced to mitigate these circumstances; nevertheless, Szreter's critique raises the question not only of whether growth reduces poverty or ill-being, but the responses (and their political aetiology) to the health challenges posed by disruptions associated with structural transformations during economic development. People may not only be left out of the accumulation of goods, but the conditions under which they live may worsen. So, despite greater material welfare, their well-being may deteriorate. In this approach, what is interesting is not that growth fosters poverty reduction, but that political actions are required to counteract adverse trends and to capitalize on the opportunities for improving welfare through public action.

It seems then that the conceptual accounts of the agricultural growth–poverty relationship do not provide a clear pointer on what we may expect from an empirical standpoint, particularly in the Indian context. In the next section, we review what the empirical literature can tell us on this relationship.

## 3. What Do We Know about the Agricultural Growth–Rural Poverty Relationship in India?

There is large empirical literature that addresses the relationship between agricultural growth and rural poverty in the Indian context. In this section, we offer a selective review of this literature, concentrating on the studies that are considered to be seminal and drawing from our previous work (in Table 1, we provide a more complete list of empirical studies that have been undertaken in this area, along with their key findings). The first empirical studies that attempted to validate the applicability of the trickle-down hypothesis for rural India were Ahluwalia (1978) and Saith (1981). Both studies use comparable periods for their empirical analysis—Ahluwalia used data from 1957–58 to 1973–74, and Saith from 1956–57 to 1973–74 (see Figure 1 for the different periods which various authors used to estimate their agricultural productivity–poverty relationships). Calculating two variants of the rural headcount index—the first one is derived by using the all-India poverty line for various years, and the second as a weighted average of the individual state-level poverty estimates—along with Sen's Poverty Index, Ahluwalia finds that rural poverty first declines from over 50 per cent in the 1950s to around 40 per cent in 1960, rises to a peak in 1967–68, and then declines again. Ahluwalia attempts to explain this movement in rural poverty using a simple Ordinary Least Squares regression where the rural poverty measure is regressed against the average and past year level of per capita real net domestic product (NDP) in agriculture, a constant term, and a time-trend. The coefficient on per capita real agricultural NDP is negative and significant—and both the sign and the significance of the latter is robust to the omission of the time trend and the substitution of current per capita NDP instead of an average of current and past values. Thus, Ahluwalia finds that there is a clear negative relationship between agricultural performance and rural poverty. Conducting the analysis at the individual state-level, Ahluwalia finds some support for the trickle-down hypothesis as agricultural performance has a poverty-reducing effect in seven of the 14 states considered, where about three-fourths of the rural population live in poverty.

**TABLE 1**

**A summary of key studies on trickle-down in rural India**

| Authors | Title | Date | Period covered | Unit of analysis | Findings |
|---|---|---|---|---|---|
| Ahluwalia | Rural Poverty and Agricultural Performance in India | 1978 | 1957–58 to 1973–74 | India Rural | Poverty falls after agricultural productivity rises |
| Griffin and Ghose | Growth and Impoverishment in the Rural Areas of Asia | 1979 | 1960–61 to 1973–74 | India Rural | Poverty rises |
| Saith | Production, Prices and Poverty in Rural India | 1981 | 1956–57 to 1973–74 | India Rural | Poverty rises |
| Datt and Ravallion | Why Have Some Indian States Done Better than Others at Reducing Rural Poverty? | 1998b | 1957–58 to 1990–91 | Indian states | Poverty falls in states with rapid farm yield growth and good initial conditions of irrigation and literacy |
| Datt and Ravallion | Farm Productivity and Rural Poverty in India | 1998a | 1958–59 to 1993–94 | Indian states | Higher farm productivity reduced rural poverty |
| Ravallion and Datt | How Important to India's Poor is the Sectoral Composition of Economic Growth? | 1996 | 1951–91 | Indian states | Poverty falls in rural and urban sectors related to rural agricultural growth |
| Ravallion and Datt | Why Has Economic Growth been More Pro-Poor in Some States of India than Others? | 2002 | 1960–61 to 1993–94 | Indian states | Elasticity of poverty with respect to non-agricultural production low in states with poor initial conditions |
| Datt and Ravallion | Is India's Economic Growth Leaving the Poor Behind? | 2002 | 1960–61 to 1993–94 | Indian states | |
| Fan, Hazell and Haque | Targeting Public Investments by Agro-ecological Zone to Achieve Growth and Poverty Alleviation Goals in Rural India | 2000 | 1970 –94 | Districts and NSSR | Differential returns to public investment by AEZ |

| Author | Title | Year | Period | Unit | Findings |
|---|---|---|---|---|---|
| Fan, Hazell and Thorat | Interlinkages between Government Spending, Growth and Poverty in Rural India | 1999 | 1970–94 | Indian states | High returns in terms of agricultural production and poverty reduction from public spending, including roads and agricultural research |
| Fan, Thorat and Rao | Investment, Subsidies, and Pro-Poor Growth in Rural India | 2004 | 1966–88 | States | Subsidies drive poverty reducing growth in the early stages, but agricultural research, education and infrastructure investments are productive throughout |
| Palmer-Jones and Sen | What has Luck Got to Do with It? A Regional Analysis of Poverty and Agricultural Growth in India | 2003 | 1960–94 | Districts and NSS regions | Initial conditions should include agro-ecological zones, since this conditions possibilities of irrigation |
| Foster and Rosenzweig | Agricultural Productivity Growth | 2003, 2005 | 1970–2000 | Villages as in NCAER data-set | Non-farm employment increased faster in areas of low agricultural productivity growth |

**Source:** Prepared by the authors.

FIGURE 1

**Periods used by different authors to assess the growth–poverty
relationship in India**

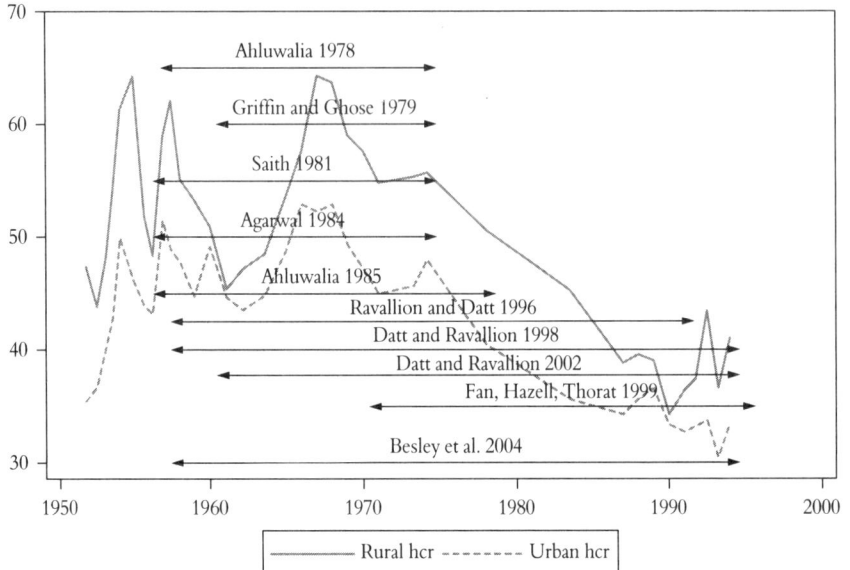

**Source:** Prepared by the authors.
**Note:**   Besley et al. (2004) use various end periods up to 2000, but appear to use 1993–94 for
their main regression Palmer-Jones and Sen (2003), is not a time series analysis.

Saith's empirical approach differs from Ahluwalia's in two important
ways—first, he uses the deviation of all-India agricultural production from
its fitted trend level instead of using the *level* of agricultural production, and
second, he adds a variable to capture the effect of inflation on rural poverty—
the deviation of the consumer price index for agricultural labourers from its
trend value. In addition, he uses a linear time trend as an explanatory variable.
He finds that agricultural output (or rather, the cyclical component of this
variable) has a statistically significant negative effect on rural poverty, while
inflation has a positive effect. The coefficient on the time-trend is positive and
significant. Saith interprets the positive coefficient to suggest that the time-
trend captures structural processes in Indian agriculture (labour-saving mechanization and the increasing power of the kulak class to influence the setting
of agricultural prices are examples of such processes) which has led to increasing poverty with the spread of the Green Revolution in India. More provo-
catively, Saith argues that the increase in poverty trend as well as the negative

impact of the inflation variable on rural poverty can themselves be related to the process of agricultural growth. As Saith (1981: 205) notes:

> ... the apparently beneficial impact of agricultural growth indicated by the negative coefficient of the agricultural production variable in the regression equations has to be adjusted for the significantly damaging impact on poverty of the price variable and of the basket of loosely identified 'trend' variables causally associated with the growth process.

Viewed from a modern time-series econometrics perspective, these two studies were clearly lacking in many respects. The number of observations used (as few as 12 in some regressions), the use of a linear time-trend along with detrended variables in the right hand side without checking for the non-stationarity of the series, and the non-reporting of standard diagnostic tests would be considered serious flaws today. But perhaps more interesting were the strong inferences that the authors drew from sparse data and very simple regressions. This is particularly true of the Saith study, where an entire theory of immiserizing agricultural growth is provided from a simple regression on a time-trend! Nevertheless, these two studies set the stage for much of the empirical analysis that was to follow in providing two very clear and starkly contrasting views of the applicability of the trickle-down hypothesis to rural India.

The next important step forward in the modelling of the agricultural growth–rural poverty relationship was provided by Datt and Ravallion (1998b) (henceforth DR). A key constraint that had been faced by researchers in this area was the lack of comparable survey data on household living standards both across states in India and over time. This constraint was relaxed when Özler et al. (1996) assembled a rich data-set which contained measures of absolute poverty and mean consumption for several Indian states for a large number of years. The measures were based on consumption distributions from 21 rounds of the National Sample Survey (NSS) from the period 1957–58 to 1990–91. DR use this data-set to exploit across state and over time variations to examine why some Indian states have done better than others in reducing poverty.

Before we discuss the DR study, it is instructive to look at simple plots of crop yield and rural poverty using aggregate Indian data for the period 1949–98 extracted from the Özler et al. data-base (Figure 2). It is fairly obvious that since the late 1960s to about 1990, there is a clear negative relationship between food crop yield and the rural headcount ratio. However, such a negative relationship is not apparent in the period between 1949 and the late 1960s and in the post 1990 period. Thus, if trickle-down has occurred at all in rural India, it seems to be mainly confined to the Green Revolution period of the late 1960s to late 1980s.

FIGURE 2

**Crop yields and poverty in India, 1949–98**

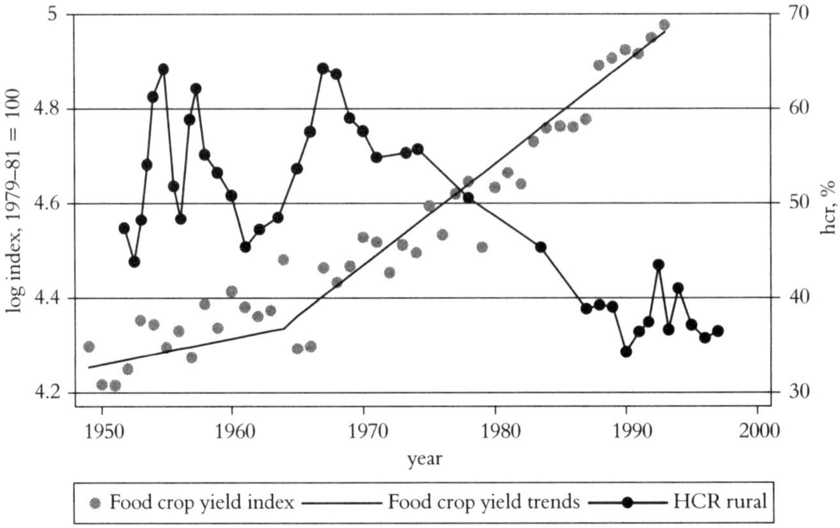

year

● Food crop yield index ——— Food crop yield trends ——●—— HCR rural

**Source:** Authors' calculations from Özler et al. (1996).

DR link the changes in rural poverty (measured alternately by the head-count ratio, the poverty gap and squared poverty gap) in a particular state to initial conditions prevailing in the state in 1960 (the starting date of their analysis), growth in farm output per acre, growth in per capita non-farm output, changes in the cost of living for agricultural labourers, and per capita state development expenditure. The initial conditions are captured by the initial irrigation rate, initial female literacy rate and the initial infant mortality rate. The period of analysis is 1960–90. Using a non-linear least squares dummy variable approach,[10] DR find that initial conditions and agricultural growth have both played an important role in poverty reduction, while the contribution of non-agricultural growth and state development expenditures have been relatively small. The key result from our perspective is the effect

---

[10] The non-linear estimation methods are necessitated by the uneven spacing of the NSS survey data on consumption that they use.

of the trend of agricultural productivity on rural poverty—DR estimate elasticities of –0.38, –0.55 and –0.70 for the rural headcount ratio, the poverty gap index and the squared poverty gap index respectively. There is strong support then for the trickle-down hypothesis—cross-state variations in trend rate of growth of average farm yields were important in explaining cross-state variations in the trend rates of rural poverty reduction. DR also find that the variables which explain the variation in poverty reduction outcomes explain the growth of average consumption across Indian states, thus indicating the lack of a trade-off between growth and pro-poor distributional outcomes.

More recently, however, Besley, Burgess and Esteve-Volart (2004) (henceforth BBEV), using the same state panel data-set as did DR, provide a less positive assessment of the ability of agricultural growth to reduce poverty in India. First, they find that the elasticity of rural poverty to per capita income is –0.6 as compared to the elasticity of urban poverty to per capita income which is –0.8. Second, using the state domestic product for the primary, secondary and tertiary sectors to assess the impact of the different sectors on poverty, they find that the secondary and tertiary sectors have a larger impact on poverty than the primary sector, with elasticities of –0.36 and –0.32 respectively as compared to –0.25 for the primary sector. The BBEV study is, however, not strictly comparable to the DR study for three reasons. First, the growth elasticities of poverty are computed using simple regressions of the log headcount ratio on log income with state fixed effects but with no other control variables. Thus, the estimated coefficients for elasticities may be subject to omitted variable bias. Second, state domestic product for the primary sector includes mining and quarrying, forestry and logging, fisheries as well as agriculture and hence may not be a good indicator of agricultural growth. In fact, BBEV do not estimate any regression where rural poverty is regressed against agricultural growth. Third, BBEV do not seem to make amends for the uneven spacing of the poverty data, in contrast to DR who do so. Thus, the BBEV study may be seen as more of an attempt to compile some descriptive statistics on the growth-poverty correlation in India rather than a fully specified econometric approach to test for the impact of agricultural growth on rural poverty.[11]

---

[11] It should also be noted that in the BBEV study, for quite a number of (relatively backward) states, primary production has a higher elasticity of poverty reduction. Further, it seems that BBEV results contrast with those reported by Datt and Ravallion (1998b), which did not find pro-poor effects of non-agricultural growth; this may of course be due to different model specification, but the data used are the same over roughly the same period.

The DR study can be seen to be a significant improvement on the earlier studies both on conceptual grounds, in its careful modelling of the inter-relationships between initial conditions, agricultural and non-agricultural growth and state-level policies that have jointly determined poverty outcomes in Indian states over time, and from a methodological standpoint, in the use of a large data-set and state-of-the-art econometric techniques. However, there were two important limitations of this study. First, the use of states as units of analysis can only be justified if there are no significant intra-state heterogeneity in rural poverty. But as Palmer-Jones and Sen (2003) show, there is considerable variation within states in rural poverty, and these vari-ations are crudely associated with differences in agro-ecological conditions which may be vastly different within a state, parts of which may be more similar to those prevailing in geographically contiguous states. Given the large intra-state variations in rural poverty, it is not obvious whether the relationship between agricultural growth and rural poverty, which has been found using Indian states as units of analysis, will be robust to a more disaggregated level of analysis.

A second limitation of the DR study is methodological, and this is related to their conceptualization of initial conditions in the modelling of the determin-ants of rural poverty. As we have noted, the DR study models the evolution of rural poverty across states and over time using a set of initial conditions— rural infrastructure, literacy and health indicators. It is arguable to what extent economic and social outcomes such as rural infrastructure and literacy should be taken to be initial conditions for a specified time-period as these variables are themselves conditioned by (earlier) policies and can be influenced by policy during the period of study. Policy responds to opportunity recursively, so that stock variables that constitute initial conditions at time *t* may have been outcomes from earlier policies. And the growth variables that are taken to be time variant (and consequently, potentially policy-induced) could be them-selves the result of a more innate set of 'initial conditions', not captured in these studies, but linked in some cases to the agro-ecological features of the region in question.

A more meaningful way of making the distinction between policies, policy-induced outcomes and initial conditions would be to treat the latter as the set of variables that are unchangeable and unmodifiable and hence truly exogenous to policy, while variables such as irrigation, literacy and rural infra-structure would be regarded as being outcomes of 'policies', past and present, and, of course, private action through markets. Agro-ecological factors char-acterize an important set of initial conditions in this context, and some Indian states are characterized by relatively homogenous agro-ecological properties that are favourable to agricultural growth—given appropriate supportive policies—which may partly account for their better performance in terms of both agricultural growth and poverty reduction, and hence the associations found in state-level analyses. Some states may have poorer average performance even though their performance in some regions of the states is impressive. Thus, by leaving out agro-ecological 'initial conditions', DR may be attributing causation to a variable that is itself an outcome of a complex interaction between initial conditions that facilitate pro-poor growth and policies that favour such processes of growth.

Palmer-Jones and Sen (2003) (henceforth PJS) address the limitations of previous studies, including that of DR. First, they examine whether the relationship between agricultural growth and rural poverty holds at the regional (sub-state) level when there is significant intra-state heterogeneity in rural poverty. Second, they estimate a model of agricultural growth that attempts to clarify the role of agro-ecological conditions in explaining variations in agricultural growth in India. PJS' empirical specification is different from DR in that they regress poverty measures computed at the NSS regional level from the 1987–88 and 1993–94 NSS consumption expenditure surveys on the growth of agricultural productivity in the period between 1962 and 1990 along with other control variables. Thus, the PJS approach is cross-sectional in contrast to the DR study which uses panel data. The cross-sectional approach is necessitated by the lack of comparable poverty measures at the regional level prior to the 1983–84 NSS consumer expenditure survey.

We present the primary set of results from the PJS study in Table 2. Column (1) presents an OLS regression with headcount poverty regressed only on agricultural growth. The results indicate a strong negative effect of agricultural growth on rural poverty, and the standardized coefficient suggests that a 1 per cent increase in the former leads to a 0.59 per cent decrease in the latter. Agricultural growth by itself accounts for 34 per cent of the variation in rural poverty. In Column (2), variables that capture social factors and agrarian structure are added. These are SC, ST, Lit, Ag_lab and Sm_farm. SC is the proportion of individuals belonging to 'scheduled castes' in total population, ST is the proportion of individuals belonging to the scheduled tribes in total population, and Lit is the number of individuals defined to be literate as a proportion of total population. Agrarian structure is captured by the proportion of agricultural labourers and small and medium farmers in the total population, which are denoted by Ag_lab and Sm_farm respectively.

TABLE 2

**The relationship between agricultural growth and rural poverty**

| Independent variables | (1) | (2) | (3) | (4) | (5) |
|---|---|---|---|---|---|
| Constant | 64.1*** | 51.9*** | 44.1*** | 23.3** | 0.12*** |
| | (15.96) | (5.31) | (4.84) | (2.38) | (3.26) |
| Ag_growth | −1,046.5*** | −1,009.3*** | −986.4*** | −535.5*** | −0.41*** |
| | (5.54) | (4.95) | (4.73) | (−2.79) | (3.20) |
| ST | − | 0.13 | 0.20* | −0.13 | 0.16 |
| | | (1.17) | (1.85) | (1.24) | (1.18) |
| SC | − | 0.27 | 0.46** | 0.31* | 0.02 |
| | | (1.24) | (2.28) | (1.74) | (0.17) |
| Lit | − | −0.39* | | −0.17 | −0.26 |
| | | (1.92) | | (0.96) | (1.56) |
| Sm_farm | − | 0.20 | 0.20 | −0.01 | 0.08 |
| | | (1.46) | (1.35) | (0.42) | (0.53) |
| Ag_lab | − | 0.22 | 0.002 | 0.19 | 0.19 |
| | | (1.49) | (0.26) | (1.57) | (1.59) |
| HCR 72–73 | − | − | − | 0.61*** | − |
| | | | | (5.09) | |
| SE of Estimate | 12.35 | 11.53 | 11.82 | 9.48 | 0.045 |
| Adj. R-square | 0.338 | 0.423 | 0.394 | 0.610 | 0.290 |
| No. of Obs. | 59 | 59 | 59 | 59 | 59 |

**Source:** Palmer-Jones and Sen (2003).
**Notes:** Dependent variable for columns (1) to (4) is the average of the headcount ratios in the 1987–88 and 1993–94 surveys; dependent variable for column (5) is the average of the squared poverty gap computed from the 1987–88 and 1993–94 surveys.
* significant at the 10 per cent level,
** signficant at the 5 per cent level,
*** significant at the 1 per cent level.

While only the coefficient on literacy is statistically significant at the 10 per cent level, the coefficients on all these variables have the expected sign— regions with higher proportion of households belonging to scheduled castes and scheduled tribes, agricultural labour and small and medium farmers, and characterized by low rates of illiteracy are more likely to be poor. Given that households belonging to scheduled castes and scheduled tribes are also likely to be illiterate, PJS estimate equation (2) with Lit omitted from the set of regressors (column [3]). As expected, both the variables SC and ST are now statistically significant. It is interesting to note that in these additional regressions, the coefficient on agricultural growth remains highly significant, with very little change in the coefficient value itself. PJS also test whether the negative and significant relationship between agricultural growth and rural poverty could be attributed to a spurious correlation—regions which had witnessed high agricultural growth in the period 1962–90 may already have had low poverty rates at the beginning of the period which remained low during the period. They address this possibility by controlling for poverty rates in 1972–73 (HCR 72–73), the only year towards the beginning of the period for which we have regional rural headcount ratios. The regression results are presented in column (4). It is clear that even when controlling initial levels of poverty, the negative and significant impact of agricultural growth on end-of-period rural poverty remains. Finally, to test for the robustness of the results with respect to the poverty measure, they replace the headcount ratio with the squared poverty gap, which measures the intensity of poverty, as the dependent variable. The results, which are remarkably similar to those for column (1) (allowing for the different units of the dependent variable) are presented in column (5) of the table. Agricultural growth not only has a negative impact on the proportion of people below the poverty line, it also seems to lead to an appreciable fall in the intensity of poverty. The finding that agricultural growth has had a negative effect on rural poverty in India seems sufficiently robust to alternate specifications. There is clear support, then, for the trickle-down hypothesis in the rural Indian context.

To test for the role of agro-climactic factors in influencing irrigation development and therefore, agricultural growth, PJS estimate a production function type regression where agricultural growth in 1962–90 is regressed on its determinants, including the level of irrigation in 1962 and the growth of irrigation in 1962–90, along with the other inputs to agricultural production (chemical fertilizers, tractors and use of male labourers). There is a clear positive effect of both the level and growth of irrigation on agricultural growth. Finally, PJS regress the level of irrigation in 1962 at the district level dummy variables constructed from mapping Indian districts to the 19 agro-ecological zones that characterize Indian agriculture.[12] They find that much of the variation in irrigation infrastructure across the country can be explained by varying agro-ecological factors, and that agro-climactic factors explain much of the variation in irrigation development independent of policies that operate at the level of the individual state and not linked to initial agro-climactic conditions.

The PJS study confirms the DR finding that states which experienced rapid agricultural growth consequently achieved poverty reduction. However, the PJS study suggest that the success of these states is due to a high proportion of favourable agro-ecological conditions and that where these conditions have not been present, neither poverty reduction nor agricultural growth have been achieved to the same degree.

[12] Agro-ecological zones (AEZs) are relatively homogeneous geographical regions that have characteristics that suit them for the design and use of similar agricultural technologies. There are

A criticism of the PJS study is that it does not address the additional complexities in econometric analysis that arise when there may be possible spatial relationships between agricultural growth and rural poverty. For example, there may be spillovers that occur due to learning processes based on information dissemination or to the intrinsic characteristics of these technologies that may make these technologies appropriate in regions with a certain type of resource endowments as compared to other regions (Byerlee and Traxler 2001, Conley and Udry 2002). Palmer-Jones and Sen (2006) allow for the possibility that rural poverty in India, and its principal proximate correlate, agricultural growth, are spatially correlated. Using spatial econometric methods, they explore the determinants of rural poverty and agricultural growth, and show that such methods provide us more consistent estimates of the relationships between rural poverty and agricultural growth and between agricultural growth and its major inputs than classical regression methods. They find that there is significant spatial dependence in the growth rates of agricultural output so that high rates of growth in one region are associated with similar high rates of growth in adjoining regions. An important policy implication of this study is that agricultural development may be hindered by inappropriate 'jurisdictions' since many water resource developments in India in the semi-arid and arid regions require inter-state cooperation which is becoming increasingly difficult to achieve.

## 4. Government Expenditures, Growth and Rural Poverty: A Critique of the Fan–Hazell–Thorat Oeuvre

A key question for a policy-maker is where to allocate scarce investible resources to obtain the highest rate of poverty reduction. Given the large literature that we have reviewed on the determinants of agricultural growth and rural poverty in India, there are surprisingly few studies that have examined the *effectiveness* of different types of public spending in bringing about

---

certain biophysical limitations on the agricultural possibilities that the AEZ classification attempts to capture. Biological productivity—bio-mass per unit area per unit time—is likely to be high where extremes of temperature are absent, soils are fertile and there is ready access to water whether through ample and well-distributed rainfall or relatively cheap and productive irrigation. The 19 zones identified in the categorization used in the PJS study were derived by an overlay of maps of bio-climate, length of growing period and soil scape (NBSS and LUP 1992). See PJS for more details.

economic growth and poverty reduction in rural areas. Most of the earlier work has tended to focus on *one* type of policy intervention relating to growth and poverty reduction like public investment in education and health, food for work programmes, price decontrols and so on (an exception is the use of CGE models for policy simulations [Narayana et al. 1990]). Fan, Hazell and Thorat (2000) [henceforth FHT] provide the first systematic quantitative analysis of the rates of return on different types of public investments towards increasing agricultural growth and reducing rural poverty in India. In further studies, Fan and Hazell explore whether the effectiveness of different types of public investments in reducing rural poverty via agricultural growth differs across agro-ecological zones. We review Fan et al. (2000) study in the next section.

# 5. The Relationship between Public Investments, Growth and Rural Poverty

The FHT paper examines the effectiveness of different types of public investments within one framework and within a single econometric model. The work has two strengths—a unifying conceptual framework for the determinants of agricultural growth and rural poverty, allows for both direct and indirect effects of public investments on growth and poverty; and a simultaneous equations system approach to modelling growth and poverty rather than the use of single equation methods, which are open to the standard criticisms of omitted variable bias and the endogeneity of the independent variables. Thus, the economic model proposed in the FHT paper can be seen as being more sophisticated both from the point of view of capturing the complex interrelationships between key economic variables and, from a methodological standpoint, in the use of more robust econometric methods.

The key relationships modelled are the determination of rural poverty and agricultural productivity. Rural poverty (the headcount ratio) is taken to be a function of agricultural productivity, rural wages, non-agricultural employment, the rural-urban terms of trade, the proportion of rural households that are landless, and one year lags of rural population growth and GDP growth. Most of the variables included are self-explanatory and are common to other econometric models of rural poverty. An increase in the terms of trade can lead to an increase in rural poverty in the short run if most households are net buyers. But it may have a positive impact on rural poverty reduction if higher food prices leads to increased investment in agriculture and, consequently, higher demand for agricultural labourers in the long-term. Rural population growth is expected to increase rural poverty if there is no commensurate increase in rural employment. The lagged GDP growth captures the remaining income effects on poverty. Agricultural productivity growth is defined as total factor productivity growth and not as growth in land or labour productivity as is often the case in the literature. Total factor productivity growth is hypothesized to be a function of current and lagged government spending on agricultural research and extension, the percentage of irrigated cropped area to total cropped area, road density, percentages of villages electrified, the literacy rate of the rural population, and stocks of government investment in health, rural development and soil and water conservation. A lagged GDP term is included to control the effects of overall economic growth on productivity growth. A rainfall index is also included.

Rural wages, the proportion of landless households, the terms of trade and non-agricultural employment are all taken to be endogenously determined. Rural wages are a function of total factor productivity, road density, the percentage of irrigated cropped area to total cropped area and stocks of government investment in health, rural development and soil and water conservation. A lagged GDP term is included to control the effects of overall economic growth on rural wages and non-agricultural employment growth. Landlessness is modelled as being determined by total factor productivity growth, lagged rural population growth and non-agricultural employment. The terms of trade are modelled in a simple manner as a function of total factor productivity growth both at the national and state levels and the weighted average of the world prices of rice, wheat and corn. In the case of non-agricultural employment growth, the latter is taken as a function of total factor productivity growth, road density, percentages of villages electrified, the literacy rate of the rural population and stocks of government investment in health, rural development and soil and water conservation.

The next set of relationships modelled are the determinants of public and private investment, road density, literacy and village electrification. Public irrigation is modelled as a function of current and past government investments in irrigation and the degree of electrification (since a higher degree of electrification leads to a higher use of pumps for irrigation); private irrigation as a function of public irrigation and the degree of electrification; road density as a function of current and past government investments in rural roads; rural literacy as a function of current and past government investments in education and village electrification as a function of current and government investments in power.

Finally, government investments in research, roads, irrigation, education, soil conservation, power, development expenditures and health are taken to be endogenously determined as functions of past values of state GDP and the terms of trade.

There are 19 equations with 19 endogenous variables. The system is fully determined. The system of equations is estimated using Full Information Maximum Likelihood methods using data for 14 major Indian states over the period 1970–93.[13]

The specification of the rural poverty determination equation allows for both direct and indirect impacts of public investments. Public investments increase total factor productivity growth and, hence, reduces poverty. By increasing total factor productivity growth, it also increases agricultural wages and, lowers agricultural prices and both these contribute to the poverty reduction impact of public investment. At the same time, by increasing landlessness through the increase in total factor productivity, public investments also contribute to an increase in rural poverty. The net effect of public investment is an empirical issue found to be strongly positive in the Indian case by FHT. The disaggregation of public investment into expenditures on research, irrigation, roads, education, power, soil and water conservation, rural development and health allow for separate rates of return calculated for each type of expenditure. Table 3 summarizes the results on the rates of return for each type of public investment.

**TABLE 3**

**Rates of return on public investments by type**

| Expenditure variable | Marginal impact (per 100 billion rupees at 1993 prices) | | | |
| | Poverty (% point) | Rank | Total factor productivity (% point) | Rank |
|---|---|---|---|---|
| Research and development | –0.45 | 2 | 6.01 | 1 |
| Irrigation | –0.05 | 7 | 0.61 | 4 |
| Road | –0.65 | 1 | 2.37 | 2 |
| Education | –0.22 | 3 | 0.62 | 3 |
| Power | –0.003 | 8 | 0.12 | 8 |
| Soil and water | –0.12 | 5 | 0.43 | 6 |
| Rural development | –0.13 | 4 | 0.49 | 5 |
| Health | –0.09 | 6 | 0.38 | 7 |

**Source:** Authors calculations based on FHT (2000).

[13] However, the years 1971, 1974–76, 1978–82, 1985–85 and 1991 were dropped due to missing values.

Public investment in roads delivers the highest impact on poverty reduction and the second highest on productivity growth. Public investment in research and development has the highest impact on productivity growth and the second highest on poverty reduction. In contrast, expenditure on power has the least impact on poverty reduction and productivity growth. Surprisingly, expenditure on irrigation and health have relatively minor impact on poverty reduction. The results suggest that if the government is interested in obtaining the maximum impact on productivity growth and poverty reduction in rural areas, it should re-allocate its expenditures from irrigation, health, and power to research and development and road construction.

There are six important weaknesses of the FHT study. First, the data used in the paper are subject to significant problems. FHT use extrapolation methods for several missing observations in the data and, thus, a large part of the data is constructed artificially (and some years are dropped).

Second, the estimation method itself—full information maximum likelihood—has advantages over single equation methods in a system of inter-linked equations, but that it can accentuate measurement bias of the estimated equations if some variables are measured with error (which is highly likely in their case, given the nature of data construction in the FHT study) is a disadvantage.

Third, the estimated equations have not controlled individual, specific, unobserved fixed effects (even though the data has been transformed to first differences, first differencing may not remove these fixed effects if there has been gradual institutional change in Indian states and Chinese provinces that differ across states and regions). Thus, unobserved time-invariant effects relating to differences in institutional contexts of states in India may not have been controlled and can potentially bias the effects of the other explanatory variables.[14] For example, in a state such as West Bengal where important changes have taken place over time in land tenure institutions, the estimates of rates of return in the FHT model may be biased if it is simply picking up the productivity enhancing and poverty reducing effects of such institutional change.[15] The omission of unobserved fixed effects may lead to an *over-estimate* of the rate of return to public investments.

---

[14] See Besley et al. (2004) for a summary of quantitative work that shows the different effects of state-level institutions on growth and poverty in India.

[15] As Banerjee et al. (2002) show, tenancy reforms in West Bengal had a clear positive effect on agricultural productivity.

Fourth, a surprising omission of the FHT study is that it does not allow for the possibility that research and development in one state or province may have significant spillovers in neighbouring states—farmers in other states may adopt new technology introduced in one state, especially if the farmers are located in similar agro-climactic zones that cut across more than one state, and find the new technology to be suitable for their climactic conditions. There is an extensive literature that documents this type of intranational spillovers. There may also be international research and development spillovers—for example, through the availability of international germplasm. As Alston (2002: 317) notes, 'studies that ignore interstate and international spillovers are likely to obtain seriously distorted estimates of returns to agricultural research'.

Fifth, the explanatory power of the model at least in the FHT study is low—the $R$-squares are below 0.5 in most cases. Thus, more than half of the variation in the dependent variables are unexplained. Most of the equations specified do not seem to originate from a precise theoretical framework and can be subject to criticisms of omitted variable bias or incorrect specification. There is a significant amount of ad-hocness in the specifications for total factor productivity growth and the terms of trade. For example, why should public stocks in irrigation, roads, electrification and so on matter for *productivity* growth, which is a residual in the production function, and not for aggregate agricultural growth itself? And why should the terms of trade not depend on demand side factors as is widely assumed to be the case for developing countries? Similar questions can be raised in the specification of public investment and stock determination equations.

Finally, the robustness of the results are open to question. Several of the variables which have statistically insignificant coefficients are retained in the policy simulations and can change the results (given the size of the coefficients) if omitted. There has been little attempt to undertake robustness tests of the policy simulations that is common in work of this nature. The question that emerges is how sensitive the results are to alternate specifications of the equations when insignificant coefficients are set to zero.

For these reasons, the precise estimates of the rates of return to public investments that are obtained in the FHT study need to be treated with a certain degree of caution. There is need for further empirical work that re-examines the FHT findings with better data, further diagnostic testing, more sensitivity analysis under alternate assumptions and improved specification of the equations, including the incorporation of unobserved fixed effects and intranational and international spillovers.

These criticisms notwithstanding, the FHT study provides a very useful starting point for those researchers interested in assessing the benefits and costs of different types of public expenditures in reducing rural poverty through the effects of these expenditures on agricultural and non-agricultural growth. For policymakers, the FHT study provides counter-intuitive results on which type of public expenditures to prioritize. If one were to take the broad conclusion of the study to be that research and development, along with road construction, matters most for rural poverty reduction, and that investing in health, irrigation and rural development are less important for rural poverty reduction, this may mean a significant re-allocation of public investments for many state governments in India.

More recently, an influential set of studies by Dorward et al. (2004b)[16] report results extending the previous work (Dorward et al. 2004a) with state-level data on poverty, agricultural production and public investments so as to estimate decade-wise returns starting from 1960. They use rather oddly the periods 1967–70, 1971–79, 1980–89 and 1990–97. These do not coincide with the periodization of the Green Revolution given in Smith and Urey (2002) who refer to various periodizations, including a first phase of the Green Revolution between 1967 and 1979 and a second phase between 1980–83 and 1993–94. Another periodization referred to is that of 1966–76 and 1977–87. Fan et al. (2004) find different returns in their different periods, which they report as 1960s, 1970s, 1980s and 1990s (p. 36, Table 1). Again, the different estimated returns are reported without standard errors and no tests of pooling such as constraints on coefficients of the same variable across periods seem to have been conducted. Under these circumstances, it is not clear whether it is worth discussing such differences unless their statistical significance can be established.

# 6. Impact of State Investments on Rural Poverty by Agro-ecological Zones

The claim that returns are higher in less favoured regions by Fan et al. (2000) has been quite widely noted. However, the empirical work on India on which it is based has been disputed by Palmer-Jones (2003). It is surprising that using three different ways of categorizing districts into agro-ecological zones

---

[16] This has been referred to frequently by Timmer 2005 and others in the Operationalising Pro-Poor Growth group of publications, including DFID (2005), World Bank (2005b) and Byerlee et al. (2005).

(as Hazell and Fan [2003] note) gives the same conclusion, namely that marginal returns are higher in less favoured regions.[17] Palmer-Jones shows that the explanation of the Fan and Hazell method to estimate the returns for different regions of India is unsatisfactory and, in their reply, Hazell and Fan admit to 'an unfortunate misprint' in their paper. They clarify their method, but this shows that it is likely that the regression coefficients estimated for different regions, the values of which are the basis for the claim that less favoured regions show higher returns, are likely to be imprecise and to have high standard errors. This means that it will be difficult to establish that any differences are statistically significant. It turns out that when the relevant coefficients and their standard errors are reported, they are indeed often statistically insignificantly different from zero. This is clearly the case in poverty equations reported in Table 8 of Fan and Hazell (2000).[18] This means that any claims about differences are not based on the usual requirements of statistical significance, and calls into question the robustness of the Fan–Hazell–Haque findings that the returns on public investments in terms of poverty reduction are higher in the less favoured areas.

[17] Fan, Hazell and Haque (FHH) (2003) use 14 AEZs according to an ICRISAT classification (FHH 2000: 414, Table 1); one of these zones is predominantly irrigated and the other 13 are classified according to predominant agricultural production pattern. Fan and Hazell (2000) report a different 20 AEZs scheme proposed by the Indian Council of Agricultural Research (NBSS and LUP 1992) in 1992, and classify them into predominantly irrigated and low and high potential rainfed zones for their estimation of marginal effects. Their claim that their growth model is not biased fails to recognize the heterogeneity of agro-ecological conditions within districts (see Palmer-Jones 2003: 428, Table 2).

[18] Fan et al. (2002) report regression coefficients for the whole sample (not by region) which are reported as significant at the 10 per cent level only, even though coefficients and their standard errors for the different regions are not given.

Further, Hazell and Fan (2003) claim that the same procedure is successfully used by Fan et al. (2002) on China. However, the China study estimates growth and poverty equations at the province level, aggregating provinces into three regions to estimate the returns to public investments for different regions. In the India study all except the poverty equation are estimated at the district level, but the poverty equation is estimated at the NSSR level after aggregating over districts within the NSSR. These are then aggregated to the three regions (irrigated, favourable and unfavourably rainfed) to estimate the marginal returns to public investment. As we point out, when standard errors are reported they are relatively large especially for the poverty equation, reflecting heterogeneity. In fact, the poverty equation coefficients on growth are not significant in either irrigated or high potential rainfed zones (Fan and Hazel 2000: 1461, Table 8), and it seems rather unlikely that they are statistically significantly different from, although they are smaller than, the coefficient for the low potential rainfed areas.

# 7. Are Agricultural Growth and Non-farm Employment Growth Substitutes or Complements?

The growth-linkages literature argues that agricultural growth generates both backward and forward production linkages along with consumption linkages that make agricultural growth and non-farm output growth in the rural sector complementary. With increased incomes ensuing from agricultural growth being spent on the products of local non-farm business, one would expect that in non-farm employment, growth will occur in regions with strong agricultural growth, thereby providing another route for agricultural growth to reduce rural poverty. Much of the earlier empirical literature that studied the role of the non-agricultural sector in poverty reduction in India did not differentiate between non-farm rural economic growth and urban economic growth, lumping these two distinct components of the non-agricultural sector into one broad category. Thus, Ravallion and Datt (1996) find that the primary and tertiary sectors had strong poverty reducing impacts in rural areas but not the secondary sector. Datt and Ravallion (2002) and Ravallion and Datt (2002) find that non-farm output growth had a discernible negative effect on overall (rural and urban) poverty at the state level for the 15 major states, and that non-agricultural economic growth was less effective in reducing poverty. None of these studies estimate the effect of the non-farm *rural* sector on rural poverty—so we cannot say how poverty reducing non-farm rural economic growth has been compared to agricultural growth.

A second limitation of the earlier empirical literature is that the studies do not make a distinction between the impact of agricultural growth on traded and non-traded goods in the non-farm rural sector. The growth-linkages story applies to non-traded goods, as a higher demand for these goods will increase their prices as well as the incomes of those individuals who work in this sector. But in an open economy, where capital is mobile between regions, agricultural growth can decrease the incentive of industrialists to locate themselves in the region if this leads to an increase in rural wages compared to other regions. In this case, agricultural growth and non-farm employment growth are not complements, but substitutes. This provocative neoclassical account of the inverse relationship between agricultural growth and non-farm employment growth is presented in two recent papers by Foster and Rosenzweig (2003, 2005) (henceforth FR).

FR support their account of the inverse relationship between agricultural development and rural industrialization by examining a panel of several thousand households in about 250 villages surveyed by the NCAER in 1971, 1982 and 1999. FR first compute an index of High Yielding Variety (HYV) seed yields using a Laspeyres weighted index for four HYV crops—corn, rice, sorghum and wheat. FR find that villages with higher HYV yield in 1971 tend to show slower crop yield growth in 1971–99. During the period 1971–99, there was a sizeable increase in share of non-farm income in total income. Much of this increase was in wages and salaries and not non-farm business income. This in turn was due to a substantial increase in factory employment, particularly in the villages in the lower quintiles of crop yield growth. FR also find econometric support for the simple negative correlation between village factory presence and HYV yield, observed in the descriptive statistics. Thus, the evidence from the NCAER village surveys suggests that rural industrialization took place most significantly in villages where agricultural growth was the slowest.[19] The empirical evidence that FR adduce support their neoclassical account of rural industrialization, where the latter is a substitute for agricultural growth.

Though FR do not directly examine the implications of their findings for rural poverty, it is clear that if one were to agree with their results, rural poverty decline may be possible if rural industrialization occurred in regions where agricultural growth was not strong. This would suggest that rural poverty rates may converge across regions over time, providing an optimistic scenario for the possibility of rural poverty reduction in areas where initial conditions may be unfavourable to agricultural growth.

The findings drawn from the NCAER data-set, which FR use, do not, however, seem to be entirely supported by other studies that use NSS data.[20] For example, Kijima and Lanjouw (2005) find no evidence of increase in total employment within the non-farm sector in the 1990s. Using a regional panel data-set, they also find that poverty reduction is clearly associated with changes in agricultural wages and employment levels than with the expansion of non-farm employment opportunities. This apparent difference between the Kijima–Lanjouw study and those of FR can be partly attributed

---

[19] However, because their data-set starts in 1971, it excludes the rapid agricultural productivity growth that starts in the mid-1960s (Figure 1).

[20] It may be noted that when we (PJS) included non-farm employment growth in our models of poverty at the end of the 1980s, this variable does not have a significant coefficient; details are available from the authors.

to differences in data definitions and partly in the different sampling methods used in the NCAER and NSS data-sets.[21] FR do not describe their data-set in detail, and it is not clear where their high-growth villages are located. Are they clustered or scattered? Are they in low potential or high potential areas? Clearly, a more careful look at the data is necessary before one can be convinced about the reliability of the data, and therefore, the robustness of the ensuing empirical analysis.

## 8. Does Poverty Measure What We Think It Does, and Can It Be Used to Measure the Impact of Agricultural Growth on Poverty?

Empirical work on trickle-down and poverty generally uses money-metric measures derived from the NSS CES and poverty lines originally suggested by the Technical Committee and then adapted by the Expert Committee of the Planning Commission (GOI 1979, 1993). Based on the cost of a household normative calorie consumption level for the rural and urban sectors separately in 1973–74, state poverty lines were computed for 1960–61 and updated using the State Consumer Price Indexes for Agricultural Labourers (CPIAL) for the rural sector and the CPI for Industrial Workers (CPIIW) for the urban sector. Datt and Ravallion (1998a) adjusted these CPIs for the cost of firewood, and computed poverty from the published group data using the POVCAL program available from the World Bank,[22] and it is these poverty measures that have been used by DR, FHT, FHH and BBEV.[23]

The official poverty measures have recently come under considerable criticism from a number of perspectives. For a number of years it has been criticized on the grounds that there has been a growing gap between the National Accounts measures of consumption and those found in the CES (Bhalla 2000; Bhalla and Das 2004; Ravallion 2000). Others have drawn

---

[21] As FR note, the NCAER data-set is a panel of the same villages surveyed in three waves beginning in 1971 and ending in 1999. In contrast, the NSSO do not necessarily survey the same villages, and the villages surveyed in later rounds of the NSS employment surveys may be more representative of the country as a whole at the time of the survey than the NCAER villages which may have become less representative over time.

[22] http://www.worldbank.org/LSMS/tools/povcal/index.htm

[23] PJS used official poverty lines to compute HCRs and so on from the unit records of the 43rd and 50th rounds. Due probably to discrepancies in the data distributed to users with that used by the Planning Commission, poverty and other aggregate measures are not usually the same.

attention to a growing gap between the calorie norms on which poverty lines were set and the estimated consumption of calories by households at the updated poverty lines (Meenakshi and Vishwanathan 2003; Patnaik 2004; Rath 1996, 2003; Ray and Lancaster 2005).[24] Deaton and associates have criticised the official poverty lines on the grounds that they are updated using Laspeyres consumer price indexes (the CPIAL for the rural sector and the CPIIW for the urban sector) with long out-of-date base weights. After calculating new spatial and inter-round CPIs from the unit records of the 43rd, 50th and 55th rounds, Deaton concludes that there are some obvious discrepancies for some state poverty lines (rural Andhra Pradesh is too low), and generally between urban and rural poverty lines for each state with official urban poverty lines being relatively too high with regard to rural poverty lines (Deaton and Tarrozi 1999; Deaton 2003c). Deaton also argues that inter-round inflation of the official poverty lines is too high (based on his UV CPIs [Unit Value Consumer Price Index] between the 43rd and 50th rounds), as one would expect from the use of the Laspeyres indexes as opposed to a more appropriate cost of living index like the Fisher or Tornqvist.

It is not clear why these criticisms do not apply to the poverty lines and poverty calculations made from them for earlier rounds using the Özler et al. (1996) data. Indeed, it is clear that the discrepancy of the unreasonably low rural poverty line for Andhra Pradesh derives from a peculiarity in the CPIAL for Andhra Pradesh between 1960 and 1973–74, rather than in the base poverty line for rural Andhra Pradesh computed for 1960 by the Expert Group (Dubey and Palmer-Jones 2005b).

Further consideration of these methods of computing poverty lines suggests that none of them (the official poverty lines [PLs], calorie norm anchored poverty lines or Deaton's UV CPI based PLs) corresponds to the expected cost of attaining a common standard of living in different states or sectors or over time (Dubey and Palmer-Jones 2005b). This is clear from economic theory that the concept of poverty can be formalized as:

$$z = \min_q(q,\ p_q,\ e_1,\ e_2, \ldots,\ e_n,\ \bar{u})$$

where $q$ are the goods consumed; $p_q$ are the prices of goods $q$; and $\bar{u}$ is the reference poverty level standard of living; $e_{-1}, e_2, \ldots, e_n$ are other variables that are likely to affect the determination of $u$ from the $q$ goods consumed.

---

[24] See also Palmer-Jones and Sen (2001), where an explanation is offered for this apparent decline in calorie consumption at a common real expenditure level.

These 'environmental' variables are not exhaustive of those that may affect the transformation of goods into well-being. For example, it neglects the implications of the physical effort required to produce goods or gain income to buy the goods consumed. An agricultural labourer, or miner or other such manual labourer will need to consume more calories to produce income or goods than an office worker. The characteristics model of consumption (Gorman 1953; Lancaster 1966), and the household production model (Becker 1965; Pollak 1978) are relevant here, as are models which include 'productive consumption' (Suen and Mo 1994), extended perhaps to allow for 'effort intensity' (Palmer-Jones and Jackson 1997; Jackson and Palmer-Jones 1999). These approaches do not, however, pay explicit attention to variations in intra-household allocations or to person-specific characteristics that affect the transformations of goods available at the household level into individual well-being. There is insufficient information about the transmission in such variations to the welfare achieved by the individuals who make up that household, though an understanding of the bargaining approach can clearly contribute to our concepts of the intra-household distribution of well-being within households(Sen 1987; Haddad et al. 1997).

This line of argument suggests that the money-metric poverty does not measure spatial, sectoral or temporal differences in ill-being, and, consequently, the dependent variables that have been used in the analysis of agricultural-growth-poverty linkages have little meaning, even if one could adjust for changes in prices by using appropriate CPIs. The UV CPIs computed by Deaton are not satisfactory not only because they neglect 'environmental' variables. The other serious problems are (a) that they do not include appropriate prices for non-UV items which constitute between 20 and 60 per cent of expenditure around the poverty line; (b) unit values have serious deficiencies as prices relevant to the poor since they are calculated for the whole population. This can be readily remedied by computing them for the lower end of the expenditure distribution, and by incorporating 'quality' dimensions although there is need to separate the efferts of quality changes from price changes in affecting the welfare; and (c) Deaton's method probably seriously underestimates the additional cost of urban living compared to rural living around poverty lines.[25] Futher problems with the official methods as also with Deaton's methods are that poverty lines are computed

---

[25] Deaton's method leads him to conclude that official urban poverty lines are relatively too high compared to rural PLs. If he had anchored his PL on the all-India Urban PL for the 43rd round instead of the all-India Rural PL for that round then he would have conclude that the official rural poverty lines are too low relative to the urban. What he really finds is that by his method

at the state level, while there is considerable intra-state variations in prices (for example, UV CPIs differ significantly between NSSR within states [Dubey and Palmer-Jones 2005a]), and also between towns of different size within states and indeed within NSSR (Dubey and Palmer-Jones 2005c).

If any or all of these criticisms of poverty calculations have some validity then one should not use the poverty aggregates derived from them as indicators of well-being measured by a common yardstick rather than being partly due to changes in the yardstick. It might be more reasonable under these circumstances to use other indicators of ill-being such IMRs, CMRs, Maternal Mortality, child anthropometry and so on. Not surprisingly these other indicators are not very highly correlated with money-metric poverty (even when calculated using what adjustments we found possible to the Deaton type PLs (ibid.).

Further, these criticisms of poverty measures for the last 20 years or so, cannot be made without giving rise to doubts about the comparability among earlier measures used in the litereature. For example, if the CPIAL and CPIIW, which have been used to inflate poverty lines over time are inappropriate for the 1980s and the 1990s, then they are almost certainly unsatisfactory for earlier rounds. This is surely unreasonable, but while adjustments to more recent poverty lines and calculations can be made using the unit records from the NSS CES, this is not possible for surveys prior to the 38th round which took place in 1983.[26] Maybe other corrections could be attempted based on more modern under-standings of appropriate inflators.

---

official PLs for the rural and urban sectors are too far apart. However, our criticism is that his method uses the behavioural Engel non-food share of expenditure of the rural sector to compute the non-food share of the urban sector, adjusting only for differences in prices of UV items. We suggest that (*a*) one should compute a separate non-food share appropriate to urban living (because compared to rural areas, urban areas require higher necessary expenses to attain a similar standard of consumption, for example, of housing); (*b*) the CPIs appropriate to non-UV items (mainly non-food items) are likely to be different from those of UV items (mainly food) since in different periods they have had quite different inflation rates and they differ spatially if one is to take the sub-group indexes of the CPIAL and CPIIW as indicators. All this is discussed in Dubey and Palmer-Jones (2005b).

[26] Computing Deaton type PLs for the 38th round does not alter most of the conclusions that have been reached based on these recalculated PLs. It is, however, interesting to note that the inter-round CPI between the 38th and 43rd rounds is not significantly lower than the OPL inflator, as found between the 43rd and 50th rounds. This is partly because the latter may underestimate inflation between these rounds as it ignores the higher inflation of non-food items in this period. It is also the case that both our and Deaton's inflator between the 50th and 55th rounds are not notably different to the OPL inflators.

# 9. Conclusions

The large body of work that has been undertaken on trickle-down in rural India has had a significant impact on development policy and thinking in the past four decades. There are several features of this work that are worthy of mention. First, in the empirical literature on agricultural growth-rural poverty, four issues stand out:

(*i*) How important were initial or underlying conditions in enabling agricultural productivity rise?

(*ii*) How important was government spending in transforming economic growth in to improvements in well-being?

(*iii*) How important was the non-farm economy in poverty reduction associated with agricultural productivity rise and how was this connected to the agricultural productivity rise?

(*iv*) Can poverty measures be constructed over time and space which capture patterns and trends of the economic well-being of the poor?

The empirical literature has progressed from simple econometric attempts to establish whether trickle-down is observed or not to more complicated models that attempt to understand the causes of trickle-down, and how these causes may be linked to initial conditions like the presence of rural infrastructure, educational attainment or favourable agro-ecological factors. While the empirical evidence here seems to be sufficiently robust to draw strong inferences on the causal forces of trickle-down, the same cannot be said about the studies that we have reviewed, which provide primacy to public investment in agricultural research and roads as the most important way that public policy can reduce rural poverty. Neither is the debate on whether agricultural growth and rural industrialization are substitutes or complements in their effects on rural poverty settled. We would argue that much of the attention of empirically oriented economists must now turn to the vexed issue of whether we can expect the expansion of the non-farm sector to bring about poverty reduction in rural areas, where agro-ecological factors are not favourable to agricultural growth and, therefore, becoming the primary driver of poverty decline.

There are also important questions that can be asked about the processes and practices of development policy analysis. For example, could more have been learnt sooner had policy analysis, conceived broadly as 'evidence-based policy discourses', been conducted in better ways? Could/should the analysis of existing data have been conducted in different ways, and or by a wider range of institutions? Were data production and dissemination up to the job, especially in the statistics of poverty? Should major policy shifts draw on a relatively narrow range of empirical studies by a small number of institutionally related organizations?[27]

Notwithstanding these and other questions arising from the recent work on agricultural growth and poverty in recent years, it is clear that the future will be unlike the past in many ways; agriculture is much more commercialized than it was in between the 1960s and the 1980s; state institutions for agricultural research, extension, input supplies and finance, output marketing and so on are more than matched by private sector organizations in these sectors, and civil society (often with a pro-poor orientation) is arguably somewhat stronger.

To end, we have the following propositions that we think emerge from our review:

(*i*) The evidence that agricultural growth has been important for poverty reduction seems fairly robust, even if often flawed; however, the nature and significance of its role will vary according to initial conditions, and it is not clear that agriculture-led poverty reduction can be transferred to less favoured regions.

(*ii*) Most important among initial conditions will be the agro-ecological conditions, but population density and the existing levels of ill-being, perhaps education, farm size distribution and other characteristics of the local agrarian structure are also likely to be crucial.

(*iii*) Spatial patterns in agricultural development and rural poverty may be more important than the temporal differences highlighted in earlier work.

(*iv*) Policies implemented by administrative jurisdictions (such as states in India) will have some impact on both the nature and extent of agricultural growth and its impacts on ill-being, but these will be conditioned by the initial conditions and vary within jurisdictions.

(*v*) Money-metric poverty may not be an appropriate indicator of patterns and trends of ill-being and should be supplemented if not supplanted by other measures of ill-being in policy analyses.

(*vi*) The policy significance of quantitative analyses of large-scale data-sets suggests that wide participation in both the production and the analysis of these data should be fostered.

---

[27] For example, the recent shift from an emphasis on the social sector in the 1990s back to the more conventional infrastructure and agricultural research and development policies characteristic of earlier decades.

**Richard Palmer-Jones,** School of Development Studies, University of East Anglia, Norwich NR4 7TJ, UK, Tel: +44(0)160 359 2807, Fax: +44(0)160 345 1999, E-mail: r.palmer-jones@uea.ac.uk

**Kunal Sen,** The School of Environment and Development, The University of Manchester, Oxford Road, Manchester UK M13 9PL. E-mail: kunal.sen@manchester.ac.uk

# References

Agarwal, B. 1984. 'Women, Poverty and Agricultural Growth in India', *Journal of Peasant Studies*, 13(4): 165–220.

Ahluwalia, M. 1978. 'Rural Poverty and Agricultural Performance in India', *Journal of Development Studies*, 14(3): 298–324.

Alston, J. 2002. 'Spillovers', *The Australian Journal of Agricultural and Resource Economics*, 46(3): 315–46.

Banerjee, A. V., P. Gertler and M. Ghatak. 2002. 'Empowerment and Efficiency: Tenancy Reform in West Bengal', *Quarterly Journal of Economics*, 110(2): 239–80.

Bardhan, P. K. 1970. 'The Green Revolution and Agricultural Labourers', *Economic and Political Weekly*, 5(29–31).

Barrett, C. B., M. R. Carter and P. D. Little. 2006. 'Understanding and Reudint Pesistent Poverty in Africa: Introduction to a Special Issue', *Journal of Development Studies*, 42(2): 167–77.

Becker, G. S. 1965. 'A Theory of the Allocation of Time', *The Economic Journal*, 75(299): 493–517.

Bell, C., P. B. R. Hazell and R. Slade. 1982. *Project Evaluation in Regional Perspective*. Baltimore: Johns Hokins University Press.

Besley, T. and R. Burgess. 2002. 'The Political Economy of Government Responsiveness: Theory and Evidence from India', *Quarterly Journal of Economics*, 117(4): 1415–51.

Besley, T., R. Burgess and B. Esteve-Volart. 2004. *Operationalising Pro-Poor Growth—A Country Case Study on India*, Final Report. Washington DC: World Bank.

Bhaduri, A. 1968. 'New Agricultural Policy', *Frontier*, 1(13): 12–13.

Bhalla, S. S. 2000. 'Growth and Poverty in India—Myth and Reality', mimeo, New Delhi: Oxus Research and Investments; http://oxusresearch.com

Bhalla, S. S. and T. Das. 2004. *Why be Afraid of the Truth? Poverty, Inequality and Growth in India, 1983–2000*. New Delhi: Oxus Research and Investments.

Byerlee, D. and G. Traxler. 2001. 'The Role of Technology Spillovers and Economies of Size in the Efficient Design of Agricultural Research Systems', in J. M. Alston, P. G. Pardey and M. J. Taylor (eds), *Agricultural Science Policy: Changing Global Agendas*. Baltimore: Johns Hoppins Press.

Byerlee, D., X. Diao and C. Jackson. 2005. 'Agriculture, Rural Development, and Pro-poor Growth: Country Experiencs in the Post-Reform Era', *Agriculture and Rural Development Discussion Paper No. 21*, Washington DC: World Bank.

Byres, T. J. 1979. 'Of Neo-populist Pipe Dreams: Daedalus in the Third World and the Myth of Urban Bias', *Journal of Peasant Studies*, 6(2): 210–40.

———. 1981. 'The New Technology, Class Formation, and Class Action in the Indian Countryside', *Journal of Peasant Studies*, 8(4): 405–59.

Chambers, R. 1983. *Rural Development: Putting the Last First*. London: Longman.

Conley, T. and C. Udry. 2002. 'Learning about New Technology: Pineapple in Ghana', Working Paper, Yale University.

Datt, G. and M. Ravallion. 1998a. 'Farm Productivity and Rural Poverty in India', *Journal of Development Studies*, 34(4): 62–85.

————. 1998b. 'Why Have Some Indian States Done Better than Others at Reducing Rural Poverty?', *Economica*, 65(257): 17–38.

————. 2002. 'Is India's Economic Growth Leaving the Poor Behind?', *Journal of Economic Perspectives*, 16(3): 89–108.

Deaton, A. 2003a. 'Adjusted Indian Poverty Estimates for 1999–2000, *Economic and Political Weekly*, 37(4): 322–26.

————. 2003b. 'Prices and Poverty in India, 1987–2000', *Economic and Political Weekly*, 37(4): 362–68.

————. 2003c. 'Health, Inequality, and Economic Development', *Journal of Economic Literature*, 41(1): 113–58.

Deaton, A. and A. Tarrozi. 1999. 'Prices and Poverty in India', Mimeo, Princeton University.

Deaton, A. and V. Kozel. 2005. 'Data and Dogma: The Great Indian Poverty Debate', *World Bank Research Observer*, 20(2): 177–99.

Delgado, C., J. Hopkins and V. A. Kelly. 1998. *Agricultural Growth Linkages in Sub-Saharan Africa*. Washington DC: International Food Research Institute (Research Report 107).

DFID (Department for International Development). 2005. *Growth and Poverty Reduction: The Role of Agriculture: A DFID Policy Paper*. London: Department for International Development (DFID).

Dorward, A., J. Kydd, J. Morrison and I. Urey. 2004. 'A Policy Agenda for Pro-Poor Agricultural Growth', *World Development*, 32(1): 73–89.

Dorward, A., S. Fan, J. Kydd, H. Lofgren, J. Morrison, C. Poulton, N. Rao, L. Smith, H. Tchale, S. Thorat, I. Urey and P. Wobst. 2004a. 'Institutions and Economic Policies for Pro-Poor Agricultural Growth', DSGD Duiscussion Paper No. 15, Washington and London: IFPRI and Imperial College Centre for Development and Poverty Reduction.

————. 2004b. 'Institutions and Policies for Pro-Poor Agricultural Growth', *Development Policy Review*, 22(6): 611–22.

Dreze, J. and A. Sen. 1989. *Hunger and Public Action*. Oxford: Clarendon Press.

Dubey, A. and R. W. Palmer-Jones. 2005a. 'Poverty in India since 1983: New Poverty Counts and Robust Poverty Comparisons', Mimeo, Norwich: School of Development Studies, University of East Anglia (electronic).

————. 2005b. 'Prices, Price Indexes and Poverty Counts in India during 1980s and 1990s: Calculation of UVCPIs', Mimeo, Norwich: School of Development Studies, University of East Anglia.

————. 2005c. 'Prices, Price Indexes and Poverty Counts in India during 1980s and 1990s: From CPIs to Poverty Lines?', Norwich: School of Development Studies, University of East Anglia (electronic).

Evenson, R. E., C. Pray and M. Rosegrant. 1999. *Agricultural Research and Productivity Growth in India*. Washington DC: International Food Research Institute (Research Report 109).

Fan, S., L. Zhang and X. Zhang. 2002. *Growth, Inequality, and Poverty in Rural China: The Role of Public Investments*. Washington DC: International Food Research Institute (Research Report 125).

Fan, S. and P. Hazell. 2000. 'Should Developing Countries Invest more in Less Favoured Areas? An Empirical Analysis of Rural India', *Economic and Political Weekly*, 35(17): 1455–64 .

————. 2001. 'Returns to Public Investment in the Less-Favoured Areas of India and China', *American Journal of Agricultural Economics*, 82(4): 1217–22.

————. 2003. 'Agricultural Growth, Poverty Reduction and Agro-ecological Zones in India: An Ecological Fallacy?', *Food Policy*, 28(5–6): 433–36.

Fan, S., P. Hazell and S. Thorat. 1999. 'Interlinkages between Government Spending, Growth and Poverty in Rural India'. IFPRI, Washington DC, Research Report 110.

Fan, S., P. Hazell and S. Thorat. 2000. 'Government Spending, Growth and Poverty in Rural India', *American Journal of Agricultural Economics*, 82(4): 1038–51.

Fan, S., P. Hazell and T. Haque. 2000. 'Targeting Public Investments by Agro-ecological Zone to Achieve Growth and Poverty Alleviation Goals in Rural India', *Food Policy*, 25(4): 411–28.

———. n.d. *Role of Infrastructure in Production Growth and Poverty Reduction in Indian Rainfed Agriculture*, Washington DC: IFPRI for The Indian Council for Agricultural Research and the World Bank.

Fan, S., S. Thorat and N. Rao. 2004. 'Investment, Subsidies, and Pro-Poor Growth in Rural India', Draft Report Submitted to DFID, Washington DC: IFPRI.

Fogel, R. 1994. 'Economic Growth, Population Theory and Physiology: The Bearing of Long-Term Processes on the Making of Economic Theory', *American Economic Review*, 84(3): 369–95.

Fogel, R. W. 1991. 'Review of "Sickness, Recovery, and Death: A History And Forecast of Ill Health" by Riley, J. C.', *American Historical Review*, 96(3): 827.

Foster, A. D. and M. R. Rosenzweig. 2003. 'Agricultural Productivity Growth, Rural Economic Diversity, and Economic Reforms: India, 1970–2000', paper presented at the D. Gale Johnson Memorial Conference, University of Chicago, Chicago, 25 October.

———. 2005. 'Rural Non-farm Employment Generation and Rural Out-migration in South Asia', paper presented at the Handbook of Agricultural Economics Conference, Bellagio, Italy.

Government of India (GOI). 1979. *Report of the Task Force on Projection of Minimum Needs and Effective Consumption*. New Delhi: Perspective Planning Division, Planning Commission.

———. 1993. *Report of the Expert Group on Estimation of Proportion and Number of Poor*. New Delhi: Planning Commission, Perspective Planning Department.

Gorman, W. M. 1953. 'Community Preference Fields', *Econometrica*, 21: 63–80.

Griffin, K. 1974. *The Political Economy of Agrarian Change: An Essay on on the Green Revolution*. London: Macmillan.

Griffin, K. and A. K. Ghose. 1979. 'Growth and Impoverishment in the Rural Areas of Asia', *World Development*, 7(2): 361–83.

Guha, S. 1994. 'The Importance of Social Intervention in the England's Mortality Decline: The Evidence Reviewed', *Social History of Medicine*, 7(1): 89–110.

Haddad, L., J. Hoddinott and H. Alderman (eds). 1997. *Intrahousehold Resource Allocation: Methods, Models and Policy*. Baltimore: Johns Hopkins University Press.

Harriss, B. 1987. 'Regional Growth Linkages from Agriculture and Resource Flows in Non-farm Economy', *Economic and Political Weekly*, 22(1–2): 31–46.

Harriss, J. and B. Harriss. 1989. 'Agrarian Transformation in the Third World', in D. Gregory and R. Walford (eds), *Horizons in Human Geography*. Totowa: Barnes and Noble.

Hart, G. 1989. 'The Growth Linkages Controversy—Some Lessons from the Muda Case', *Journal Of Development Studies*, 25(4): 571–75.

———. 1993. 'Regional Growth Linkages in the Era of Liberalization: A Critique of the New Agrarian Optimism', World Employment Programme Research, Working Paper No. 37, Geneva: International Labour Organization.

Hazell, P. and A. Röell. 1983. *Rural Growth Linkages: Household Expenditure Patterns in Malaysia and Nigeria*. Washington DC: International Food Policy Research Institute (Research Report 41).

Hazell, P. and C. Ramasamy (eds). 1991. *The Green Revolution Revisited: The Impact of High-Yielding Rice Varieties in South India*. Baltimore: Johns Hopkins University Press.

Hazell, P. and S. G. Fan. 2003. 'Agricultural Growth, Poverty Reduction and Agro-ecological Zones in India: An Ecological Fallacy?', *Food Policy*, 28(5–6): 433–36.

International Fund for Agricultural Development (IFAD). 2001. *Rural Poverty Report, 2001: The Challenge of Ending Rural Poverty*. Oxford: Oxford University Press.

Irz, X., L. Lin, C. Thirtle and S. Wiggins. 2001. 'Agricultural Productivity Growth and Poverty Alleviation', *Development Policy Review*, 19(4): 449–66.

Jackson, C. J. and R. W. Palmer-Jones. 1999. 'Rethinking Gendered Poverty and Work', *Development and Change*, 30(3): 557–83.

Johansson, S. R. 1994. 'Food for Thought: Rhetoric and Reality in Modern Mortality History', *Historical Methods*, 27(3): 101–25.

Johnston, B. W. and J. W. Mellor. 1961. 'The Role of Agriculture in Economic Development', *American Economic Review*, 51(4): 566–93.

Kijima, Y. and P. Lanjouw. 2005. 'Agricultural Wages, Non-farm Employment and Poverty in Rural India', mimeo, World Bank.

Kydd, J. and A. Dorward. 2001. 'The Washington Consensus on Poor Country Agriculture: Analysis, Prescription and Insitutional Gaps', *Development Policy Review*, 19(4): 467–78.

Kydd, J., A. Dorward, J. Morrison and G. Cadgisch. 2004. 'Agricultural Development and Pro-Poor Economic Growth in Sub-Saharan Africa: Potential and Policy', *Oxford Development Studies*, 32(1): 37–57.

Ladejinsky, W. 1969a. 'The Green Revolution in Bihar—the Kosi Area: A Field Trip', *Economic and Political Weekly*, 14(26).

———. 1969b. 'How Green is the Green Revolution', *Economic and Political Weekly*, 14(39).

———. 1977. *Agrarian Reform as Unfinished Business: The Selected Papers of Wolf Ladejinsky*. Oxford: Oxford University Press.

Lancaster, K. 1966. 'A New Approach to Consumer Theory', *Journal of Political Economy*, 74(2): 132–57.

Lele, U. and B. Bumb. 1994. *South Asia's Food Crisis: The Case of India*. Washington DC: World Bank.

Lewis, A. 1954. 'Economic Development with Unlimited Supplies of Labour', *The Manchester School*, 22(2): 139–91.

Lipton, M. and R. Longhurst. 1989. *New Seeds and Poor People*. London: Unwin Hyman.

McKeown, T. 1976. *The Rise of Modern Population*. London: Edward Arnold.

———. 1979. *The Role of Medicine: Dream, Mirage of Nemesis?*. Oxford: Blackwell.

Meenakshi, J. V. and B. Vishwanathan. 2003. 'Calorie Deprivation in Rural India', *Economic and Political Weekly*, 38(4): 369–75.

Mellor, J. W. 1966. *The Economics of Agricultural Development*. Ithaca: Cornell University Press.

———. 1976. *The New Economics of Growth: A Strategy for India and the Developing World*. Ithaca: Cornell University Press.

Mellor, J. W. and G. Desai (eds). 1985. *Agricultural Change and Rural Poverty: Variations on a Theme by Dharm Narain*. Baltimore: Johns Hopkins University Press.

Narayana, N. S. S., K. S. Parikh and T. N. Srinivasan. 1990. *Agriculture, Growth and Redistribution of Income: Policy Analysis with General Equilibrium Model of India*. North Holland: Allied Publishers.

NBSS and LUP. 1992. *Agro-ecological Regions of India* (2nd editon). NBSS Publication No. 24, Nagpur: National Bureau of Soil Survey and Land Use Planning.

Özler, B., G. Datt and M. Ravallion. 1996. 'A Database on Poverty and Growth in India', http://www.worldbank.org/poverty/data/indiapaper.htm

Osmani, S. R. 1993. 'Growth and Entitlement: The Analytics of the Green Revolution', UNU-WIDER Research Paper 108, Helsinki.

Palmer-Jones, R. W. and C. Jackson. 1997. 'Work Intensity, Gender and Sustainable Development', *Food Policy*, 22(1): 39–62.

Palmer-Jones, R. W. 2003. 'Agricultural Growth, Poverty Reduction and Agro-ecological Zones in India: An Ecological Fallacy', *Food Policy*, 28(5–6): 423–31.

Palmer-Jones, R. W. and K. Sen. 2001. 'On India's Poverty Puzzles and the Statistics of Poverty', *Economic and Political Weekly*, 36(3): 211–17.

———. 2003. 'What has Luck Got to Do with It? A Regional Analysis of Poverty and Agricultural Growth in India', *Journal of Development Studies*, 40(1): 1–31.

———. 2006. 'It's Where You are that Matters: The Spatial Determinants of Rural Poverty in India', *Agricultural Economics*, 34(1): 1–14.

Patnaik, U. 2004. 'The Republic of Hunger', Public Lecture on the occasion of the 50th Birthday of Safdar Hashmi organized by SAHMAT (Safdar Hashmi Memorial Trust), 10 April, New Delhi.

Pollak, R. A. 1978. 'Welfare Evaliaton and the Cost-of-Living Index in the Household Production Model', *American Economic Review*, 68(3): 285–99.

Rath, N. 1996. 'Poverty in India Revisited', *Indian Journal of Agricultural Economics*, 51(1–2).

———. 2003. 'Poverty by Price Indexes', *Economic and Political Weekly*, 10 April: 4260–68.

Ravallion, M. 2000. 'Should Poverty Measures be Anchored to the National Accounts', *Economic and Political Weekly*, 35: 3245–52.

Ravallion, M. and G. Datt. 1996. 'How Important to India's Poor is the Sectoral Composition of Economic Growth', *World Bank Economic Review*, 10(1): 1–25.

———. 2002. 'Why Has Economic Growth been More Pro-Poor in Some States of India than Others?', *Journal of Development Economics*, 68(2): 381–400.

Ray, R. and G. Lancaster. 2005. 'On Setting the Poverty Line Based on Estimated Nutrient Prices: Condition of Socially Disadvantaged Groups during the Reform Period', *Economic and Political Weekly*, 40(1): 46–56.

Saith, A. 1981. 'Production, Prices and Poverty in Rural India', *Journal of Development Studies*, 19(2): 196–214.

———. 1990. 'Development Strategies and the Rural Poor', *Journal of Peasant Studies*, 17(2): 171–244.

Sen, A. K. 1985a. 'A Sociological Approach to the Measurement of Poverty: A Reply (Poor, Relatively Speaking)', *Oxford Economic Papers*, 37(4): 669–76.

———. 1985b. *Commodities and Capabilites*. Amsterdam: Springer.

———. 1987. *Gender and Cooperative Conflicts*. World Institute for Development Economics Research, Helsinki: World Institute for Development Economics.

Sen, A. and Himanshu. 2004a. 'Poverty and Inequality in India—1', *Economic and Political Weekly*, 18 September: 4247–63.

———. 2004b. 'Poverty and Inequality in India—2', *Economic and Political Weekly*, 25 September: 4361–75.

Singh, I. 1990. *The Great Ascent: The Rural Poor in South Asia*. Baltimore: Johns Hopkins University Press for the World Bank.

Smith, L. D. and I. Urey. 2002. *Agricultural Growth and Poverty Reduction: A Review of Lessons from the Post-Independence and Green Revolution experience of India*. London: DFID.

Stewart, F. (ed.). 1987. *Macro-policies for Appropriate Technology in Developing Countries*. Boulder: Westview Press.

Suen, W. and P. H. Mo. 1994. 'Simple Analytics of Productive Consumption', *Journal of Political Economy*, 102(2): 372–83.

Szreter, S. 1988. 'The Importance of Social Intervention in Britain's Mortality Decline', *Social History of Medicine*, 1: 1–37.

———. 1994. 'Mortality in England in the Eighteenth and the Nineteenth Centuries: A Reply to Sumit Guha', *Social History of Medicine*, 7(2): 269–82.

———. 1997. 'Economic Growth, Disruption, Deprivation, Disease, and Death: On the Importance of the Politics of Public Health for Development', *Population and Development Review*, 23(4): 693–730.

———. 2004. 'Industrialisation and Health', *British Medical Buletin*, 69(1): 75–86.

Thirtle, C., L. Lin and J. Holding. 2004. 'Explaining the Decline in UK Agricultural Productivity Growth', *Journal of Agricultural Economy*, 55: 343–66.

Thirtle, C., L. Lin and J. Piesse. 2003. 'The Impact of Research-led Agricultural Productivity Growth on Poverty Reduction in Africa, Asia and Latin America', *World Development*, 13(12): 1959–75.

Timmer, P. C. 2005. 'Agriculture and Pro-Poor Growth: An Asian Perspective', Working Paper No. 63, Washington DC: Global Centre for Development.

UNDP. 1990. *Human Development Report*. Oxford: Oxford University Press.

World Bank. 2005a. *World Development Report 2006: Equity and Development*. New York: Oxford University Press.

———. 2005b. *Agricultural Growth for the Poor: An Agenda for Development*, Washington DC: World Bank.